The Maggie Greville Story

PAM BURBIDGE

The Book Guild Ltd

First published in Great Britain in 2022 by
The Book Guild Ltd
Unit E2 Airfield Business Park,
Harrison Road, Market Harborough,
Leicestershire. LE16 7UL
Tel: 0116 2792299
www.bookguild.co.uk
Email: info@bookguild.co.uk
Twitter: @bookguild

Copyright © 2022 Pam Burbidge

The right of Pam Burbidge to be identified as the author of this
work has been asserted by her in accordance with the
Copyright, Design and Patents Act 1988.

All rights reserved. No part of this publication may be
reproduced, transmitted, or stored in a retrieval system, in any form or by any means,
without permission in writing from the publisher, nor be otherwise circulated in
any form of binding or cover other than that in which it is published and without
a similar condition being imposed on the subsequent purchaser.

Typeset in 11pt Adobe Garamond Pro

Printed and bound in the UK by TJ Books LTD, Padstow, Cornwall

ISBN 978 1914471 476

British Library Cataloguing in Publication Data.
A catalogue record for this book is available from the British Library.

Maggie the unknown star was born on 20th December 1863.

Born as Margaret Helen Anderson, Maggie became one of the key London hostesses and the confidante of international royalty, politicians and aristocrats, as Margaret Greville, the wife of Ronald Greville.

This book is dedicated to my daughter Antonia, my son-in-law Benjamin, and my three grandchildren, Barnaby, Huxley and Lawrence, who provide a constant supply of fun in my life.

PREFACE

The Maggie Greville Story

When I arrived at Polesden Lacey to work as a Volunteer some years ago, the information and stories which were provided to me, as the background to the key participants, and the ownership and development of Polesden Lacey, included some inventive, mistaken and strange storylines. The people who passed on this information did so without being aware of how much misinformation existed.

I was able to participate in new research when the National Trust commenced a new strategy of opening up some closed doors; by that I mean Simon Jenkins' (Past Chairman of the National Trust) encouragement of being more friendly and outward-looking, innovating and enabling research, to profile what the National Trust could offer. The opportunity to be involved became possible.

I offer the real truth of Maggie Greville's life: her background; William McEwan's management of Maggie, including some of her time at Polesden Lacey and Charles Street, London; and pass it on, as I now do.

I uncover Maggie's mother's and father's participation in her journey from her birth, and Maggie's husband's involvement after her marriage (particularly by Ronnie's connections) for a number of years, through to her reign as the Chatelaine of Polesden Lacey from 1907 until her death in 1942.

It is always possible for mistakes to occur when writing and compiling a life story, but I can now provide much of the real story and background of Maggie

Greville, who became such a major force in the social world from Edwardian times to the 1940s. With factual references, long-time research in archives, studying original legal documents and by creating new archival information, and with help from friends and colleagues who have supported me and offered new research, I have been able to write *The Maggie Greville Story*, with much information not previously known.

In writing this book, I wish to show that when Maggie was born (illegitimately), a star arrived, albeit in an inconspicuous manner. When Maggie grew up, her ability to become a major player in society and life became apparent; her father provided much of the stage and circumstances to manage and ensure her role.

William McEwan tutored, educated, encouraged and advised Maggie for nearly fifty years. His fortune and his hard work were rewarded, with Maggie Greville's continuing success as a major player in an international world.

Maggie had many sides to her character: difficult, acerbic (at times) and critical (although never of the British Royal family); inquisitive, intelligent, kind and more generous than most people could imagine. She was helpful, considerate and incredibly thoughtful. She was described by one of her friends of being able to "sum people up in an instant" (Osbert Sitwell).

Her education in her early years, was sufficient to allow her to understand what she needed to absorb, learn and assimilate, into the grown-up world which she joined, with the aid of her father (and his money); including the transition into the Marlborough House Set by her marriage, which furnished a major stepping stone.

Maggie made one particular bad judgement (more of this later – no doubt there were some other smaller mistaken perceptions of people and life), but she made up for this particular mistake with the overwhelming supply of direct help to people, charities, causes, and the British government in both World War I and World War II.

I hope you enjoy reading how Maggie progressed through different stages of her spectacular life, which contributed to her becoming a person who made a difference.

Unravelling the real Maggie Greville story was not simple, as so much had been done to obscure Margaret's early life. But Maggie (and I call Margaret Greville "Maggie", as her friends always did) enjoyed a special journey, from a relatively quiet starting point, to her eventual secure position as one of the key hostesses in Edwardian society, and beyond, to the middle of World War II.

She was more than a society hostess. She was a lady who enjoyed a political salon, and whose connection to the British Royal family endures to this day.

I find as I complete this book that I am surprised at how much Maggie gave. Going back some years, I was advised of many criticisms about Maggie. Why? I ask why was so much done to obscure the truth about Maggie? She possessed an exceptional ability to be kind.

The book has been written to amuse, illuminate and prove Maggie's life story, and place her in a world encompassing decades of interaction in society, amongst international royalty, maharajahs, aristocrats, politicians, and with everyone whom she met and worked.

In assessing Maggie Greville, it is apparent that she connected, curated and maintained her royal connections without falter.

Maggie's Salon at Polesden Lacey commenced in 1907. Her position as an Edwardian hostess was initiated earlier in London, by her marriage in 1891 to Ronnie. The guidance and financial support her father gave to Maggie, created an enduring base for the whole of her life.

Maggie Greville was far more than an Edwardian hostess. Maggie's politics, her staging of meetings away from London (many of her guests were political, some international, some lawyers, ambassadors and decision makers on the world stage), were significant.

The nature of Maggie's Salon was different to some of the other society hostesses in her time. Cosmopolitan, quiet briefings and discussions in the country, involving politicians, provided a discreet place without eavesdropping or spying; enabled by luxurious surroundings, amazing food and a superb wine cellar, political negotiations were comfortably settled.

The Long Walk (a famous part of the gardens at Polesden Lacey) provided a walk with a stunning view, which enabled politicians and diplomats to have discussions without interruption, and without being overheard. A glance at the Visitor Book reveals the truth. Maggie has been underrated for so many years.

Servants who worked for Maggie never gossiped. They needed their jobs and their homes; dismissal was for many servants unthinkable.

Misinformation and unsubstantiated criticism can now be removed.

Political discourse, combined with an ability to elicit change, sometimes, in a number of political situations, and Maggie's grasp of what was really important internationally, allowed her to host discreetly (at times) a political caucus of some magnitude. Maggie continued to entertain guests in 1942 in the summer at the Dorchester Hotel in London, not long before she died.

Remarkable? Fascinating? Exciting at times. Occasionally mistaken. Sometimes sensational and often adventurous!
Welcome to *The Maggie Greville Story*.

Pam Burbidge

FAMILY DATES FOR MAGGIE GREVILLE

The Chatelaine of Polesden Lacey

William McEwan
Born 16th July 1827
Christened 19th August 1827
Died 12th May 1913

Helen McEwan (née Anderson)
Born 15th January 1837
Christened 15th February 1837
Marriage between Helen Anderson and William McEwan
26th November 1885
Died 3rd September 1906

Margaret Helen Greville (née Anderson)
Born 20th December 1863
Christened 8th April 1864
Marriage between Margaret Anderson and Ronald Greville
25th April 1891
Died 15th September 1942

Ronald Greville
Born 14th October 1864
Died 5th April 1908

Contents

One	Origins and Beginnings	1
Two	Who Was Maggie?	13
Three	Two Marriages	20
Four	Life as a Married Lady	33
Five	Entertaining Royalty – the Country House	38
Six	Two Deaths	56
Seven	Maggie's Life After Ronnie Died	66
Eight	Maggie and Her Servants	75
Nine	Managing Polesden Lacey	92
Ten	Maggie the Collector	109
Eleven	Maggie's Travels	128
Twelve	Third Death	138
Thirteen	Maggie the Hostess	142
Fourteen	Maggie's Charity Work	154
Fifteen	Formal Offer to George and Mary in 1914 of Polesden Lacey	171
Sixteen	The Year of Three Kings	181
Seventeen	Pre-Second World War	188
Eighteen	Fourth Death	196
Nineteen	Donation of Jewellery to the Queen Mother	204
Twenty	The Closure of a Star Performance	215
Acknowledgements		233
Endnotes		237
RAF Explanations		255
Further Bibliography		257

Maggie Greville: the image was taken by James Lafayette (James Stack Lauder) on 5th October 1900 at his Studio (179 Bond St, London)

© Victoria and Albert Museum, London

ONE

Origins and Beginnings

The real story of Margaret Greville and William McEwan (father) is so intertwined that in order to provide the truth, and at the same time remove misinformation from Maggie's background, it is essential to commence with describing the beginning of William McEwan's life, and follow his journey from his early working days to his success as a businessman and a brewer, and to the philanthropist he became. I provide the background of McEwan's care and management of his future wife, Helen, so she could participate in society in London.

Importantly, William McEwan stage-managed Maggie and her introduction to Edwardian society, thus providing the first magic key in Maggie's ascending social life after he married Maggie's mother, Helen, when Maggie was twenty-one years old. The second magic key was the introduction and marriage to Ronald Greville, which was the vital stepping stone for Maggie to become a star in Edwardian society. The third magic key we will talk of later, as this was the final piece of the jigsaw which was needed to ensure Maggie's continuity as a key hostess in society throughout the world.

William McEwan was "the man who made a fortune" from hard work, studying and careful planning. He was not a man to do anything without thinking first. He did not act spontaneously. He executed his carefully worked out plans after meticulous investigations and analysis. His background was "comfortable" and he benefited from a reasonable education.

The Maggie Greville story commences with the birth of William McEwan

(Maggie's father) in 1827 in Alloa. McEwan grew up in Alloa. His work took him from Alloa to Glasgow and on to Honley before he knew what he wanted to do in life. His father worked hard, and William McEwan inherited the same innate ability. He had to make money, by earning it, and by learning/studying/improving his education, as an adult. He became a self-made successful man (a millionaire) from his hard work.

William McEwan was born in Alloa, Clackmannanshire, on 16th July 1827, (died 1913). His parents were John McEwan (died January 1832), who married Anne Jeffrey on 19th May 1822 at St Ninians – near Stirling. John McEwan was a successful businessman, a ship captain and owner. He paid the builder Ramsay Traquair to erect a house at 15 Forth Street, Alloa (during 1827–29), for his family.[1] Written invoices and receipts exist showing the costs for this house, including furniture. Also, receipts were retained for plants for the garden, including fruit trees and other shrubs. All costs were paid outright, and no loans existed.

William McEwan was one of five children: Janet, who was born on 17th March 1823; Anne, who was born on 10th March 1826; William, who was born on 16th July 1827; Peter, who was born on 21st January 1830; and John, who was born (four months after his father died) on 21st April 1832. The death of John McEwan (father) when William was four years old did not result in his mother Anne becoming poor, sad though it must have been for all of the family.

John McEwan owned shares in four ships, which were the *Mary*, the *Fame*, the *Anne* and the *Catherine*. All four of these ships were "coasters", which were used to carry goods regularly between Alloa/Grangemouth to Glasgow and Newcastle upon Tyne and other ports. They were less than ninety tons and were registered at Lloyds.[2]

After William McEwan's father died, the share in the ship named *Fame* was retained by the executors of the will on behalf of William's mother Anne, which meant that she received income. John McEwan had been in partnership with Robert Crawford from 1814, and this partnership continued in William's mother's name after her husband died. A new version of the ship named *Fame* was built at Duncanson's Yard in Alloa in 1835. This ship was known to exist in 1853, and it was tracked in voyages between Scotland and Belgium, and also Sweden. William McEwan grew up in reasonable comfort, and he attended Alloa Academy (established 1825).

Additionally, two more ships were purchased, and they travelled south across the channel to Calais and back along the east coast, visiting a number of ports going north until arriving back in Scotland.

William McEwan had three jobs after completing his education at Alloa Academy. He did not particularly enjoy these jobs, but he learnt about bookkeeping, trading, foreign payments and how companies were managed, all of which provided sensible business experience.

McEwan's first job was at the Alloa Coal Company, where he worked from 1843 to 1845 for Mr Mackie. His time there was very much involved with bookkeeping entries, and foreign and home trading, profit and loss accounts.

McEwan moved to Glasgow for his second job, commencing in January 1845, at TL Paterson, a commission agent and merchant (wool). His job in Glasgow was as a clerk, and his time there was not happy.[3]

McEwan described his employer as "mean", and the other employees as well as McEwan worked in hard conditions, working for what McEwan described as a "pittance" of £30 per year. He struggled financially. He was supported by the delivery of "ham, eggs, tea and apples from home" and in one year he received £9, sent from his relatives in Alloa. Being poor at this time did not prevent McEwan from extending his education at the Mechanics Library and Commercial Reading Club. He studied German, ancient and modern history (Professor Reid of Glasgow). He took dancing lessons. He visited the theatre and attended concerts, and did a small amount of travelling.

Whist being poor, he continued to improve himself. His behaviour was never casual. His careful planning (one of his personal character traits) helped him to survive, but without these gifts from home, life would have been very hard.

William McEwan demonstrated probity in his behaviour (mostly), although he kept some details of his personal life from society (permanently). He detailed in his notebooks every expense: precise company accounts and the financial details of his working and personal life. His was a thinker and a planner. He extended his knowledge hugely by reading, but he criticised his own reading as being "too loose" at times.

He visited home sometimes (an arduous trip in the late 1840s). He did not enjoy his time in Glasgow very much, but he furthered his education, and when he wanted a change of employment for better circumstances, he was given a first-class reference (in spite of his employer's meanness and nastiness); his employer stated that McEwan "is a person of the most strict probity, integrity and steadiness and possesses an excellent knowledge of accounts".

McEwan, in moving to a new employer, was hoping to widen his business knowledge and deal with foreign trade, not just British business. He believed he was joining a company in Huddersfield owned by Mr Shaw. His journey in August 1847 was really difficult, but when he arrived in Huddersfield, he was extremely downhearted to discover that although he thought he was to work in that town, instead he was sent to work in a village named Honley in Yorkshire. His dismay included the realisation in his view, that Honley was "a village without society". But he did settle down to life in Honley and joined various societies, made friends, and attended local concerts and fetes and enjoyed days out.

Again, he furthered his education: McEwan studied French, attended the Mechanics Institute, read extremely widely and tried to understand politics and the economy, though he said he remained "lamentably ignorant" on this subject. He was one of the founders of the Honley Reading Society. While working in Honley he travelled much more, and his salary improved gradually, eventually reaching £100 per year.

His travels included visiting large cities: London, Manchester, Liverpool and Leeds. He visited important historical places, such as St Paul's, the Tower of London, Greenwich and the Great Exhibition of 1851.[4] He continued to enjoy the theatre, and he was becoming "a better dresser", as he could spend money on finer clothes than had previously been possible. By this stage of his life he was making contributions to charities, which he continued throughout his life. He was now in a position to save money from his wages, even allowing for his more relaxed lifestyle.

What is interesting and amusing retrospectively is that at this time, he did not have much interest in drinking alcohol. While his records show purchases of occasional bottles of sherry or ginger wine, mostly when entertaining friends, drinking was not a main requirement or interest. In 1848 he stayed at the Temperance Hotel in Perth, and also later at the Temperance Hotel in Huddersfield. In 1850 he took out memberships to two temperance societies, the Huddersfield Total Abstinence Society and the Teetotal Society.

In 1851 (November), William McEwan returned home to Alloa after his time working in Yorkshire. Within one week he joined his uncles John and David Jeffrey at their brewery in Edinburgh (the Heriot) and he began to learn the trade of brewing. His decision made, he never looked back. Clever, astute and thorough in everything he did, his plan to join his uncles must have been on his mind for some time.

McEwan's time at the Heriot brewery was spent working there, but more than this, he studied brewing. He travelled and visited different brewing companies:

Oil painting on canvas, The Right Hon. William McEwan MP (1827-1913) by Walter William Ouless RA (St Helier 1848 - London 1933), at Polesden Lacey, Surrey

© National Trust Images /Jonathan Gibson

Bass, Allsopp and more. He declared in letters home to his mother that he had stated on these visits that he had "no connection with the trade". He was comfortable about lying on these visits. He analysed methods of brewing, and at this time he demonstrated his character of being "a thinker and a planner".

He worked for and with his uncles from 1851 to 1856, at their brewery in Edinburgh (the Heriot), and made time during those years to investigate how he could open his own brewery. The rest of the family were aware of his intentions during these years.[5]

In 1852 he visited both Bass & Allsopp Breweries in Burton upon Trent. He wrote after his inspections to these breweries, in a letter to one of his uncles that, "I had however to put conscience altogether out of the question for the nonce and declare I was not connected with the trade".

In his letter he talked about his analysis of every detail of production undertaken by both companies. He discussed the gravity of beer, the work done by yeast, that no refrigeration was involved at any stage, the fermentation process into "squares", the conservation process, followed by being racked into casks, and normally retained for three months prior to sending the beer out to the customers (public houses/hotels).

After five years working for and with his uncles, having made it well known that he wished to establish his own business, he borrowed £2,000 to establish his own brewery. He was twenty-nine years old, and in 1856 he achieved his ambition.

This decision, as with all of McEwan's decisions, was not made lightly. His brother-in-law (James Younger was married to his sister Janet and was heir to the George Younger Brewery in Alloa). James researched several places in Liverpool for McEwan to set up as a brewery, but they proved to be unsuitable. McEwan's own brother John had also been searching for suitable premises, but none proved to be adequate. McEwan took the brave decision in 1856 to borrow the sum of £2,000 so he could create and establish his own business.

The location of his brewery was researched intensively. He required access to pure Edinburgh water, and research showed that a constant supply of this water from fresh springs was available underneath the land he chose – several springs of "Fresh Edinburgh Water", hence the name of the business is explanatory. The Fountain Brewery was situated between the Caledonian Railway and the Union Canal. McEwan wanted to produce several different beers, not one beer, so this supply of water mattered to him. He wished to use trains and barges to transport his beer (more of his backing of the industrial revolution later), as well as local dray deliveries.

The precision of his planning with high standards enabled him to produce, manage and deliver effectively his products. He understood perfectly how to calculate his costs to achieve profit; his training and his studying, combined with his acumen and intelligence, meant that he fully comprehended how his business could achieve success. As "the thinker and the planner", he left nothing to chance.

He borrowed £500 in April 1856 from another uncle, Thomas Jeffrey, a farmer. He needed this money early in the year in order to organise his plans/architect/drawings, and his intended land purchase. On 2nd October 1856 he borrowed the rest of the money he needed: £500 from his mother, and £1,000 from the Union Bank of Scotland via James Finlay.[6]

The letter from the bank offering the land is dated 2nd October 1856, offering to "feu" William McEwan fourteen thousand square foot of land, at a ground rent of £40 per year. He accepted instantly. His two-year search for a perfect site was over.

McEwan wanted to offer a selection of beers. Nothing McEwan did was without pre-planning. His ability to think out carefully his requirements enabled his business to flourish.

One of his letters shows his prompt payment of interest to his uncle Thomas Jaffery; the letter stated, "Dear Uncle, I enclose a draft on the Bank of Scotland Stirling for £12.10/- being 6 months interest on £500 due this day. I am dear uncle, yours truly", dated 17th November 1856. His agreements and contracts with his agents show just how thorough he was.

Every aspect of the machines which were built, was ordered/checked and proved to be perfect for his requirements. The repayments (interest due until the debts were paid) on the £500 owed to his uncle Thomas, the £500 he borrowed from his mother and the £1,000 from the Union Bank of Scotland, were paid back punctiliously. Later his larger loans were paid back totally.

McEwan organised the building of the brewery (his brewery – the Fountain Brewery), arranged for the machines he ordered to be built, hired the men and the boys and, importantly, hired the agents. Good agents were needed to sell beer successfully. The Fountain Brewery, Fountainbridge, was completed

The Front of Fountain Brewery Edinburgh

by December 1856. McEwan "fussed" and demanded near-perfect results for everything he ordered, and if any of his suppliers delivered late or did not finish on time, he reduced payments to them. He was fastidious and precise in his demands, as he was ultimately with his products.

His letters show how carefully his planning and execution of his criteria to build the brewery was managed. He covered every detail, from insurance in the early stages of setting up his business to the completion of all requirements for the building and machines he had installed; and the hiring of men and boys to work for him; followed by precise, detailed arrangements with agents to sell his beer, the transportation of his beer and understandably, the system of accounting he put in place (something he understood totally).

His details regarding specifications for everything he ordered were precise to the tiniest of details, and in a letter dated 15th December 1856 to Messrs Haldane & Rae, Edinburgh (so close to his schedule for completing his brewery): "Please make for me this week, 5/½ inch cocks with screwed tails, and coupling screws and rings all on one pattern – also a ¾ inch cock with screwed tail… It will be great favour if you can let me have these by the end of the week".[7]

McEwan benefited from some aspects of the industrial revolution, just as he was starting his business. The development of the patent mashing machine in 1853 by William Steel (although not absolutely perfect at the time of McEwan's purchase – it was improved by William Steel over a four-year period) gave McEwan the ability to mix water and malt prior to it being sent to the mash tun. It was a clever machine which saved a huge amount of time and labour, and it became popular with many brewers. A letter dated 2nd January 1857 confirmed McEwan's purchase of this machine: "Dear Sir, I beg to enclose my cheque on the British Linen Co here for £8.8.6 being amt [*amount*] due to you for Patent Right on mashing machine. Please acknowledge receipt".

Another letter dated 13th April 1857 (he had been able to sell his beer from the middle of January 1857 to the British market) concerned his first direct sale from his own company to a client in Australia (Mr Clelland). In this letter he explained to his agent Robert Brown of Glasgow that, "I have in my time made a great deal of ale for the Australasian market and know well what is wanted there. I shall be glad to make brewing of Pale Ale for Mr. Clelland, but I hope he will extend his order to 10 hds as to take the whole of it off my hands. I could make the ale to be delivered early in May…"

McEwan had many competitors and there were many different brands of beer available from other brewers. In addition to the home market, McEwan produced Export beer; India Pale Ale did form a successful part of William McEwan's sales, but the major part of his success (whilst still acknowledging the role of India Pale Ale) was in taking over approximately fifty per cent of the regular beer-drinking market between the lowlands of Glasgow and Edinburgh, and in capturing approximately ninety per cent of the market in the North East of England.

Men working in shipping, mining, armaments and other factories wanted two/three pints of beer at the end of their working day before going home for the meal their wives would have ready for them. Other very successful businessmen/entrepreneurs, such as William Armstrong, employed thirty thousand men (eventually) in the dock areas of the North East/Newcastle upon Tyne (shipping and armaments). The market was there, and while McEwan did have other competitors, he managed with his analysis (using a chemist to ensure his ale achieved the right balance) to produce a large range of successful beers for the home market, and also some for the international market.

With regard to McEwan's Export ale, McEwan worked out that the beer when it arrived in India (or elsewhere abroad) needed to "peak on arrival" – in other words, when the beer reached its destination country, the recipe he used would just reach the "ready stage". Too often, other brewers' beers previously sold internationally were "spoiled" by the time they arrived abroad. It took six weeks for McEwan's beer to reach India (until the Suez Canal was opened up in 1869), so his recipe involved ingredients which allowed the beer to "peak" on arrival. Because the men working in India were unhappy with the available drinking water, beer was welcomed, but it needed to be in good condition on arrival.

It should be noted that Louis Pasteur established for the first time in 1876 information re yeast cultures and fermentation.[8] What became known as pasteurisation was not yet established. Therefore, it was necessary for brewers to analyse and produce their beer with their own "safe" recipes.

Also, while McEwan successfully exported to India, Australia and New Zealand and also Malta, until the Suez Canal was opened up, a long journey would mean his stock/costs and profit were tied up for long periods, and while these countries did contribute to a proportion of his sales and profits, his faster, easier profit lay in capturing the more "local market", as suggested above. After the Boer War, so post-1902, the South African market became another country for receipt of his ales.

McEwan worked steadfastly; he always knew the best way after analysis to get over faults/mistakes/problems with the variety of beers he produced.

He never accepted second best, and with his constant "hands-on" policy of running his business, he gradually became a key player in quite a large group of brewers, although he was never the largest producer. However, he did become a successful brewer, consistently selling his beers, taking his profits and building up a large portfolio of investments (worldwide), in addition to investing in art and antiques, when he realised, he was wealthy enough to do so.

He had produced and continued to produce many different beers, some of which were: India Pale Ale, Export Beer, Scotch Ale, McEwan's Best Scotch, McEwan's 60/-. 70/-, 80/-, Champion Ale.

William McEwan banked half a million pounds, and retained forty-three per cent of the voting shares, when he incorporated his company on 24th July 1889, the registration date for William McEwan and Company, Limited, by the solicitors Morton, Smart & Macdonald, WS Edinburgh.[9] McEwan invested this sum in worldwide stocks and shares; half a million pounds became 1.5 million pounds, which he bequeathed to Maggie in 1913 when he died – possibly worth approximately eighty to one hundred million pounds today?

At the time of his death (1913) McEwan owned shares in twelve railway companies. His investments in these companies included the Caledonian Railway, which he used regularly to transport his beer (£88,400 probate). He invested in four more British railway companies: the Great Western, the North Eastern, the London and Western Railway (£133,125 probate, largest of his rail share holdings), and the Midland Railway.

Also, he invested in foreign railway companies, which were: the Pennsylvania Railroad company, the Nashville Florence & Sheffield Railway, the Northern Pacific Railway company, the Baltimore & Ohio Railroad company, the Atcheson, Topeka & Sante Fe Railway, the Great Northern Railway (USA), and the Union Pacific Railway (£122,300 probate).

In addition to shares in his own company valued at £326,250 (probate) the rest of his investments were in chemical and industrial companies, with his largest shareholding in other shares in the Hudson's Bay Company (£246,250 probate). His shrewdness brought success, but with the majority of his shares in railway stocks, had he made been mistaken in backing the Industrial Revolution, Polesden Lacey would be a different place today. Maggie's inheritance from McEwan included more than money; there are seventeen paintings at Polesden Lacey bequeathed by McEwan, and some other artefacts.

Continuing the story of McEwan's beer; in 1930, seventeen years after McEwan's death, Younger's and McEwan's announced the beginning of a merger, technical, financial and distributive, and by 1931 Scottish Brewers became one company.[10]

On 1st May 1960 Scottish Brewers merged with Newcastle Breweries, and were named Scottish & Newcastle Breweries (S&N). In 1995 Scottish & Newcastle purchased Courage, and became named as Scottish Courage (renamed Scottish & Newcastle in 2006).

Scottish Courage had acquired Hartwell (Finland's major beverage company) in 2000, thereby becoming part owners of Baltic Beverages Holding (BBH), which included some interest in Russia, Ukraine, Kazakhstan and the Baltic countries of Latvia, Lithuania and Estonia. The remaining fifty per cent of BBH was owned by Carlsberg, and they took one hundred per cent control of the company in 2008.

In 2008, the Carlsberg Group and Heineken together, bought Scottish & Newcastle. In 2006 Wells of Bedford merged with Young's of Wandsworth, and in 2011 Wells and Young's bought the Scottish McEwan's and Younger brands from Heineken. In 2015 Wells and Young's became known as Charles Wells.

It was announced on 19th May 2017 that Marston's had acquired Bombardier, Courage, Young's and McEwan's beers, by taking over Charles Wells. The brewery story continues to evolve today.

William McEwan was a Christian and gave regularly to church funds. McEwan gave to charity as a poor man and as a rich man. As William McEwan became wealthy, his generosity to the arts/charities, and becoming a benefactor to Edinburgh, became important to him and the city. He asked advice as to how she should invest his profit in art, when he found he had sufficient funds to become a collector. He was advised that Dutch art was most sound for investment purposes, as well as being recognisably fine. As he began his collection of paintings, he also found time to be a benefactor.

In 1885 he purchased two paintings by Frans Hal – *A Dutch Lady* and *A Dutch Gentleman* – and gave them to the National Gallery of Scotland, where they are still on show today. In 1892 he paid £5,775 for the Rembrandt painting *Woman in a Bed* and gave this to the same gallery and it is still on show.[11]

McEwan bought nearly all of his paintings through the dealer Lesser; Adrian Lesser (123 New Bond Street and 14 Westbourne Terrace, London). McEwan began seriously collecting for himself by 1893, but he had begun, as shown above, to be interested in art from 1885 (but possibly much earlier). Additionally, McEwan used Agnews, after Lesser's death in 1911, to buy his paintings. Though it does seem that McEwan really trusted Adrian Lesser; the purchase of *The Golf Players* (now known as *The Colf Players*) by Pieter de Hooch in 1894 (cost £1,575), and the purchase of the *Introduction* by Gerard ter Borch in 1896 (cost £3,000) were both bought via Lesser's gallery.

In 1886 McEwan was elected a Liberal Member of Parliament for Edinburgh Central, with a majority of 1,524 over his closest rival. McEwan polled 3,760 votes. In 1892 McEwan again won the seat and polled 3,733 votes. At the 1895 election McEwan was returned unopposed and remained as an MP until 1900.

In 1897 McEwan realised that although the new Medical School for Edinburgh University had been completed (architect Sir Rowan Anderson), the university totally lacked funding for the graduation hall which was required; he was also aware that money from other sources seemed not to be forthcoming. He announced that he would pay for the whole project. It was suggested to him that the likely cost was expected to be in the region of £40,000.

The actual cost for this building, known today as McEwan Hall, was £115,000. This included all building costs, the magnificent, huge electric organ, and the amazing decorative work by William Mainwaring Palin. The building is stunning, and at its opening night on 2nd December 1897, students led a torchlight procession into the building. The following day, the official opening of the building took place with William McEwan being made an honorary LLD (Doctor of Law), and he was made a Burgess and Guild Brother of the city, after he persuaded the university to allow civic functions in the hall. Both Maggie and her husband Ronnie attended this ceremony.

As McEwan became successful, his careful management of his profits allowed him to be a benefactor, and to indulge in art purchases, which he was advised "should increase in value".

TWO

Who Was Maggie?

Parallel to McEwan's business becoming established and successful, the importance of McEwan's relationship with a lady named Helen Anderson, (1837–1906), followed by the birth of Margaret Helen Anderson, McEwan's daughter – Maggie (1863–1942), generated new and permanent extensions to McEwan's life.

We need to begin by looking at where and how Maggie's mother Helen lived and grew up in order to establish Maggie's real background on her mother's side.

Maggie's grandparents (her mother Helen's parents) were Helen Lawrence (died 1889), from Charlestown, Dunfermline, and Thomas Anderson (1808–63), an agricultural labourer and later a farm foreman, from Merryhill. Maggie's grandparents were married on 2nd June 1832. As a family they lived in Dunfermline and then Torryburn.[12] They produced twelve children.

Helen, Maggie's mother, was born on 15th January 1837. Note use of Helen for both Maggie's mother's and her grandmother's names. Maggie's grandmother moved by 1871 (a while after her husband had died) to Edinburgh with the family.

However, Helen (Maggie's mother-to-be) and her older sister Margaret (born in 1833) had already left the family home for work, possibly initially in Dunfermline, but by or before 1863, they had reached Edinburgh.

While Maggie's future mother Helen, was working in Edinburgh, she met William McEwan, possibly as late as the very beginning of 1863, or it may have been earlier. Helen's education meant that her choice of jobs was limited; she would have benefited from some education, but this would have ceased when she was twelve or thirteen years old.

There is currently no absolute proof of exactly where Helen worked after arriving in Edinburgh. It is likely she did some domestic work or possibly worked as a young cook at McEwan's brewery? But, at the time of writing this book, proof has not yet been obtained regarding where Maggie's mother Helen worked. Suggestions/theories and misinformation stating that Helen worked directly for McEwan as a housekeeper, are not of help and are incorrect.

Proven facts are what I offer, not conjecture, which produces inaccuracy. While I provide up-to-date information about Maggie and her mother (which is the result of the last ten years of research), the date for Maggie's mother Helen arriving in Edinburgh, or where she worked, is not precisely known (at the time of writing).

But Helen did arrive in Edinburgh. Helen and William McEwan met, and their relationship flourished (both of them were unmarried). Helen became pregnant, and William McEwan did not choose the most straightforward of ways to manage Helen's pregnancy. From the moment Helen became pregnant, and prior to and after Maggie's birth, truth was not the first option for anyone close to Helen Anderson or William McEwan.

William McEwan managed some complicated and discreet arrangements so Helen could give birth to their child, Margaret Helen (Anderson). McEwan was not present at the birth of his only child. William McEwan and Helen Anderson were unmarried, so there was no legal impediment to a marriage. What did McEwan do? As a thinker and a planner, he worked out carefully anything he wished to do ahead of time, both in his business/professional life and his personal life.

William McEwan's relationship to Helen Anderson was important to him, but in 1863, he was not ready to make public that Helen was pregnant or marry Helen when she was pregnant. A marriage at that time in such circumstances would have raised comments. McEwan would realise that his position in Edinburgh society might be questioned socially, if he made public that his lady Helen was pregnant. His connections in commerce and industry were likely to be affected.

Marrying Helen in 1863 would not have earned approval from his family, given the differences in their backgrounds. There were no impediments to marrying, only the social and business pressures of criticism, which might be attached to McEwan. McEwan made arrangements for Helen to give birth to their child in London, away from the eyes of Edinburgh society.

Helen Anderson, Mrs William McEwan (d.1906)

© *National Trust Images, Collections-Public*

McEwan arranged for William Murray Anderson to come off the payroll at the brewery, and he asked Murray Anderson to accompany Helen Anderson to London and to stay with her while she was resident in London, and for the time she gave birth – to Margaret Helen Anderson. It can be seen from brewery ledgers that William McEwan recorded that he was taking cash amounts of money (legitimately) from the business, during the time Helen Anderson and Murray Anderson were living in London.[13] This money was needed to pay for the various expenses during those important months and was a discreet way of managing and paying for the birth of McEwan's only child. The money would pay for all of the costs associated with living in London, fees for health/hospital care and general expenses, until both Helen Anderson and William Murray Anderson returned (separately) to Edinburgh, from London.

William McEwan chose William Murray Anderson to be Helen Anderson's companion when she gave birth to Margaret Helen Anderson; the coincidence of their surnames enabled McEwan to manage this arrangement. McEwan must have decided that, Murray Anderson was reliable and trustworthy. Helen Anderson gave birth to Margaret Helen Anderson on 20th December 1863.[14] Margaret Helen Anderson was born in a cottage at 4 Wellington Place, just opposite Lords cricket ground in Marylebone. Her father was named as William Murray Anderson, who was described as a commercial traveller. William Murray Anderson played a successful and satisfactory role, which enabled the documentation to be established.

Maggie's grave can be seen in the Ladies' Garden at Polesden Lacey. Maggie's grave has the incorrect birth date for her (chiselled into the short side of her grave), near the gate to the Rose Garden, of 2nd March 1867. Totally untrue. Pure fabrication. A number of reasons for this, some involving the background I have described above. Certainly, Maggie never provided the correct date to Ronnie (he was nine months younger than Maggie), whereas she pretended to be three years younger than he was. Additionally, Maggie provided varying birth dates on different occasions for passenger shipping lists, when embarking on her travels, which helped the confusion to be continued during her busy lifetime of travelling.

When Maggie was baptised on 8th April 1864 at St Stephen the Martyr,[15] Marylebone, London, her mother was named as Helen Anderson and her father was named as William Anderson (no Murray on this occasion), with his occupation described as a gentleman on this date. Maggie is listed in the baptism book as entry 424, page 53, and named Margaret Helen Anderson.

So, the leading Edwardian hostess, who subsequently became Margaret Greville, was born as the one and only daughter of Helen Anderson on the 20th December 1863, with the father named (above) as William Murray Anderson.

After Maggie's baptism had taken place, Murray Anderson returned to Edinburgh, and resumed work at McEwan's brewery at Fountainbridge. Later he became the foreman cellar man.

Who was William Murray Anderson?[16] He was born in July 1830 and his birth was recorded at Selkirk Old Parish Register, and his parents were Mercer Anderson and Janet Waugh. William Murray Anderson (1830–98) was married for the first time on 18th June 1852 to Ann McPherson. He was at that time described as a labourer. Ann died on 5th January 1892. His second marriage to Wilhemina Campbell took place on 7th April 1893 in Edinburgh. At this stage of his career, he was described as a cellar man. Murray Anderson had by this time, become the Brewery Cellar Man (Foreman) at the Fountainbridge Brewery. Murray Anderson died in 1898 and his second wife Wilhemina survived him.

Helen, Maggie's mother, returned to Edinburgh in 1864 after giving birth to Margaret; Helen said she had been married, and was a widow. This may have been accepted, but she was not married and she was not a widow. William McEwan was not married.

On her return to Edinburgh, Helen took over a small property, and offered accommodation – she had three rooms to rent. Certainly by/before 1868 she was established at 14 Maitland Street, Edinburgh. By 1876 Helen Anderson had moved to 4 Atholl Place, where she had nine rooms to rent. Helen was able to make money, and care for Maggie.

She remained there until 1885. Helen employed two servants at both of her addresses.

McEwan lived in Glasgow and Honley after leaving Alloa, in rented accommodation, whilst working for two of his three different employers. He continued to rent accommodation in Edinburgh, while he worked for his uncles John and David Jeffrey at the Heriot Brewery (1851–56): William McEwan lived at Melville Street from 1854, and by 1863 he was residing at 17 Shandwick Place until 1871/73.[17] By/before 1873 McEwan was residing at 43 Manor Place and remained there until 1885. All three addresses were lodgings, providing privately rented rooms, until his new house 25 Palmerston Place was built. He had three servants working for him at this time.

A map of Edinburgh (1893–94) clarifies the proximity of their residences to each other. Certainly, for twenty years William McEwan and Helen Anderson lived close to each other, at one side of Edinburgh and close to the brewery.

From McEwan's private notebook, it is now known that McEwan paid tuition fees for Maggie, at the McIntosh School. (Eleanor Docherty, The McEwans and their Legacy: McEwan Journals, Scottish Brewing Archives: SBBA Vol 21, 2021-ISSN 2515-3099). There is also a listing for dancing lessons in McEwan's private notebook. It should be noted that this is a small book "he kept about his person".

While Maggie lived with her mother Helen (post-1863), McEwan was able to supervise and influence Maggie's formative years. Maggie learnt from her father the management of money; wealth was not only for pleasure but was the tool to improve the lives of many people. McEwan provided to Maggie, by example and tuition, the principles and tenets of her upbringing.

McEwan was able to continue to manage his situation of caring for Helen and Maggie, whilst remaining unmarried, until it suited him to marry Helen in 1885.

The purchase of a house in Edinburgh for William McEwan began in 1881. He paid £800 for the land on 11th March to the builder.[18] McEwan continued to make payments to Gilroy and other contractors until the house was completed in 1885.

25 Palmerston Place was on the corner of Chester Street and Palmerston Place. Applications to build the house were submitted from 1881, when the site was purchased by the builder George Gilroy of Brandfield Street, Edinburgh. Gilroy was also the builder who had constructed Fountain Brewery for McEwan in 1856. Gilroy continued to be employed to carry out repairs and maintenance at the brewery.

The initial interior work for the new house was carried out in 1883 and 1884. From detailed notes reference the building of this house, some small additional items were completed, such as stained-glass windows in July 1885, by Dickson & Walker, and some ironwork paid for in December of that year to Thomas Gibson & Sons, so by the end of 1885 the house was completed. Some small final payments after completion were made in 1886 by McEwan. The cost for the total build was over £15,000. 25 Palmerston Place had/has five floors: the dining-room floor, which included a library, a billiard room, a pantry, a toilet for the family and another toilet for servants; the drawing-room floor included, in addition to the main room, two bedrooms, a dressing room and a bathroom; the bedroom floor had three bedrooms, two dressing rooms and a bathroom; the attic floor had one servant's bedroom, two other rooms, a cistern room and the cupola over the main staircase. There were two sets of stairs, main and separate stairs for the servants. The basement floor had a lot of storage: a large kitchen, scullery, wash house, servants' hall, housekeeper's room, bedroom, wine cellar, servants' toilet and storage rooms which ran under the pavement of Palmerston Place.

Although William McEwan had organised a house to be built in Edinburgh, it is uncertain if this house was lived in/much used. But the house was kept by McEwan after he moved to London, after his wedding to Helen (in London). The house, 25 Palmerston Place, was William McEwan's first owned house since leaving the family home.

McEwan purchased a separate coach house in Rothesay Terrace in 1886. Post-1886, McEwan, William, Helen and Maggie rarely stayed at 25 Palmerston

Place, preferring to stay in hotels when visiting Edinburgh after the move to London. It was simpler and cost-effective, rather than having a number of servants employed and in situ for a property infrequently used.

It has been confirmed by a letter written by William McEwan's nephew (William McEwan Younger) that both McEwan and Maggie stayed at the Royal Hotel, Edinburgh, for the magnificent opening of the McEwan Hall on 2nd December 1897, and this hotel, according to press reports, was McEwan's normal choice.

Maggie inherited the property from her father when he died. Later Maggie donated the house to Edinburgh University. The house was used as a university hostel for a number of years. More recently, the house has been acquired by the Palmerston Trust (from 2011), providing religious activities, and is managed as a spiritual centre.

It is possible that building the business, Edinburgh society and the differences in their backgrounds, contributed to the various reasons for William McEwan waiting until Maggie was twenty-one years old before deciding to ensure Maggie's future (by marrying Helen, Maggie's mother). The marriage ensured a satisfactory place in society for his family. However, he did leave this decision until rather late.

THREE
Two Marriages

William McEwan adored Maggie; he was involved in her upbringing, and without his marriage to Helen Anderson in 1885, what would Maggie's future have been? The doors and houses of aristocratic London, international society, both royal and political, and many more important players on the world scene, would not have become her close "family". Writers, ambassadors, maharajahs, kings, queens, princes and princesses, dukes and duchesses, the British Royal family, were amongst the many who were to become Maggie's real friends. Such relationships and intimacy could never have existed without Maggie's parents marrying. This was the first magic key, which set Maggie on her route to being a star in society.

By the date (1885) of William McEwan's marriage to Helen (Maggie's mother) McEwan's brother John, had died (1875) from tuberculosis, at the Royal Edinburgh Asylum;[19] his mother died in 1879; his sister Anne died in 1882 of cancer of the stomach. Another brother, Peter, died aged thirteen (1830–44), but he was not relevant to the timing of this marriage. McEwan's sister Janet was married to James Younger, and their son William became an apprentice at McEwan's Fountainbridge Brewery in 1874. The two families remained close. Maybe one of the reasons McEwan delayed marrying Helen was simply due to Helen's different family background?

Additionally, McEwan had been busy building a large successful business from an initial outlay of £2,000, and this took a huge amount of energy and time. Also, Edinburgh society may have played a part in his delay, as Helen was not accepted in town society? Whatever his reasons for delaying the marriage until Maggie was twenty-one years old, he was certainly leaving the question of Maggie's future until rather late.

Was it the timing of being ready to leave the brewery to his nephew William (Younger) to run? Or his plan to become an MP in 1886? As a thinker and a planner, whatever the true cause for the delay, had McEwan not gone ahead with this marriage, then both Helen Anderson (mother) and Maggie Anderson (daughter) would have experienced a very different life. Maggie Greville, as she became, was able to become centre stage in society, dominated as it was by royalty and aristocrats and a political circle.

The marriage between Helen Anderson and William McEwan took place in London, at the parish church in the district of St Peter's Pimlico, in the county of Middlesex, on the 26th November 1885.[20] The wedding took place "according to the Rites and Ceremonies of the Established Church, by Special Licence". Maggie signed the wedding certificate as a witness in her name of MH Anderson. Maggie was twenty-one years old at this time. The other witness was G Nicholson.

McEwan stated that he was a bachelor and his father was John McEwan. Helen stated that her father was named Thomas Anderson. Helen also stated that she was a widow, which was untrue. The pretence of Helen having married previously was provided in this legal document. As I have stated, both McEwan and Helen were not previously married.

The timing of this marriage allowed for the introduction of Maggie with her parents to the aristocratic world, in which she later played such a major part. The marriage established a permanent change in Maggie's life. It is known that William McEwan was very close to Maggie, while she grew up in Edinburgh (personally and geographically re houses), but without the delayed marriage of her father to her mother, Maggie and Polesden Lacey's future would not have combined.

While 1885 provided the first owned house for McEwan (25 Palmerston Place, Edinburgh) since leaving home to begin his working career, it was also in 1885 that the move to London took place. The Edinburgh house may have been occupied, only briefly. It seems that the move to London was, as with all of McEwan's life, well planned.

Initially, on arriving in London, McEwan took a lease on 4 Chesterfield Gardens, Mayfair, as the base for himself, Helen and Maggie. It was from this London house that Maggie was launched into society.

Helen managed the running of a large house in London, and of looking after her husband and Maggie, in her new role in town. There are not many details of Helen's life at this point available.

Helen's attention to detail in looking after guests in her previous life would have been useful to her in her position in society. It is interesting to note later, that when Maggie (with Ronnie and without him) travelled abroad with her father – a cruise/South of France, and more trips – Helen did not usually accompany them. It is possible that Helen was less interested in foreign travel than her husband and her daughter, and did not wish to be too immersed in some aspects of a social life which were available to her. But she did make some friends, and she managed her new situation sufficiently well.

The move to London (McEwan kept ownership of the new house in Edinburgh) was, as with all of McEwan's planning, enabling not just Maggie's future, though no doubt this was a large part of his reasoning, but also, in 1886 he became MP for Edinburgh Central (Liberal). Becoming an MP is not something to be done on the spur of the moment, so it was useful to own a house in Edinburgh in addition to a London house.

The brewery was by this time being run by William Younger (McEwan's sister Janet and husband James Younger's son). William was left in charge of the brewery from 1885, "as long as he reported to William McEwan every day of his life how business was working" (wherever McEwan was in the world), then William Younger was in charge, technically becoming manager in 1886.

McEwan took a forty-four-year-long lease on 16 Charles Street from Lady-Day 25th March 1890, although Maggie's wedding reception in 1891, was at 4 Chesterfield Gardens.[21] Possibly McEwan had arranged for work to be undertaken at 16 Charles Street for some time, but he was paying ground rent of £360 per annum from March 1890 to the Berkeley estate.

Life in London for Helen and Maggie must have been very different from the years spent in Edinburgh. Being introduced into society, with McEwan's money and his ability, intelligence and shrewdness, provided the basis for Maggie to begin her journey in an aristocratic life she was not previously used to. However, her education had provided her with some skills (her father had seen to that); her inheritance of intelligence, shrewdness and ability to learn very quickly (from her father) meant that her understanding of what worked in society was quickly understood. Maggie was able to grasp what was required in any situation. She had a quick mind but also a thoroughness in her understanding of what may be needed, to encompass and to take things forward. Maggie (and McEwan and Helen) must have been aware of some criticism and opposition as the new people in town from some aristocrats. McEwan was, of course, sensible and shrewd, as well as being rich; there is some suggestion that he may have helped Edward VII with some of his finances (one of an ever-increasing number of people, during Edward VII's life). If so, McEwan was one of a number of people who contributed to the Prince of Wales/Edward VII's ability to stay afloat, in what were years of over-expenditure by the Prince/King.

This link may have been one of the reasons and ways Maggie was introduced to Ronald Greville (1864–1908), but this cannot be confirmed currently. The proximity of the Greville's London house at Cumberland Place, near to William McEwan's original home in London in Chesterfield Gardens, may have also helped their acquaintance.

It was known that before Maggie became engaged to Ronnie Greville, he had been looking for a rich wife. His parents were also looking for a wife on

Captain the Hon. Ronald Henry Fulke Greville (1864-1908) by Elliott and Fry (photographers) Baker Street, London

his behalf, as they needed an injection of funds into the family line. While the family's aristocratic line was most acceptable in society, a reduction of capital became the springboard for a search for a rich wife for Ronnie.

Questions are frequently asked about Ronnie Greville's family background, particularly Ronnie's connection to the Greville family, who owned Warwick Castle. Ronnie was descended from the second son (Algernon) of the 5th Earl of Warwick (1642–1710). Algernon did not inherit the "title, wealth or Warwick Castle". Ronnie's family continued as minor aristocrats and career soldiers over the next two centuries, firstly in England and then in Ireland. They were often short of money but made good marriages to keep afloat (hence the move to Ireland).

Ronnie's grandfather, Colonel Fulke Southwell Greville (1821–83), did particularly well and was created the 1st Baron Greville.[22] Ronnie's father Algernon (1841–1909) was the 2nd Baron Greville. Ronnie would have been the 3rd Baron Greville but he died on 5th April 1908, prior to his father dying in 1909, and therefore his younger brother Charles became the 3rd Baron. This title has ceased, as Charles had one legitimate son who had no heirs.

Ronnie was the eldest son of Baron Algernon Greville and his wife Lady Beatrice Violet Graham (born 1842, married 1863, died 1932), daughter of the fourth Duke of Montrose. They produced four children: two boys, Ronald and Charles, and two girls, Camilla and Veronique.

To provide clarity: the Greville family who owned Warwick Castle continued to own the castle until the 7th Earl of Warwick (Charles Guy, 1911–84) sold off much of the land and retired to Spain. Later, the 7th Earl of Warwick gave ownership of the castle to his son, the 8th Earl of Warwick (David Robin, 1934–96), who sold it to Tussauds in 1978 after selling off many artworks, including a Canaletto. The 9th Earl of Warwick (Guy David, born 1957) is the current holder of the title.

In Ronnie's search for a wife, he was linked to Virginia Daniel Bonynge, an American heiress; they became engaged in 1889.

Virginia Bonynge was presented at court after arriving in London in 1886.[23] A lady named Louise Mackay was also presented at court in 1886. She was married to John William Mackay.

Derogatory rumours were spread by the Bonynge and the Mackay families about each other as they entertained London society. A small book criticising the Bonynge family was circulated, and disparaging newspaper articles were published and sent to both families and acquaintances, while they were participating in the social scene. The two families had become wealthy from their businesses in America, and wanted to establish themselves in the Court Circle in London.

Virginia's social position was affected; news emerged that Virginia's real father was William Daniel, who had killed a man/or possibly shot a man but not killed him (newspaper articles suggest varying stories about this) while prospecting for gold, and he had been imprisoned in San Quentin.

Virginia's mother, Rodie Daniel, petitioned for his release and divorced Daniel (while he was in prison). Daniel died after his release in a place named Battle Mountain near Austin. Later, Rodie married Charles Bonynge, who adopted Virginia when she was five years old.

Virginia's stepfather, Charles Bonynge, and John William Mackay became enemies after falling out when they were in America. Mackay's business interests were in mining and cable/telegraph lines, and he had employed Bonynge as a broker. The arrangement ceased, and Bonynge attacked Mackay for his business schemes. This led to blows in the Nevada Bank in San Francisco in January 1891. Extreme social rivalry between both (wealthy) families continued when they were in London.

This news of the real background to Virginia's family reached Ronnie a considerable time after he became engaged to Virginia. *The New York Times/Town Topics* published numerous aspects of their backgrounds. Ronnie was presented with these details before/by 1891, and he asked the Bonynge family to tell him the truth regarding Virginia's parentage. On discovering that Virginia's mother Rodie was divorced, and that Virginia's real father had killed or injured a man, and had been imprisoned, Ronnie broke off the engagement without speaking to Virginia. Ronnie stated that "There had never been the slightest blemish on his lineage and his pride in his name meant that it was impossible to sully it with even such a remote slur". Some newspaper articles suggest that the dowry being offered by Virginia's stepfather Charles Bonynge to the Greville family was insufficient, but this may have been suggested to cloud what really happened.

Virginia did marry; she married Lord Deerhurst in March 1894, at the Church of All Saints, Kensington, as reported by *The New York Times*. It was also stated at the time that she brought a dowry of four million dollars to the marriage. Her stepfather gave her some stunning jewellery on her wedding day.

Had Ronnie made a mistake? Possibly not? In a very short timescale after breaking his engagement to Virginia, Ronnie became engaged to Maggie.

Were the Greville family (including Ronnie) aware that Maggie had been born illegitimately? Did McEwan present to the Greville family and London society a dignified family profile? Was McEwan's marriage to Helen in 1885 sufficiently far back to 1891 and therefore accepted without consideration? Was much known about this in London society? Certainly, people in Edinburgh society were aware of some of Maggie's background. Did McEwan help the Prince of Wales/King Edward VII out financially, as I suggested above? Did this provide a connection for the families? Did the promise of a large dowry (as invested stocks) provide the springboard for an agreement to the marriage? As the McEwan family had lived in London since 1885, they were known in town.

The second magic key was the marriage in 1891 of Margaret Anderson (Maggie) to Ronald Greville (Ronnie) on 25th April, at St Mark's, North Audley Street, London.[24] The Greville family were content for Ronnie to be married into a moneyed family, and for Maggie, Ronnie's connections brought the second magic key to the next stage in her life. She had the backing of her father William McEwan financially, and she was socially and mentally prepared for the transition into the finest of society, which she achieved by this marriage.

Maggie met Ronnie while she lived at Chesterfield Gardens, Mayfair. The wedding reception for her marriage to Ronnie was held there, and managed by her mother Helen, and naturally her father.

The Greville family did not possess an excess of money at this time, although the aristocratic line stretches back for many generations.

Who was Ronnie and what did he bring to the marriage? What he brought was considerable in one way, but not in another way. While Ronnie did not have much money: Ronnie had the connections!

Ronnie joined the Army after attending Rugby School. He was at Rugby School from 1874 to 1880. It is now established that, although it has previously been suggested that Ronnie met George Keppel whilst he was at Rugby, I can confirm that this is incorrect.[25] Rugby School have confirmed that, while Ronnie did attend Rugby, George Keppel did not. Their paths to meet were either because of Sandhurst – although possibly George graduated in a different year to Ronnie, (George initially joined the Gordon Highlanders and later the Norfolk Artillery) or in a social setting. Ronnie was, of course, in the 1st Life Guards.

It is not known how soon Ronnie joined the army after leaving school. Ronnie's army record states that he joined the Argyle and Sutherland Regiment as an ensign/cornet, but no date was recorded. On Ronnie's army record, it is stated that he was a 2nd Lieutenant in the 1st Life Guards, but there is no established date.[26]

However, the army has recorded that on 21st July 1886, he was promoted to 1st Lieutenant in the 1st Life Guards. The army also recorded that he became a Captain on 21st July 1892; this was an automatic time promotion. Ronnie did not travel abroad with the army. Ronnie was not involved in any campaigns; he did not hold any medals and was not given any staff appointments or manage campaigns. He resigned his commission on 24th June 1896.

This information was confirmed by the archivist at the Combermere Barracks, Windsor, where Ronnie was based and where his army records are held. As a member of the Household Cavalry, he was also stationed for some of the time at the Hyde Park Barracks (also known as the Knightsbridge Barracks), an extremely convenient place for a social life in town.

When Maggie met and married Ronnie, he was a Lieutenant, and he became a Captain just over a year after they were married.

King Edward VII (1841-1910)

What were his connections? Colonel in chief of Ronnie's Regiment (1st Life Guards) was Edward VII (from 1880 as Prince of Wales, then as King from 1901, until his death in 1910). Maggie, in marrying Ronnie, married into the Marlborough House Set.

Edward (as Prince of Wales) was given the lease of Marlborough House. and an annual income of £100,000 per year, when he married Princess Alexandra of Denmark in 1863. As Edward and Alexandra began to entertain friends at Marlborough House, the name the "Marlborough House Set" was established. Edward enjoyed having a wide variety of friends in his inner circle, as long as they were amusing, well mannered, sporting (often connected with horse racing) and wealthy. Victorian society was surprised, as he numbered wealthy Anglo-Jewish and American families as his friends.

Edward liked to meet his male friends at Whites Club. He asked the club if smoking could be allowed in the morning room of the club, but his request was turned down. Edward, as a great smoker, was not pleased. He went on to establish the Marlborough Club, and he selected the four hundred members and twenty-two founder members himself.[27]

This club was opposite Marlborough House, and it opened in 1869 and was funded by one of Edward's financial backers, James Mackenzie, with £18,000, in May 1868. Edward treated the club as an extension of his court and was present daily when at home in London. The club operated from 52 Pall Mall and was described as "a convenient and agreeable place of meeting for a Society of Gentlemen". (Windham, Orleans and the Marlborough Clubs amalgamated on 31st December 1945, forming the Marlborough-Windham Club. Rising costs and lack of candidates for admission forced the club to close in 1953.)

Ronnie's connections enabled Maggie to become friends with many of the members of the Marlborough House Set, many of whom became frequent visitors to Polesden Lacey and Charles Street. They included Sir Ernest Cassel; the Duke and Duchess of Devonshire; Portuguese Ambassador Marquis de Soveral; Arthur Balfour; Lord Curzon; Daisy, Duchess of Warwick; Alice and George Keppel; and they are all featured in photographs taken at Polesden Lacey.

To members, the "Prince's word was law". There was a strict code of honour (not to be confused with morality): "corridor creeping" was a stock feature of smart set house parties, but divorce was utterly unacceptable. No member could have an affair with an unmarried lady. That would have been social disaster for the man and total disaster for the lady. Their places in society would no longer exist. As Alice Keppel said more than once, "you have the heir and the spare, and after that you incorporate any further children into the family, without commenting on a likeness".

Culinary standards and correct modes of dress were very important. When staying at a country house for the weekend, the customary group photograph always featured Edward sitting in the centre, the hostess on his right and his mistress/es on his left but not immediately next to Edward.

Who Paid for Everything?

William McEwan, the entrepreneur, philanthropist and benefactor, a thinker and planner, did nothing spontaneously. Without William McEwan, Polesden Lacey would not exist today. Maggie Greville bequeathed Polesden Lacey to the National Trust, but William McEwan made the fortune that enabled her to do so. McEwan the brewer became McEwan the financier.

Once William McEwan became wealthy, he used his money to provide education, culture and support to a number of people and institutions.[28] He looked after his own family, in particular his brother John, who suffered real ill health until his death in 1875. McEwan paid £115,000 for the McEwan Hall, Graduation Hall, Edinburgh (in spite of being told it would cost approximately £40,000). He gave two Frans Hals paintings and a Rembrandt painting, *A Woman in a Bed*, to the National Gallery of Scotland (still on show today).

McEwan ensured Maggie's future by enabling her marriage to Ronnie, and in paying for the wedding, and providing the house in Charles Street. McEwan guaranteed an income for life for both Maggie and Ronnie. McEwan continued to finance Maggie's life, so the purchase of Polesden Lacey in Maggie's sole name was achieved, and he provided the continual finance for the upkeep of two houses. McEwan continued to fund the couple's lifestyle while Ronnie was alive and endorsed Maggie's ability to continue in society for ever more after her husband had died.

A piece of gossip (the *Gazette*) suggested that Helen Anderson (Maggie's mother) paid off Ronnie's debts and gave Ronnie £10,000 prior to his wedding to Maggie. This may/may not be true. Certainly money (more than this sum) would have been invested by William McEwan to finance Maggie and Ronnie's lives.

At the time of writing, I have no absolute proof as to a precise amount of money made available to Maggie and Ronnie, when they married. I do not believe that Ronnie was given access to the money directly, because his assets when he died in 1908 suggest otherwise. McEwan provided the couple with an income from a capital sum. What precisely that sum was, is not precisely known yet.

William McEwan is responsible directly for the successful purchase of Polesden Lacey because of the use of some of his fortune, and his instruction and management of Maggie, until his death in 1913.

McEwan created the platform for Maggie to gain connections in society, and to rise to the highest social level available. Ronnie enabled the transition, but without McEwan, Maggie as a young lady could not have offered Ronnie the stepping stone he required, which was a cash injection and guarantee, to maintain his lifestyle and position in society in 1891.

As the daughter of a lady/manageress of private rented accommodation, marrying Ronnie Greville, was certainly a successful move for Maggie, and beyond her younger aspirations, although not necessarily beyond her father's expectations. Clearly her father's success in business, politically and socially, made this dream possible. McEwan had left until rather late his marriage to Maggie's mother, Helen. But the marriage was part of the catalyst for bringing Maggie to live in London, and the springboard (supplied by William McEwan) for Maggie's new life beginning to reach up through the levels of society as it then existed.

Ronnie not having too much in the way of finance was not a problem; McEwan intended to, and did, finance Maggie's life as a married lady.

The second magic key for Maggie was provided by the wedding which took place at St Mark's, North Audley Street, on 25th April 1891 at 2.30pm.[29] The church was filled with palms and numerous flowers. There were four bridesmaids: Ronnie's sister Veronique, Miss Colville, Miss Hodgkinson and Miss Parker. There was a young page who carried Maggie's train, and he wore a white satin Tudor-style outfit.

The best man was Captain John Glynn Richards Homfray, a friend and fellow officer in the Life Guards. Both Ronnie and Richard Homfray had similarities in their backgrounds. Ronnie was from Ireland, and Richard Homfray from Wales. Both belonged to declining aristocracies. Homfray's family lived in Penllyn Castle, Cowbridge, South Wales. They were both interested in horse racing and both became amateur jockeys. While Ronnie was not very successful, Homfray was involved in breeding, and he raced his own horses with moderate success. Homfray named one horse Land League (a yearling he bought from the 4th Earl of Dunraven) and the horse won thirty-nine races out of fifty-nine. Land League ran in the Cambridgeshire Handicap in 1907, one of Newmarket's most important races.

Maggie's wedding dress was made of white satin, trimmed with lace and orange blossom.[30] Her veil was made of fine lace and held on her head by five diamond stars Ronnie had given her. Ronnie also gave Maggie a diamond and ruby heart which she wore on the day. The bridesmaids wore pink bengaline dresses and white (transparent) hats. Helen McEwan wore a sapphire blue dress, decorated with small pink roses, and a long-skirted coat. Ronnie's mother, Lady Greville, wore a dark bengaline dress with jet and which had sleeves of moss green. Her bonnet was decorated with shaded pansies.

McEwan gave Maggie diamonds: a tiara made up of three rivieres, all stunning; also, he gave her a diamond spray which could be worn as a brooch, or taken apart as three separate hair or dress ornaments. Helen McEwan gave Maggie a beautiful travelling bag made of dark crocodile skin, and fitted with every personal item a lady would need; it also included writing equipment.

Lord Greville (Ronnie's father) gave Maggie a bracelet of emeralds and diamonds (alternative and equal in size), and Ronnie's mother Lady Greville gave a beautiful cross of turquoise set in diamonds. There is a full list of jewellery which Maggie received on her wedding to Ronnie, and of the fabulous jewellery she acquired in her life, detailed in Chapter 18. There were many other wedding gifts, including some given with such thought: a total of 468 men from McEwan's brewery gave the "Silver Monteith Bowl" to the couple, and a pair of candelabra. The 1st Life Guards gave Ronnie a tankard, and Maggie was given a pretty fan by them.

McEwan also provided, a lease of a house in Deanery Street (Mayfair) for the newly married couple (owned by the Concurry family). McEwan gave a dinner for five hundred of his workmen at the Music Hall in Edinburgh, to celebrate his daughter's wedding.

Maggie's and Ronnie's wedding reception was held at 4 Chesterfield Gardens (the house McEwan leased when he brought Helen and Maggie to live in London in 1885). The house was filled (both in the entrance hall and the main reception rooms) with palms, white flowers almost everywhere, and roses and orchids. The wedding breakfast was sumptuous.

After all of the celebrations were completed, Maggie and Ronnie departed for the first part of their honeymoon at Oatlands Park, Weybridge, Surrey. A little later they travelled abroad, and Maggie's famous portrait (at the top of the stairs in the Central Hall at Polesden Lacey) was painted by Carolus-Duran in 1891, while they were in Paris on honeymoon.

Later, William McEwan provided Maggie and Ronnie with number 11 Charles Street as a permanent home, after the couple had temporarily used the house in Deanery Street. Work on 11 Charles Street was undertaken.

William McEwan acquired number 16 Charles Street for Helen and himself in 1890, as stated above.

FOUR

Life as a Married Lady

Maggie with her background could never have been a debutante, but Ronnie's grandmother, the Duchess of Montrose, presented Maggie at Court on 17th May 1892, in the afternoon. This meant that Maggie was on the Court list. The season included presentations at Court, the Derby, Royal Ascot, Henley, Goodwood, Cowes Regatta, Court functions and debutante balls, filling many dates in diaries.

Maggie settled down to life as a married lady in society, although some social opposition existed, and was enacted towards her as she was without an old aristocratic background. However, as she entertained the future King Edward VII, and was included totally in the Marlborough House Set, acceptance began to be established. She became a successful hostess, backed by McEwan and with Ronnie's social contacts.

Married life for Maggie was comfortable (McEwan ensured this).

Ronnie provided the background/the stage set in terms of connections, and Maggie participated and transitioned (with her father's backing) into the beginning of the "career" she was to establish as an aristocratic hostess.

Ronnie's resignation from the army in 1896 was due to Maggie's encouragement to him to stand for Parliament. He had already tried to win the Barnsley seat in 1895 in the General Election and failed, although he was considered to have done quite well.

On 10th November 1896 Ronnie Greville won the Bradford East by-election, which was caused by the death of the previous MP, Mr Byron Reed – Conservative.[31] The results were: Captain Greville, Conservative, 4,921 votes; Mr Alfred Bilson, Liberal, 4,526 votes; and Keir Hardie, Labour, 1,953 votes. When the result was announced, Ronnie was cheered as he proceeded from the town hall to the Central Conservative Club. The Constituency had witnessed the highest turnout ever recorded.

In his election address to the voters of Bradford East dated 28th October 1896, Ronnie stated that, "In respect to legislation for the amelioration of the lot of the working classes, I heartily endorse the past policy of Conservatism, which, in the face of adverse Radical opposition has secured for the working men the free right of combination, absolute equality before the law, the whole beneficial system of Factory Legislation which is their chief protection against unscrupulous employers, abolition of the Truck Acts, and the foundation of the National System of Education."

Ronnie did look after his constituency. Maggie visited the area on a number of occasions to help and to show care for the locals, including attending fetes. An example of Maggie's activity in Bradford East took place on Saturday 16th January 1904. Maggie hosted an "at home" in the constituency at the Great Northern Victoria Hotel.[32] Maggie had chosen the hotel for convenience and comfort for her guests; Maggie received 350 ladies as her guests, who were "her personal friends among the workers. After being received by Mrs Greville, the large company sat down to tea".

The programme of music consisted of six artistes: a soprano, Miss Maud Sugden; a contralto, Miss Elsie Bradley; a tenor, Mr Vincent Ward; a bass player, Mr Harry Horner; a "refined humourist", Mr GW Stocks; and accompanist Mr C Stott. The occasion followed the annual dance of the Eastern Division of the Primrose League.

Five hundred members attended the dance. Ronnie was a member of the Grand Council of the League, which was part of the social side of the Conservative Party.[33] The league was formed as a result of Disraeli's death; he recognised the need to attract more working-class voters. The primrose was Disraeli's favourite flower. Lord Randolph Churchill was one of the founders of the league in 1883, which was established to reach out to these voters.

Ronnie spoke in Parliament eleven times, usually to ask a question (recorded). He was not known as a great speaker. His only full speech was made in seconding the address to the throne, on 17th February 1903. He remained an MP until he resigned just prior to the general election of 1906; electioneering began from 12th January and lasted until the result on 8th February 1906. Thereafter, Ronnie appeared to enjoy his life without too many commitments.

Maggie had by now developed her position in society. She was comfortable with the blessing of being in the Marlborough House Set, and with her intelligence, shrewdness and intuition, she was able to entertain kings, queens, princes, princesses, dukes, duchesses, maharajahs, earls, lords, ladies, politicians and friends with ease. Her father's money made everything possible. Her father's influence and his acumen ensured a passage of success in society.

Ronnie provided the coded access of a place in the Marlborough House Set. His aristocratic line, including his background, appeared to be first-class, enabling this transition; however, without McEwan's money, Maggie would not have been able to create and manage the position of an increasingly pivotal hostess in society. Maggie's father continued to provide financial support and advice to Maggie throughout his life (and, after his death, by his bequests to Maggie).

Maggie's father gave her (and Ronnie) number 11 Charles Street as a permanent home a short while after they were married. Work was undertaken on this house by C Mellier, a fashionable architect and decorator. The location of the house was (and is, as it remains today), in one of the most fashionable and acceptable parts of London for society; for entertaining and to be entertained. The street can be accessed from the south-west side of Berkeley Square.

Maggie and Ronnie had many friends in the Marlborough House Set. Weekends away at country houses with Prince Edward and the rest of the set became "the new normal" for Maggie and Ronnie. No doubt it was while Maggie visited other large country houses, that she learnt (although Ronnie would have been aware from an early age), what a weekend spent in the country really meant.

They wished to acquire a country house for their entertaining. It was not enough to only have a house in London, no matter how fashionable the area was.

Maggie travelled with her father and sometimes Ronnie, during the early years of her marriage. In 1899 William McEwan commissioned the yacht SY *Rona* for a holiday, which included the Prince of Wales, Grand Duke Michael and Grand Duke Cyril of Russia, Countess de Torby, Alice and George Keppel, Sydney Greville (Equerry to the Prince of Wales), Duchess of Manchester and Alex Colebrooke, plus McEwan and Maggie, and Ronnie for some of the trip.[34] Maggie, in her handwritten journal (written in March, April and May of that year), stated that she had become very comfortable with her position.

The yacht *Steel Screw Steamer Schooner* had been built in 1893 by D & W Henderson & Co, Glasgow, at the Meadowside Yard. The ship was initially owned by AHE Wood of Rugby, followed by Baron Ferdinand de Rothschild's ownership by 1895 and sold on to Arthur Dupree in 1899 (as reported by *The Scotsman*, 19th May 1899). In later years the ownership of the ship continued to evolve.

Ronnie came out from England for some of this trip. Ronnie was with Maggie at the beginning of the journey (28th March) and when the SY *Rona* reached Catania, Sicily (4th April). Ronnie departed on 24th April to return to England from Constantinople. Maggie did not note on which ship Ronnie travelled back to England. Maggie's journal began as the yacht SY *Rona* journeyed through the Mediterranean Sea from France (Monaco), then moved on to Italy, Ajaccio, Sicily, Corfu, Greece, Constantinople, Corsica and Sardinia.

Maggie made a comment in her journal of this holiday: "Ronnie left for England – and I went to… and, after luncheon I accompanied…". No comments were made of how much she might miss Ronnie, just that he departed. This suggests the marriage worked comfortably for both of them but was not necessarily overladen with romance? Her father continued to travel with her, and all of the costs were paid by McEwan. There is a gap in these pages from 6th April to 23rd April – missing pages.

A newspaper article (*The Scotsman*, 19th May 1899, as above) confirmed that William McEwan was back at the Houses of Parliament the previous night and had recovered from a chest infection while away on this cruise.

William McEwan was a Liberal MP from 1886 to 1900, as member for Edinburgh Central.

From this article we learnt that Crete was one of the places that McEwan visited with Maggie and their guests. It seems that the two weeks of missing pages must have included this particular visit to the island.

The newspaper article said that Crete was undergoing change, which was an understatement, as the Great Powers (Britain, France, Italy, Austria-Hungary and Russia) intervened in 1897 as the Ottoman Empire had lost control of the island. It was declared autonomous with suzerainty granted to the Ottoman Empire, until the island passed to Greece in 1913, following the close of the Balkan Wars. As a place to visit, it must have been beautiful in 1899: quite wild yet stunning.

Aristocratic travel was usually undertaken in the winter months (from just after Christmas until the end of April/very beginning of May), in order to be back in London for the season to commence.

With Ronnie as her husband, Maggie engaged with the position society offered her, which was assisted by McEwan's expertise and money. Any jealous criticisms from old aristocratic families were insufficient to affect her social standing, given the longevity of the Greville family line of which she had become part. Aristocrats, whoever they were, had made money, even if this had been accomplished a long time previously: from land ownership (in Great Britain and elsewhere), mining, industrial companies run by their families, and ownership of companies established abroad, and also large country estates. The source of their finances had to come from (possibly from long-standing ownership) the contribution of hard work, from people who were employed by them.

While the aristocrats did not like talking about money, they used it. They assumed they had it. Maggie now had an unassailable security blanket which allowed her to elevate her position as an important hostess in society; with William McEwan's guaranteed money, combined with Ronnie's background, her place on the foremost stage of society was set. Plus, there was the bounty of Edward VII's blessing. No aristocrat would have wanted to exclude themselves from the court through unsociable behaviour towards Maggie and Ronnie by being too negative.

A stunning black and white photograph of Maggie was taken by Lafayette (James Stack Lauder) on 5th October 1900 at his studio, 179 Bond Street, London.[35]

Lafayette was an extremely fashionable and important society photographer. Maggie was seated and was wearing a beautiful dress, which has been recreated and is usually on show at Polesden Lacey.

This particular photograph appeared in several publications: 5th October 1901, *Candid Friend*, page 894; 11th February 1903, the *Car*, front page; 16th April 1904, the *Queen*, front page; and 18th May 1912 in *Gentlewoman*. Confusion has previously existed about the dating of the photograph, but I can confirm 1900 as being correct, therefore Maggie was thirty-seven years old. Lafayette photographed most of the guests at the Duchess of Devonshire's 1897 Ball (a famous and extraordinary Ball) at Devonshire House in Piccadilly. Maggie's photograph at that event was taken by Alice Hughes, another society photographer who was available.

FIVE

Entertaining Royalty – the Country House

Maggie entertained most of the key members of society in London, but by 1900 she was aware that she needed a country house. Other aristocrats entertained in their country houses at the weekend. Maggie wanted to be able to do this too. The weekend (Saturday to Monday) was a way of entertaining each other away from London, but more importantly entertaining royalty. Edward VII and Alice Keppel, along with members of the Marlborough House Set, stayed with Maggie and Ronnie when they entertained at Reigate Priory; Maggie and Ronnie rented the house (for a number of weekends) from Lady Henry Somerset (née Somers) – who had inherited the house in 1883 from Charles Somers, 3rd Earl – from time to time. This meant they had a foothold in this part of Surrey for entertaining, which allowed them the opportunity to house hunt for a permanent country home.

The Reigate constituency interviewed Ronnie in 1903 as a possible successor to the Hon Roland Cubitt for a seat in Parliament. Although Ronnie stated that he was not interested in January 1904 in winning that seat (he telegraphed a formal denial). However, it appears that the committee, which included Sir Trevor Lawrence and others, had considered Ronnie, and had gone as far as to issue a statement on the prospect of Ronnie being accepted for the constituency. Ronnie, of course, was the MP for East Bradford at the time. While this may be gossip, as discussions were confirmed, this part of Surrey was clearly an area which appealed to both Maggie and Ronnie.

Maggie bought Polesden Lacey on 22nd February 1907 (conveyance document) for £80,000.[36] This money was given to Maggie by her father William McEwan. The house was legally transferred to Maggie in her sole name. While Ronnie was very much alive, the money was, of course, McEwan's and he wanted to ensure his daughter retained his money (and therefore her property) in her own legal right.

Edward VII and Alice Keppel (and other guests staying for the weekend) were taken to see this house while staying at Reigate Priory (as Maggie and Ronnie's guests for the weekend), and they inspected the building work. The date for this visit was 19th May 1907. The guests were all members of the Marlborough House Set.

The architects Mewes & Davis oversaw approximately eighteen months work to modify, extend, refurbish and upgrade Polesden Lacey. With their guidance and management, the house was transformed into Maggie's new country house. Most of the work was undertaken by White Allom (an interior decorating company and an antique reclamation company), and Jackson's the Plasterers, who upgraded the ceilings, coving and décor.

Meves and Davis completed the Ritz Hotel, Piccadilly, London in 1906 (a newly built property). It was one of the earliest substantial steel-frame structures in London, the Savoy Hotel extension of 1903–04 being the first in the capital.

The site for the Ritz was originally the home of the Old White Horse Cellar (a famous coaching inn), followed by the Walsingham House Hotel and the Bath Hotel on this same site, which were demolished in 1904. Mewes & Davis designed the outside and inside of the Ritz, totally. A plaque is fixed to the front right-hand wall of the hotel, confirming their names as architects to the Ritz, with the completion date of 1906.

Background to Polesden Lacey

The various owners of Polesden Lacey provide a fascinating background to the timeline of the property. The position of Polesden Lacey and the surrounding acreage, enabled it to maintain its desirability.

The later owners were, post-1747:[37] Lord North, 2nd Earl of Guildford, who inherited Polesden Lacey from William Moore in 1746. The sale notice is dated 1747 to Captain Francis Geary; sale completed by 1748.

In 1795 the house was transferred to William (Francis Geary's son) and William provided a lease to Richard Brinsley Sheridan in 1797, which was managed by Sheridan and his wife's financial backers Charles Grey and Samuel Whitbread. Charles Grey took on the legal liability for Polesden Lacey.

Unfortunately, while Sheridan was at Polesden Lacey, he made a difference of more harm than good. Upon obtaining a lease on Polesden Lacey, Sheridan declared it was the prettiest house in England. He began to make changes to the property.

By 1813 Sheridan had made Polesden Lacey uninhabitable, because of his improvements, which allowed little of the roof to remain intact. Sheridan was lucky to be helped out by the Prince Regent – the future George IV – and the generosity of some of George's aristocratic friends, which enabled Sheridan to live at Randalls Park, Leatherhead, after he (Sheridan) had rendered Polesden uninhabitable. Sheridan later fell out with the Prince Regent after receiving this help, in 1813.

Randalls Park was a timbered house, owned by Sir John Coghill until 1812, but by 1813 it was owned by Nathaniel Bond (the timescale for Sheridan moving to Randalls Park was c.1813). By 1856 Randalls Park was owned by Robert Henderson, whose son John lived there. Randalls Park was pulled down later (date unknown). The land has been established as both a cemetery and a crematorium for some time.

Sheridan died in 1816. In 1817 Charles Grey transferred Polesden Lacey to Charles Brinsley Sheridan (RB Sheridan's son).

William Geary's father Francis Geary died in 1796. When Sheridan died in 1816, leaving a ruin, it took until 5th August 1818 for the legal work to be completed by William Geary (Francis Geary's son) so the house could to be sold to Joseph Bonsor, who bought a ruin with only 318 acres for £10,000. Bonsor was a wholesale stationer and bookseller (originally from Nottingham). Additionally, Bonsor supplied *The Times* newspaper with its paper – the source of his fortune.

Once Bonsor acquired the property, he had the ruin demolished. It was the correct approach. Bonsor asked Thomas Cubitt to build a grand house. The main body of the house was built between 1821 and 1823. There were some additional items fitted up to 1825, which included furniture.

The parkland was laid out and large quantities of trees were planted. Bonsor (who had originally spent £10,000, as stated above) paid Thomas Cubitt more than £46,900 in total for the new house, and for the parkland to be improved.

Joseph Bonsor's son Joseph (junior), inherited Polesden Lacey from his father in 1835. The house was sold to Walter Rockcliffe Farquhar in 1853 for approximately £37,000.

Walter gave Polesden Lacey to his son Thomas in 1862. Thomas Farquhar sold Polesden Lacey in 1902 to Sir Clinton Dawkins for £60,000. Dawkins died in 1905 and his widow Lady Dawkins sold Polesden Lacey to Maggie Greville in 1907.

On purchasing the house Sir Clinton Dawkins demolished most of it, as he wanted a new house for his wife Louise to entertain their friends. Sir Clinton Dawkins employed Sir Ambrose Macdonald Poynter as the architect for his new house; he was the grandson of Ambrose Poynter, one of the early members of the Institute of British Architects, which was established in 1834.

In 2014 the Cambridge Architectural Research Company (CARC) compiled a Historic Buildings Analysis Report of Polesden Lacey.[38] Using the 1935 ground-floor plan, and based on the electrical installation drawings of Higgins & Griffiths, and from archive material, CARC established that the part of Polesden Lacey which was retained by Ambrose Poynter for Sir Clinton Dawkins, and therefore designed by Thomas Cubitt for Joseph Bonsor (between 1821–23) was as follows: the Saloon (Gold Room), and as we already understand, the pillars on the south terrace; the small sitting room (Tea Room); one other small sitting room was retained, which is in front (east) of the Saloon (now incorporated into the Library). Nothing else was retained.

Poynter designed a large house in 1903 for Sir Clinton Dawkins, which included the Central Hall, the curved Dining Room, the Courtyard, the Billiard Room, the Smoking Room, and the kitchen and back-of-house/servant areas, and the Tea Room west terrace. All of these were added to the retained rooms (as above).

For the most part, a new house was built and completed by 1905 for Sir Clinton Dawkins. Possibly a little plain inside, as there were many plain white walls and flat white ceilings to the ground floor. However, if Sir Clinton had lived longer, he may well have embellished these areas.

Sir Clinton Dawkins was a fascinating man. He worked for the government, using his expertise on a number of financial committees. He also worked for Lord Curzon, who was Governor of India from 1899. Sir Clinton was headhunted by JP Morgan opening their first bank in London in 1900 and became a full partner in this branch. He continued to work for the government (part time), because they did not want to lose him. In 1902 he was made a Knight Commander of the Order of Bath, in the Coronation honours list, because of his work chairing the review of the administration of the War Office.

Dawkin's sudden death of heart disease, aged forty-six, in 1905, allowed a suitable location and house to be available for the couple (Maggie and Ronnie), who were already residing locally at the weekends at Reigate Priory and were looking for a permanent country home.

Sir Clinton Dawkins died from a heart attack on 2nd December 1905. Polesden Lacey came on to the market in 1906. Maggie Greville purchased the property on 22nd February 1907 with William McEwan's money. Ronnie's name was not on the legal document (Ronnie was very much alive). Maggie bought and owned the house in her sole name.

Margaret Greville's purchase of Polesden Lacey in 1907, is clearly stated on the Conveyance Deed of Transfer of the legal title of Polesden Lacey on 22nd February 1907 (as above). The conveyance was made between the then mortgagees of the estate (1); the personal representatives of Clinton Edward Dawkins (Viscount Milner, Cyril Earle Johnston, and Lady Dawkins) (2); and Lady Dawkins (3); and Mrs Greville (4). Clinton Dawkins had taken out a mortgage of £40,000 on 30th September 1902.

Clinton Dawkins' Will, was dated, 28th January 1903. Apart from specific bequests, he bequeathed his estate to his wife Lady Dawkins. At the date of death of Clinton Dawkins, the mortgage remained outstanding. "The sale of Polesden Lacey" to Margaret Greville was agreed by the personal representatives and Lady Dawkins at a sum of £80,000, but that £40,000 would be paid to the mortgagees and the remaining £40,000 paid to the personal representatives. The conveyance document confirms the repayment of the outstanding mortgage and the transfer of Polesden Lacey to Mrs R Greville.

The whole of Polesden Lacey estate transferred by the conveyance, comprised nine hundred acres, two roods and thirty-four perches made up of the mansion and grounds and woodlands; Polesden Farm and land described as part of a park, Goldstone Farm, Yew Tree Farm and Bagden Farm.

Polesden Lacey is situated in a stunning position on a hill and now consists of approximately 1,400 acres of parkland. After purchase in 1907, it required work for Maggie to be able to provide a sumptuous house and parkland for her guests.

As the house was reasonably plain inside when Maggie purchased it, there was work to be done to transform Polesden Lacey into the house Maggie decided she wanted. This work was organised/planned and executed by Mewes & Davis (architects), whom Maggie employed after they had completed the building of the Ritz Hotel in London (as stated earlier).

Some of Mewes & Davis' ideas used at the Ritz translated well to Polesden Lacey, for example in bathroom styles for Maggie's en-suite bathroom. The creation of the Saloon, with its panelling, was from an eighteenth-century Italian palazzo which had been demolished, and the pieces were in store in Italy, and were brought to Polesden Lacey and fitted into what was an ordinary drawing room. This glitzy (new) room reminded visitors of the London Ritz Hotel's ground-floor rooms.

William McEwan's money allowed Maggie to have the best of everything she wanted.

The £80,000 purchase price of Polesden in 1907 was the starting point for much more expenditure to bring the house up to the standard required for Maggie's entertaining: extensions were required, glamorous fixtures and fittings, with en-suite bathrooms and bedrooms and rooms to entertain in. "I want a room fit for kings, queens and maharajahs, she said to Mewes & Davis, this being (now) the Saloon, otherwise colloquially known as the Gold Room. Electrical light fittings were installed (Maggie's maids did not have to work by candlelight), and much of the house embellished by panelling.

Mewes & Davis planned and oversaw the extensions, refurbishment and additional decorative work executed at Polesden Lacey between 1907 and 1908, employing two important companies for the interior of Polesden Lacey: White Allom and Jackson's the Plasterers.

From 1907, after Maggie purchased the house, Mewes & Davis' work included a number of changes: an extension to the kitchen, modifications to back-of-house/servant areas and some modifications to the inner courtyard. The most significant changes Mewes & Davis designed for the ground floor of the house were: the creation of a Library by extending it from a small sitting room, and the addition of the Study, with windows facing south and east.[39]

The building of the new Library enabled Mewes & Davis to create Maggie's private apartment upstairs, which included her Boudoir (sitting room), her bedroom and an en-suite bathroom with two sinks (intended, as it was, to be shared with Ronnie), a bath and toilet. Maggie and Ronnie were to have a delightful bedroom overlooking the gardens on the south side. A corridor was created to provide a walkway to a room for Ronnie (as his dressing room), and a large bedroom for William McEwan (again on the south side), as he was the benefactor and financier of the whole project.

Additionally, nine of the fifteen guest bedrooms were made en suite. Many other detailed modifications were completed, to first and second floors.

High expenditure provided by a loving father.

Electricity was extended; Dawkins had already installed a generator. Some light fittings were purchased as electrical, others, such as the 1860 chandelier by Baccarat in the saloon, were acquired by White Allom and converted to electricity.

In 1880 William Armstrong electrified Cragside, Rothbury, with incandescent lamps, with the help of Joseph Swan. This was the first house in the world to have electricity (hydro-electricity), and this "fact" is accepted by historians. Some twenty-seven/twenty-eight years later, electricity was available to those rich enough to afford it. For Maggie and Ronnie's new house, central heating was extended through the house. Plumbing too offered indoor and en-suite bathrooms, if you had sufficient funds.

When Maggie purchased Polesden Lacey, the left front of the property (looking towards the front door from the front driveway) was set back very much. The right-hand side of the property was projected forward, so there was an imbalance. Mewes & Davis designed the extension to the house, by building forward the left-hand side of the property. A library was created from a small sitting room (this library became approximately two thirds longer than the pre-existing small sitting room); a small lobby was added as an entrance to the new study.

The Study has an unusual feature; it includes a small cloakroom as well as a lift (fitted in 1917), but the remarkable thing about this room is that Maggie wanted the view to the front and east of the house, and also the view from the south side of the room, overlooking the gardens, including the view across towards Ranmore.

As this room was built on, Mewes & Davis organised for a fireplace to be built along the south wall, with a window immediately above the fireplace. In order to do this, the fire had a flue which lead across to the left-hand side of the fire at an angle and travelled upwards behind the first section of the bookcase, which was on the left-hand side of the fire. The chimney itself was built to the left of the fireplace (as viewed from inside the room). So, the chimney was not above the fireplace. While this may seem to be remarkable, there are some other examples (few) in the UK. This fireplace was plain, unlike the other richer/antique fireplaces which were in place throughout the house, which were supplied by White Allom.

In France during the Belle Epoque period (1871–1914), a number of fireplaces were installed in France which work in this manner. While building them to be effective may not have been simple, they must have been reasonably successful. Mewes (and possibly Davis) would have understood how to make this fire function.

Maggie enjoyed having so much space and light in her study, and the use of this fireplace which, while unusual, must have worked. In the evenings, sitting in the Study after dinner, with one of her fascinating guests (a king, queen, maharajah, a prime minister or another politician) and having a tête-à-tête with the person she selected prior to re-joining the other guests, must have boosted Maggie's importance. Maggie must have enjoyed being able to elicit information and follow this with advice or suggestions for action, both politically and socially.

Other guests would have been in the Saloon enjoying the entertainment she provided (actors, singers, musicians and dancers, mostly from London clubs and theatres), or alternatively playing cards and billiards. The Study must have been a rather special place.

It should be noted that the lift was installed in 1917, some ten years after Maggie purchased Polesden Lacey.

The lift was useful in Maggie's early days to provide privacy, by enabling Maggie to remain in her bedroom or study, and not meeting her guests in the early morning. Maggie could talk to her staff by pressing a bell in the room to summon someone; she was able to remain in the Study without moving.

In Maggie's later years, the lift enabled Maggie to go up or down the stairs, without walking through the rest of the house when she was less able.

Maggie's Head Chauffeur, Sidney Smith, was able to bring the car to the front of the house, just outside the Study, which meant Maggie could exit by an additional outside door from the lift to a small corridor, and go out to the car with very little walking.

George Jackson & Sons Ltd were London manufacturers who specialised in mouldings and the casting of decorative plasterwork for interiors.

Previous information has suggested that Jackson's commenced as a company as early as 1780. This has been disproved by Marion May, a descendant of the Jackson family.[40] George Jackson began his career by 1805 supplying glue to businesses, and by 1811 was supplying moulds to make picture frames.

While three out of four sons worked with their father initially (a son William had emigrated to India). By 1833 another son, George, had departed from the company. John and Thomas continued to work with their father. In

1850 George Jackson died. In 1851 the partnership between John and Thomas was dissolved. John became the only member of the Jackson family to be involved with the company from 1851. John was actively involved in the Great Exhibition of 1851.

"John introduced the use of fibrous plaster into the country. He bought the patent rights in 1856 from Owen Jones, the architect, who had acquired it from the inventor, French modeller De Sachet. The plaster was combined with canvas and built up in the workshop."

In a Jackson catalogue from 1902, numerous advantages were listed for this method, including "great lightness, increased strength" (due to the fibre in the plaster) and "simplicity in fixing". In 1868 John retired; his sons John Junior and Edward Elliot ran the company until the early twentieth century. Jackson's became a limited company in 1910.

The last member of the Jackson family to be involved in the company was Edward Elliot's son, Edward Francis (known as Mr Frank).

Frank became a freeman of the City of London aged twenty-four and was a member of the Worshipful Company of Painters-Stainers. Frank married Mary Nona Holland in 1907. The Holland family were furniture makers.

Edward's son, Mr Frank, helped to run Jackson's during 1907–08, when Polesden Lacey was upgraded, extended and embellished.

In 1934 Jackson & Sons moved to Rainville Road, Hammersmith. (Mr Frank) Jackson sold the company in 1947. He died three years later.

George Jackson's as a company continues to this day. A number of different owners have acquired Jackson's since 1947 and sold the company on; the present company is now based in Sutton, Surrey. I visited the works in 2009, and I was able to see some of the original moulds dating back as far as the history of the company.

The earliest record of Jackson's work was the Royal Pavilion Brighton between 1815 and 1822. Later Jackson's worked on Buckingham House, London, helping to convert it into a palace for George IV, who became Regent in 1811 and King in 1820, so possibly this work was executed after 1820?

Years later Jackson's worked for Queen Victoria at Osborne House. Osborne House was bought by Victoria and Albert in 1845, demolished in 1848 and the new Osborne House built, much of it completed by 1851. In 1902 Jackson's were still working for Buckingham Palace. Four Royal warrants were obtained from William IV, Victoria, Edward VII and George V. This would naturally have impressed Maggie.

One of the leading modellers and wood carvers who worked for George Jackson's was Walter Stiles (1861–1938), who was great-grandfather to one of the current volunteers at Polesden Lacey.[41] The start date for Walter working at Jackson's the Plasterers is not precisely known, but certainly by 1881 (as confirmed by a census when he was living at 16 Raphael Street, Westminster). Walter worked at 49/50 Rathbone Place and lived two miles away from his work at that time. Walter became an architectural modeller by 1911.

Walter Stiles married Elizabeth Sarah Dury in 1884, and after their marriage they lived at Wendell Road, followed by Rylett Road, both in Shepherd's Bush, five miles from his work. Walter's skills were recognised, and it was claimed that "he was the best-paid man in his trade in London" although this did not make him a wealthy man. He was not known as a designer but as "a hands-on man". Walter created complex moulds and was a superb craftsman who took immense pride in his work. He created more complex moulds than many of the other workers. He carved moulds using boxwood and mixtures of whiting, glue, resin and linseed oil known as "composition" which was pressed into the moulds, which in turn created detailed moulds which were light and were easy to apply to a ceiling or wall.

Walter worked for fifty years at Jackson's, including the time Polesden Lacey was extended and refurbished for Maggie Greville. Three years after he retired, he moved in 1933 to Stoke Fleming (a village near Dartmouth), where he died in 1938.

The work executed by Jackson's the Plasterers was always of the highest standard. The company worked throughout the world. The plasterwork at Polesden Lacey, which included the Jacobean vaulted ceiling in the long south corridor, was created by Jackson's from a flat white ceiling. The design of the ceiling was copied from Chastleton House, Chastleton, near Moreton-in-Marsh, from their first-floor large wide gallery.

The ceiling in Maggie's Boudoir was copied from the ceiling of the globe room at the Reindeer Inn, Banbury (a property and room which has experienced a fascinating history).

There was a large, damaging fire at Polesden Lacey in 1960.[42] When the work to restore the house (the contents were mostly saved, but there was considerable damage to the building, particularly upstairs) was undertaken, this particular room was once again treated by George Jackson & Sons, who carried out remedial work to the plasterwork in the ceiling in October 1961. Maggie's choice of Jackson's was recognisable because of its trading history and links to Mewes & Davis.

White Allom was the other important company who worked at Polesden Lacey when Mewes & Davis made many changes to the house – changes which remain untouched to this day. I met with two directors of White Allom in 2009; they came to Polesden Lacey for a meeting I arranged. Four of us (colleagues) at Polesden Lacey met with the two directors. Charming as they were, they had no historical documents. No archive material to share with us. The company had undergone a number of changes of ownership through the years; seemingly much historical documentation was lost. What we do know is that White Allom were originally designers and were employed directly (not as subcontractors) on clients' commissions. At any one time they employed twenty to thirty traders/workers.

Thomas Allen (1804–72) was an architect and artist. He designed many buildings in London.[43] He was also a topographical illustrator. He worked with Sir Charles Barry on a number of projects, including the Houses of Parliament; he remodelled Highclere Castle, and buildings in Liverpool and Hull. He travelled extensively and produced topographical illustrations from his travels of the UK, Europe and Asia.

Thomas's son Arthur became successful as an architect; he became President of the Architectural Association and an associate member of RIBA in 1857. He created the Debenham & Storr building in King Street, Covent Garden, in 1860, and although now demolished, the first grandstand at Lord's cricket ground in 1860. He married Isabel Carrick, the daughter of Thomas Carrick (the miniaturist). They had seven children who were successful, but the most notable was Charles Carrick Allom (1865–1947).

Charles Carrick Allom was a registered architect but not a member of the Royal Institute of British Architects. He was, however, a member of associations and represented the professional work of architects and surveyors. In 1893 he founded the firm of White Allom, "which carried out interior decoration of a distinguished character". His original partner, White, disappeared from the company at an early stage. He brought together a talented and distinguished team of designers at his office at 15 George Street, Hanover Square, London. His timing was astute. Owners of country houses recovering from previous grandiose fashions in decorating (both extravagant and restrained) wanted new settings for their furniture.

Charles Allom was meticulous and traditional in his methods; he provided first-class craftmanship. He began to collect various artefacts, which became available to his clients for fixtures and fittings in the houses he was renovating or building. A number of such items were provided by his company at Polesden

Lacey. Sometimes fragments of decorative craftmanship from all over Europe were used to help with this work, and to improve and embellish his offer to his clients. He was a brilliant draughtsman and designer.

By 1904 Charles Allom was working for Prince George, Prince of Wales, at Marlborough House. In 1907 Edward VII employed White Allom to work on the Ballroom and annex, the Supper room, the East gallery and the Bow drawing room at Buckingham Palace. When Prince George (V) became King in 1910, with Queen Mary's direction, Charles redecorated the centre room, from which the Royal family make public appearances on the balcony, overlooking the Mall. He created a "chinoiserie concoction" by setting the old imperial yellow silk panels (from the Brighton Pavilion) in chinoiserie frames.

Maggie, of course, with her friendship with both Edward VII, George V and Queen Mary, would have understood the quality of the work White Allom executed. If the British Royal family used White Allom, then Maggie, with her father's infinite purse, was able to access this fine company.

Charles himself was a yachting man, sometimes beating George V in his yacht *White Heather* at Cowes! He was also a cricketer and a golfer. His home in Totteridge had a golf course and a cricket ground. He owned an art gallery in New York (the New Allom Gallery).

Charles worked on both sides of the Atlantic; he worked successfully with the Duveen Brothers in London and New York. He worked for Henry Clay Frick at the Frick Mansion, New York (1912–14); Whitemarsh Hall, Wyndmoor, Pennsylvania, for ET Stotesbury (1919); the Huntington Library, San Marino, California; the Waldorf Astoria, New York; Buckingham Palace, London; St Donat's, Wales, for William Randolph Hurst from 1925; Elvaston Castle, for the Earl of Harrington (1930); and the Detroit house of Mrs Horace E Dodge in 1931. When the Wall Street Crash arrived, his business in America declined, but the period between two World Wars was buoyant for Charles. He worked on the British Empire Exhibition in 1924/25. His work included interiors of hotels, clubs, theatres and ocean liners (particularly Cunard). Furniture was provided and manufactured, for his "new settings", with the aid of Percy Macquoid.

Charles's speciality was the reconstruction of period rooms, ceiling and cornices.

Charles continued to "restore where possible and recreate where necessary appropriate settings" and "often this involved installing old panelling as they had done for Mrs Greville at Polesden Lacey, Surrey" (plain white walls were transformed by this method).

In 1952, the company supplied the Chair of Estate and refurbished the throne for the Coronation in 1953. White Allom remained Royal warrant holders until 1960.

In 1960, Holloway Brothers acquired White Allom, a firm with an equally distinguished history in interior design. As Holloway Brothers, the company had built the Admiralty buildings on Horse Guards Parade, the Old Bailey in the early 1900s and the fountains in Trafalgar Square.

The company was also active in civil engineering and constructed several bridges across the Thames, including Hampton Court bridge, Wandsworth bridge and Chelsea bridge, and helped construct the "Mulberry harbours", the floating docks used in the D-Day Normandy landings in 1944.

Holloway White Allom became part of the John Laing construction group in 1964. By 1968 the name of Holloway White Allom was used as a separate trade name once more. In 2002 a number of its directors and senior managers bought out the company from the Laing Group.

Sadly, in 2011 Holloway White Allom closed, as it went into administration in October, although it had a turnover of sixty million pounds prior to the recession. One contract which was not paid on time caused a particular problem, and they could not maintain their debt liability. After 118 years of operating, 170 staff were made redundant. The company had completed the rebuilding of the Medieval and Renaissance Galleries at the V&A Museum in 2010.

White Allom were responsible for much interior decoration, and for importing fixtures and fittings from other properties which had been demolished, for many of their clients; Polesden Lacey was a prime example of this treatment.

In 1907–08, wall surfaces such as the Saloon (Gold Room) were covered in gold leaf (just under twenty-four carat); the Reredos in the Central Hall was fitted; the flat white walls were matured by the importation of old panels.

One of the men on the construction team for White Allom, working at Polesden Lacey, was Alfred How.[44] His daughter has stated the following about Alfred's time at Polesden Lacey: "My father, Alfred How, was employed as foreman joiner and was responsible for the joinery work to the entrance hall, library, etc. He was a skilled craftsman and often spoke of the great pleasure it had given him to work in such a fine house. The Hon Mrs Greville took a great interest in the work and my father had many conversations with her." A photograph of the construction team was sent to Polesden Lacey by Alfred How's daughter, and this provides a rare visual record of the men working in 1907–08 in the house.

The Saloon at Polesden Lacey, nr Dorking, Surrey

© National Trust Images / Andreas von Einsiedel

White Allom were commissioned by Mewes & Davis, and they were told by Maggie that she wanted "a room fit for kings, queens and maharajahs".[45] White Allom were able to produce the panelling and the ceiling paintings which had been acquired from an eighteenth-century Italian palazzo (palace).

The pieces had been stored in Italy, when the palazzo was demolished. They are now in place in the Saloon (Gold Room) at Polesden Lacey. White Allom purchased them, transported them to England and cut the panelling to fit the room. There are spares packed up and conserved in the cellars.

While it is agreed that most country houses would not have or wish to welcome such an opulently decorated room, it does seem that this was exactly what Maggie required.

Maggie did some entertaining at Polesden Lacey with her husband Ronnie, as early as 1907. In May 1907 Edward VII with Alice Keppel had made a "day visit" with some of the guests who were being entertained at Reigate Priory at that time, to see how the building work was proceeding. From late November 1907 until late January 1908, Maggie and Ronnie entertained some guests who were able to stay at Polesden Lacey.

The Visitor Book at Polesden Lacey, includes everyone in society for more than thirty years, who could or did matter.[46] Did British or international royalty dislike this room, or did they feel comfortable in it? What, I wonder, did the maharajahs think about the decoration of the room? Did they think it seemed normal and did it remind them of their palaces? Did other aristocrats like the design of this room? Would politicians have found the room uncomfortable? Certainly, some of the aristocrats who owned country houses of their own may have found this room startling or not to their taste. But a maharajah or a king or queen may not have noticed or thought about it at all, given their own palaces would have been sumptuously decorated.

It can also be noted that Maggie arranged for a curry kitchen to be built on the north side of Polesden Lacey (in the north back yard), so the maharajahs were able to bring their own chefs with them when they came to stay at Polesden Lacey. Imagine a large shed; double this in size. Add four square windows and two doors, and you can begin to appreciate the size of the kitchen. When Maggie was entertaining, the rest of the guests would enjoy French food, but the maharajahs would be happy and comfortable with their own choice of menus.

Add to this the opulently dressed aristocrats, royalty and maharajahs, including the jewellery worn by them all during the evenings, then the scene must have beaten anything MGM could have dreamt up.

The jewellery worn by the aristocrats, and the incredibly rich maharajahs and Maggie, created sensational, opulently and extremely glamorous people dressed to impress each other (and themselves), which was far beyond anything working people could imagine. This was real life to those people involved.

Some people criticised Maggie for the establishment of the Saloon in this style, especially in a country house; it worked for Maggie, and it worked for royalty and maharajahs. I have studied much of the jewellery worn by Maggie, the maharajahs, royalty and aristocrats. I visited the Al Thani Exhibition (Jewellery of the Maharajas) at the V&A (on show November 2015 to April 2016). The exhibition moved to Paris and Rome. I can state that the quality, creativity, size and quantity of such jewellery is totally astounding. All of the rooms at Polesden Lacey would be lit up by such a show of wealth and possessions. How suitable the Gold Room must have seemed at times, for such a show of opulence.

In the Central Hall at Polesden Lacey, a reredos is in place above the fireplace.

Maggie purchased the reredos from White Allom in 1907–08 (interior decorators and antique reclamation specialists).[47] They were employed to upgrade the fixtures and fittings in the mansion, as already discussed; they had acquired the reredos in the nineteenth century. Most of the contents of St

Matthew's, Friday Street, Cheapside, were sold/despatched to other churches and places of significance in London, prior to the building being demolished.

The reredos was removed from St Matthew's, Friday Street, Cheapside, prior to its demolition. Notice to declare St Matthew's redundant was made in 1881, and it was demolished in 1884. The church was designed by Christopher Wren, and it was built after the Great Fire of 1666. Notice to demolish churches in London was provided by the Union of Church Benefices Act of 1860, which allowed funds raised from selling off underused churches to be spent on parishes, which were expanding outside London. By 1938, the act resulted in sixteen Wren churches being demolished in the City of London. Hitler succeeded in the demolition of more Wren churches in World War II.

Edward Pierce/Pearce (born 1628 to 1632 – no exact birth date is known – and died in 1695) carved this reredos. In 1685, Pierce commented on a small additional improvement to his work on the reredos in his own accounts. Pierce worked extensively for Christopher Wren on buildings in London. He worked using stone, marble and wood: St Lawrence Jewry (1671–87), St Paul's Cathedral (1679–90), the Guildhall (1670–73) and St Clement Danes (1680–82).

Pierce executed carvings for some of the fountains at Hampton Court. He also worked at Sudbury Hall, Derbyshire (1675–76).

The oak reredos in the Central Hall was acquired by White Allom, a while after St Matthew's, Friday Street, Cheapside, was destroyed in the nineteenth century.[48] No visible remaining part of the church can be viewed; much of the street has disappeared into the Bank of England. In the thirteenth century, St Matthew's Church existed; was destroyed by the Great Fire of London (1666); then rebuilt and "united" with St Peter, Westcheap; and opened in 1685. St. Matthew's was "the cheapest and plainest of Christopher Wren's city churches" and cost £2,381.8s to build.

Edward Pierce was renowned as a Restoration carver and a fine sculptor; and he worked frequently for Christopher Wren. Edward Pearce created a large bust of Christopher Wren which is on show at the Ashmolean Museum, Oxford, and I viewed the bust in 2018.

The Union of Churches Benefices Act (1860) allowed many city churches to be demolished. In 1883 St Matthew's displayed placards "inviting tenders for purchase of its materials". Pierce's font and cover was sold to St Clements, Fulham Road; the pulpit to St Peter's, Reporton Road, Fulham.

There were 6 lots advertised for sale; Lot 2 included "The Handsome carved oak Altar Piece with Corinthian Columns, richly gilt, the borders and panels richly carved with fruit & flowers". The purchaser at the time of the sale is unknown; White Allom purchased it secondly and offered it to the V&A Museum in 1905, but the museum had no funds available. Sir Thomas Graham Jackson RA, a member of the museum's advisory council, advised that it should be purchased, but the director, Sir Purdon Clarke, "had reluctantly to reject it for lack of funds".

Messrs White Allom, who were by then engaged in embellishing Polesden Lacey for Mrs Ronald Greville, thereupon disposed of it to her and set it up in its present position. Had it not been acquired by Maggie for Polesden Lacey, it would almost certainly have been shipped to America, where this firm at that time was very active. Alterations to the size were made to fit the reredos above the marble and oak fireplace, which technically replaces the altar table. We do not have a purchase price for the reredos recorded anywhere.

The quantity of panelling which was brought into Polesden Lacey to change plain white walls into panelled rooms and corridors added more gravitas and style. The finish of the interior became more subtle as a house for guests to enjoy themselves, although some visitors may not think this applies to the Saloon (Gold Room).

The Tea Room walls were provided with a mural (thought to be in the style of Francois Boucher) leading on to west terrace. This mural is split into sections to fit the room. How successful was this? Why sit in a plain room when money can achieve much more style?

A library was created by extending the house, and incorporating the original small sitting room which had the influence of Louis Remy de la Fosse (1659–1726), a much earlier architect, with its classical style. Charles Allom knew how to please his clients. What the cost for all of Maggie's new work was remains unknown.

Having electricity from the beginning enabled Maggie's maids to work without candlelight. Guests were becoming accustomed to visiting country houses which had electricity during Edward VII's reign. Why stay at a house where candlelight was the only lighting system available? It was much more comfortable in a centrally heated house with electricity.

A company named Wenham & Waters Ltd installed the plumbing and the bathroom fittings.[49] Mewes & Davis copied some of their own ideas for the bathrooms at Polesden Lacey, from the bathrooms they had installed at the Ritz Hotel in London.

The house that Maggie bought was changed from a relatively plain large building into a decorative and comfortable property, because of the lighting, heating and plumbing, fixtures, combined with soft furnishings and wall decoration (the panelling alone changed white flat walls into areas proffering imposing style). Coupled with the drama of the decoration of the Saloon, Polesden Lacey was effectively changed into a house with personality. Can a house have a personality? Yes, if it reflects the owner's own taste. Maggie, via her architects Mewes & Davis, and with White Allom and Jackson's the Plasterers, created a memorable, inviting and hospitable backdrop for some of the most prestigious players in society in Great Britain and from across the world. After the completion of so much decorative work, Maggie set about collecting artefacts to dress and impress her guests, and to provide the stage set of a Salon, which was exceptional.

As Edward VII said, Maggie "had a genius for hospitality". McEwan funded the hospitality, Maggie ordered it and the result was spectacular. So, some aristocrats criticised this in the short term. No matter, the victor was Maggie. She dazzled, starred, and ran her Salon to such a successful degree, that most of the most important participants on the world stage, flocked to Polesden Lacy until the later stages of her career, as the Chatelaine of Polesden Lacey.

White Allom may have been responsible for the provision of the statuary in the grounds at Polesden Lacey. Currently we have no proof regarding these items, which add to the structure of the garden.

SIX

Two Deaths

First Death – Helen

Helen's Will is dated 30th December 1903, and it is recorded in court books of the commissariat (Edinburgh Sheriff's Court for people who were Scottish but who died outside Scotland) at Edinburgh, 29th December 1906.[50] The Will confirmation after death was recorded for 30th December 1906.

Helen died on Monday 3rd September 1906.[51] Helen's Will was valued at £20,749.3.8 pence (gross). After probate Helen's estate was valued at £19,539.4.2 pence. Helen's jewellery could not have been included in this value at this time, as the jewellery was not meant to be bequeathed permanently to Maggie or anyone else, as clarified below.

Helen bequeathed, after certain legacies were fulfilled, the residue of her estate to be divided equally between the Royal Hospital Chelsea and the Gordon Boys' Home. Helen is listed on the chapel board as a major benefactor to the Royal Hospital Chelsea, London.

Also stated in Helen's Will was a clause related to Helen's jewellery, which was "all my watches and jewellery to my said Trustees in trust to permit my daughter The Honourable Margaret Helen Greville the wife of Captain Ronald Henry Fulke Greville MP to have the use and enjoyment thereof during her life and after her death I declare that the same shall fall into and form part of my residuary estate".

"What in fact happened was that Mrs Greville purchased these items by agreement with the executors at valuation, so that she became the absolute owner of them and the Royal Hospital and the Gordon Boys' Home got their money immediately."[52] After investigations with the Royal Hospital Chelsea the archivists, who are and were very helpful, confirmed that, "A tatty page in the Royal Hospital register of funds… led us to the copy executors' accounts, which show all the receipts and payments".

"The Royal Hospital received a payment on account of £2,700 which it invested in 2.5% Midland railway debenture stock. A subsequent balancing payment (excluding the jewellery etc.) of £1,824 was invested in 3% Great Northern Railway debenture stock. The half-share of the net proceeds of the sale of the jewellery and watches amounts to £491 and is dealt with in a supplementary executors' account, and shown in the register; £400 of this was placed on bank deposit. The total amount received by the Royal Hospital under Mrs Helen McEwan's Will was therefore £5,015."

The Royal Hospital Chelsea in their records show that the fund was used for "Gardens and Convalescent and General Services at the Hospital". The Royal Hospital was not sure whether "Mrs McEwan expressed a wish to this effect in her Will or whether the Royal Hospital decided that it would be a good use for the unexpected windfall".

I can state that Helen's Will does not direct the Royal Hospital Chelsea how they should spend the money, only that the said residuary estate was to be placed "in trust for The Royal Hospital Chelsea and The Gordon Boys' Home No 5 York Street, St. James, in the County of London in equal shares".

The Gordon Boy's Home (a school "for necessitous boys" which was established in 1885 in memory of General Gordon), funded by a number of royal families in the world, along with some Indian and British Regiments and the British Navy, has confirmed that Helen's bequest £5,015 was the largest by far from a list of eight legacies they have received.[53]

From 1887, the school provided training in practical trades, with a military influence. Royal patrons of the school have continued from Queen Victoria to our present Queen. After 1943, the teaching of trades, although still taught, began to change to more academic education. In 1990 the school became co-educational and changed its name to Gordon's School. It is now a successful state boarding school. I contacted Gordon's School and the 22nd Annual Report, dated 1907, confirms this amount.

The Gordonian Officer said that "the money probably went into the general fund, rather than be allocated to a specific capital project". These legacies made a real difference to both institutions.

Helen was buried at Highgate Cemetery on 5th September 1906.

William McEwan had paid £262.10.0 for the exclusive right of burial on 1st September 1906. "The grave is on a junction where two paths meet and the plot is triangular in shape, in the centre of which is a brick vault 9" by 4" in size. The location of the grave was selected by the cemetery on behalf of the family." Other adjacent entries for plots in the cemetery show costs of £3–£4 for small spaces. Helen's burial plot demonstrated the importance of her position as the wife of William McEwan. The death was registered on 4th September (number 442) by Ronald Greville, at the sub-district of Mayfair and Knightsbridge of St George, Hanover Square, London.

The funeral took place at twelve o'clock at Highgate on 5th September.[54] On Thursday 6th September 1906 the *London Daily News* reported that "the Chief mourners had included Mr. McEwan [*husband*] and other gentlemen of the family. Among those who sent wreaths were Lady St. Helier, Lady Mildred Cook, Mr. Fitzroy Stewart, Colonel Stewart, Countess of Cork, Captain Greville and the Hon. Mrs. Greville. A memorial service was held at the same time as the funeral, at Christ Church, Albany St. [*Camden*]."

"In the Victorian period, because women were thought to be in insufficient control of their emotions, the custom arose of forbidding their attendance at funerals". Though this strict social law was gradually relaxed by the close of the nineteenth century, women mostly remained in the house, until after the funeral service and burial had taken place. Seemingly, Maggie was following this protocol, possibly under the direction of her father.

Second Death – Ronnie

In 1908, Maggie was travelling with her father (William McEwan), and while they were in Cannes, she was informed that Ronnie had become unwell. Ronnie had been staying at Colonel and Mrs Hall Walker's home, Gateacre Grange, Liverpool, in order to attend the races at Aintree and to watch the Grand National (27th March). Ronnie Greville became unwell at the races at Aintree on Thursday 26th March. His throat was causing a great deal of pain. He departed for London on Friday 27th March in order to see a consultant on Saturday 28th March 1908. Ronnie would not have missed the Grand National (27th March) unless he was in serious trouble. The race is now run on a Saturday, but back in 1908, it was run on a Friday.

Ronnie realised, unhappily, he could not remain at Aintree to see the race. He had been suffering from hoarseness and general discomfort for some time. He was informed on Saturday 28th March, that he had cancer of the larynx, and that his vocal cords needed to be removed immediately. The result of the operation "could not be foretold". If the operation had been successful, it would not have been possible for Ronnie to speak after this operation.

Ronnie replied to the London specialist, "Well, Dr -----, when you tell a man news like that, you ought to have a brandy and soda in the room." Ronnie left the consulting room, without further comment or complaint, and returned to 11 Charles Street. Maggie arrived back from Cannes on Monday 30th March, and the operation took place on Tuesday 31st March. Pneumonia followed the operation, and Ronnie died on Sunday 5th April. Newspaper reports described his death as "tranquil and painless".

The funeral took place on Thursday 9th April at St Nicholas Church, Bookham, at noon.[55] "The coffin was almost hid from view by the profusion of flowers, the widow's tribute, a cross composed entirely of violets [*Maggie's favourite flowers*], extending the whole length." On the coffin, there was an inscription which read, "Ronald Henry Fulke Greville, born 14th October, 1864. Died 5th April, 1908."

On the same day, simultaneously, a memorial service was held at St Margaret's, Westminster, for Ronnie, for those friends and relatives who could not attend the funeral in Bookham. Both services were identical in content, so the same hymns and music were played. Many aristocrats travelled to Bookham for the funeral in addition to those who attended the memorial service in town. Prince Francis of Teck, and a deputation of officers from the 1st Life Guards, attended the memorial service.

William McEwan remained in the South of France and did not attend the funeral. This raises questions. Given the care Maggie's father William took to ensure Maggie bought Polesden Lacey in her sole name in 1907, as already stated, while Ronnie was very much alive, what did McEwan really think of Ronnie? It can be suggested that McEwan was frail or not well in 1908, and did not want to travel back to England, but McEwan did not die until 1913, and seemingly was enjoying life in 1908.

Given McEwan's other measures to protect his daughter financially, it seems that his regard for Ronnie was such, that yes, Ronnie was a gentleman, Ronnie had provided the connections, hence the marriage, but Ronnie never got his hands on much capital, as Ronnie's Will proved.

McEwan was a measured man who never did anything without thinking it through. McEwan, the planner and organiser, as I verified, while he created his business, must have considered what measures he should take on hearing of Ronnie's illness. McEwan's lack of return to England when Ronnie became ill suggests that possibly McEwan knew how serious Ronnie's illness was, and yet he was not motivated to return, or did he not care? Did her father not attach sufficient importance to the possible outcome? Had Ronnie done what was required of him (in McEwan's eyes) in providing Maggie's passport to society? McEwan, because of his position in Edward VII's world, may have calculated that there was enough security established for himself and his daughter at court, and whatever the outcome for Ronnie regarding his operation, there would be not be any change to Maggie's and his position at court.

Maggie re-joined her father in Cannes nine days after Ronnie died. Maggie departed from London on 14th April to return to her father, and together they travelled on an extended tour to Italy from France. A telegram, dated 13th April 1908 and written by Jennie Cornwallis-West, expressed her sadness to Maggie about the loss of Ronnie. This confirms Maggie's return departure date (14th) for the South of France, as Jenny expressed her need (in the telegram) to catch Maggie, prior to her departure the following day.

The marriage had been a success socially and had brought McEwan's daughter into the inner Royal court. Back in 1899, when McEwan charted the yacht SY *Rona* for a cruise in the Mediterranean, Ronnie did accompany/arrive at the same time as Maggie and her father to sail and join the other guests (Monaco, 28th March 1899). He departed on 24th April (a reasonable time later). The Mediterranean cruise was completed sometime in May (no precise date known). However, Maggie's only mention of Ronnie's departure was "After luncheon Ronnie left for England – and I went to the museum and saw the Sarcophagus of Constantine a truly magnificent object – there met Pater and Ned again and we drove about visiting more mosques". Maggie's comments were not really close, loving remarks, and do not suggest much closeness to a husband who had just set off to return home.

There are a number of questions about Ronnie. Did his instincts include other relationships? With whom? Was he not really interested in ladies?

A descendant of the Greville family line, currently living in Australia, made a comment about Ronnie (which had been provided by her father) when she

Two Deaths

visited Polesden Lacey in 2019. This comment suggested that Ronnie was possibly not very interested in ladies so much.

Maggie loved children; there is absolutely no knowledge available, to state that she was unable to have children. There is (so far) no definite information known to state that Ronnie was not much of a ladies' man.

On 9th April 1908, Maggie's wreath for Ronnie was a cross, covering almost the length of the coffin, consisting of Princess of Wales odorata violets (Maggie's favourite flowers).

King Edward VII was represented at Ronnie's funeral by Major Holford. The King sent a beautiful wreath which was made of arum lilies and lilies of the valley, with an inscription stating "From the King".

The chief mourners were: Maggie accompanied by Lord and Lady Greville (Ronnie's parents), the Duke of Montrose (his grandfather), Lady Vane Tempest, Sir Evelyn Ruggles Brice, the Hon George Keppel, Sir Charles Hartopp, Lord Ilchester, Captain Dewhurst, Sir George Cotterell, Major and Mrs Heneage, Mr Holbeck, Messrs W and B Younger, and Miss Robertson. Servants and estate employees at Polesden Lacey and Charles Street were also present. There were many, many wreaths sent from so many friends – a huge list which included Grand Duke Michael of Russia, some members of the 1st Life Guards (Ronnie's old regiment), Ronnie's old constituency Bradford East Conservative Association and the Bradford East Primrose League.

After the service was held in St Nicholas Church by the Rev GS Bird, the coffin was taken to the grave (which is still situated in the grounds of the church), which had been lined with lilies, azaleas and many white flowers. All of "the funeral arrangements were carried out by Messrs Gastin and Son, Cavendish Square". Maggie received many letters of condolence after Ronnie died. One of the first people to send a letter was McEwan's sister Janet (1823–1912) from Alloa, who wrote "So grieved at the sad news deepest sympathy in your great loss may you be strengthened to bear it bravely" on 6th April 1908. Many newspapers reported both Ronnie's death and his funeral.

Ronnie owned two horses at the time of his death: Petual and Lady Desmond.

Ronnie's Will was dated 8th October 1906.[56] Maggie and Ronnie's brother, Captain the Hon Charles Beresford Fulke Greville were executors. Ronnie bequeathed "to my said wife all my watches jewellery trinkets and personal ornaments belongings apparel paper guns plate furniture and effects of every description (whether indoor or outdoor) which shall be in or about or belonging to or appropriated or ordered for no 11 Charles Street aforesaid or the stables occupied therewith or any other house belonging to my said wife absolutely". Ronnie gave "one year's wages to my servant Francis Bole free of duty in addition to any wages which may be due to him if he shall be in my service at the time of my death".

Ronnie bequeathed to his two sisters, Camilla Hay (wife of the Hon Alistair Hay) and the Hon Veronique Greville "in equal shares all money which may be in my possession at the time of my death"; including the money in his possession and at his bankers, the policies on his life and his shares in limited companies. The rest of Ronnie's estate after funeral and any other expenses and debts were met, was bequeathed "free of duty unto my said wife absolutely". The solicitors were Dowson Ainslie & Martineau, 19 Surrey Street, London, and the witnesses were Walter Dowson (solicitor) and James Hinks (clerk to Messrs Dowson Ainslie & Martineau). Probate was granted on 15th April 1908. Probate was granted quickly.

"The copy Grant of Probate dated 15 April 1908 records the value of Ronnie's estate and liabilities, as provided to the Probate Registry on the Application for a grant and his gross estate was recorded as £12,962 2s 10d with a net value of £5,834 19s 2d."[57] There are two additional handwritten sets of figures on the copy of probate, which vary; they are re-sworn figures of approximately £15,000, including his effects. The final outcome meant that Ronnie had very little money, in relation to either William McEwan or Maggie.

Because Ronnie had provided the link to enable Maggie to succeed socially, would his death signify the removal of the supporting structure for Maggie to continue in the Marlborough House Set? Maggie entered the period of up to two years' Edwardian mourning after Ronnie died. What was to become of her socially?

We can wonder whether McEwan had impressed many aristocrats, including the Prince of Wales/Edward VII, which meant McEwan had possibly helped Edward with his debts, thereby ensuring his place in society.

Was this the reason Ronnie (and his family) quickly approved Maggie as a choice of wife, bearing in mind their own diminishing finances? Especially as Ronnie had previously been engaged to Virginia Daniel Bonynge prior to marrying Maggie on 25th April 1891.

Ronnie's background and his place in the Marlborough House Set, made him a perfect and useful husband for Maggie. In the first part of the twentieth century, money and aristocracy interacted to provide families with the ability to maintain their social positions, to continue to entertain lavishly, and stop in an instant, any descent into circumstances which of their own volition, would have prevented or diminished the continuity of such a lifestyle.

Maggie and Ronnie as a couple seemed to have been comfortable with each other. Ronnie was able to continue his interest in horse racing. His social life was maintained, albeit by his father-in-law's finances. Ronnie was useful for two terms as an MP, but decided at the age of forty to remain "at home" and retire from parliament. His mother commented that she never knew what Ronnie did. Maggie, with McEwan's money and support, managed to initiate, indulge and establish her connections so satisfactorily that the period of Edwardian mourning (necessary as it was) after Ronnie died, served to present to society how capable she was of continuing forward in her own right as a significant figure. Maggie was married to Ronnie for seventeen years. We do know how much Maggie liked children. In Maggie's Will, her godchildren are all remembered.

When Ronnie died, he did not have the wealth some people might have expected. Of course, the money he bequeathed was not inconsiderable, compared to people who were really poor. But compared to many of his friends in the aristocratic world, to which he was born and lived, his bequest was not large.

This suggests that Ronnie had never been given control of a lump sum by McEwan as a dowry for Maggie, although a dowry would have been provided (as discussed in Chapter 3, under title of "Who Paid for Everything".

It seems that investments were placed by McEwan for the couple, providing an income, so that both Maggie and Ronnie had enough money to entertain well and be full members of society, but not actually provide personal control to Ronnie (as normally a husband was entitled to) over such a fund.

We now know and have proved, that when Maggie purchased Polesden Lacey in 1907, Ronnie's name was not on the deeds. It seems that Ronnie was not given control of any, or much of, McEwan's money, as would have been normal practice on marrying. If any additional proof re a dowry, surfaces between now and the printing of this book, I will amend this last statement prior to publication.

Maggie's Dogs

William McEwan owned one dog; a white Collie named Phyllis (no dates known).
Maggie enjoyed the company of seventeen dogs, throughout her time and life, at Polesden Lacey.

Her dogs were: Tyne, a white collie who died in 1904; Tokio, a Japanese spaniel, from 1898 to 1906; Mutzu, a Japanese spaniel who died in 1908; Prince Chang, a Pekinese, from 1903 to 1914; Pe-Tu (Mrs Bunn), a Pekinese, from 1905 to 1916; Sailor, a retriever, from 1905 to 1917; Pungie, a Pekinese who died in 1918; Anthony, a white collie, from 1905 to 1921; Caesor, an Airedale who died in 1923; Rip, a West Highland terrier who died in 1928; Lokui, a Pekinese, from 1907 to 1923; Cho, a Pekinese, from 1908 to 1924; Jose, a Cairn terrier who died in 1936; Glen, a Cairn terrier, from 1933 to 1940; Dougal, a West Highland terrier, from 1925 to 1938; Ian, a Cairn terrier, from 1927 to 1933; and Billy, an Airedale who died in 1936.

Maggie loved her dogs. As she had no children during the seventeen years of her marriage to Ronnie, the dogs were very important to her. They are buried in their own graveyard, in juxtaposition to Maggie's grave in the Ladies' Garden.

Another dog buried at Polesden Lacey is Mr Snooks, who is not buried alongside Maggie's dogs. Mr Snooks belonged to Baron Emile-Ernest de Cartier de Marchienne, who was the Belgian Envoy Extraordinary and Minister Plenipotentiary to Great Britain from 1927 to 1946 (and a real friend of Maggie's). The Baron was not ambassador but was Head of the Belgian Legation. In 1815 the Congress of Vienna established diplomatic ranks. Until the twentieth century most diplomatic missions were legations. Ambassadors were only exchanged between great powers, close allies and related monarchies. In 1960s the last of the legations became embassies.

The Baron stayed at Polesden Lacey on different dates from 1927 up to 1942 (April). He stayed increasingly often in later years (1939/1940/1941/1942), with many weekend dates in 1941.

When Mr Snooks died, Maggie offered a plot in her dog cemetery to the Baron for Mr Snooks. The Baron believed that Maggie's cemetery was a private sanctuary and space for her dogs, so the Baron declined. Instead, he asked for a quiet location in the grounds at Polesden Lacey. Maggie agreed and suggested that the Baron should discuss a suitable place with Henry Smith, the head gardener. In 1938, Mr Smith recorded that, the Baron was "tearful" when he talked to him about choosing a resting place for Mr Snooks. The two men chose a quiet spot which is set in a green space set amongst some trees (so hidden from obvious view) south-east of Polesden Lacey house, not far away from the south lawn in the direction of theatre lawn.

Edward VII's Dog Caesar Is Buried at Marlborough House

Edward VII owned a fox terrier named Caesar.[58] The King was very fond of this dog. For some years, there have been a number of suggestions that King Edward's dog Caesar was buried at Polesden Lacey. This is completely untrue.

Maggie owned an Airedale dog named Caesor (as above), who died in 1923.

Edward VII's fox terrier, Caesar, was known as a noisy dog. Queen Alexandra did not like the dog much.

When Edward VII died, the dog was clearly sad at the loss of his owner. Caesar walked along with Edward VII's cortege in the funeral procession, immediately behind the carriage carrying Edward's body, taking his place ahead of several kings!

After Edward VII died, Caesar did not eat and became unwell. The dog really missed his owner. Although Alexandra had not cared much for the dog when Edward was alive, she felt sorry for him. She managed to get him to eat properly again, and looked after him.

When Caesar died in 1914, Queen Alexandra organised a grave for the dog, with a headstone showing an image of the dog which is in place in the grounds of Marlborough House. A photograph of the grave can be viewed on the Marlborough House website. Two different dogs and two different timescales.

SEVEN

Maggie's Life After Ronnie Died

It was necessary and vital that Maggie fulfilled her role as a grieving widow. Up to two years of mourning was expected to be adhered to, by aristocratic ladies in Edwardian society. Going out and attending parties and balls was not an option immediately available to a society lady in mourning. Black had to be worn for the first year. Gradually in year two, some white could be introduced into clothing, followed by some grey and mauve. This was followed by beginning to be able to attend society functions, gradually. However, from the Visitor Book at Polesden Lacey, I can confirm that Maggie did commence entertaining again by June 1908, firstly some family members, followed by from July to October small numbers of friends, although weekend guest lists were never large at this time. To hold large gatherings in society would have been disrespecting standards. Maggie would not wish to be seen to break the rules.

In Maggie's second year of mourning, Edward VII and Alice Keppel stayed with Maggie at Polesden Lacey for the weekend; articles were placed in the press announcing Edward VII was to visit Maggie Greville for the weekend.

This was the next (third) magic key in Maggie's life: King Edward VII's continuing kindness to her. He included Maggie in the Marlborough House Set after Ronnie died. Edward VII brought Alice Keppel and fifteen members of the Marlborough House Set, for the weekend of June 5th and 6th 1909, to Polesden Lacey (more than a year after Ronnie died), thereby enabling the continuity of Maggie in the Marlborough (Edward's) House Set and the Royal Court.

What was Edward's reason? Maggie was among some of the richest people in aristocratic circles. Edward VII later said Maggie had "a genius for hospitality". Did Edward VII like her (not sexually, but for what she managed to do and provide in society)? Edward's comforts in life mattered to him, especially after his hard upbringing.

The official photograph of this particular weekend of the house party is on display at Polesden Lacey. The importance of this weekend for Maggie cannot be overstated.

Maggie needed three magic keys to manage her life. The first magic key in her life, was McEwan finally marrying her mother Helen. The second magic key was Maggie's marriage to Ronnie. The third key was provided by Edward VII. He enabled Maggie to continue to be a member of the Marlborough House Set, which allowed her to extend her position in society, and become the international hostess (the Chatelaine of Polesden Lacey) until she died in 1942, even though she had lost her husband. This last key was absolutely vital to Maggie.

Was Maggie just lucky? Or was it her intelligence or her gift for generosity which we know Edward VII enjoyed? Or was the reason because of McEwan's continuing support financially to Edward, along with McEwan's calculating management of both his and Maggie's place in this world? Was this a time when McEwan was even more active in helping out Edward VII financially?

William McEwan had demonstrated his total commitment to planning/thinking/managing all of the details of his new business (the brewery) at every stage. He did nothing spontaneously (as already stated re the building of his company), so why would the challenge of ensuring Maggie continuing to remain a central player in society be beyond him?

McEwan, the master planner, was unlikely to allow chance or a casual laissez-faire attitude to prevail, regarding his or his daughter's place in society, having spent years building a fortune and becoming a millionaire from a loan of £2,000. I can see nothing happening casually or by chance in McEwan's life from my study of what he created and accomplished, except possibly for the news of Helen's pregnancy, when it became known during their relationship in 1863.

Without denying that Ronnie was a support to Maggie when she married him, thereby enabling her entrée into the Marlborough House Set, it was McEwan who brought Maggie on a journey, which began in secret in London at her birth, followed by his management of her in Edinburgh. Although McEwan was not married to her mother Helen until Maggie was twenty-one years old.

McEwan arranged Maggie's education, including dancing lessons, and provided and taught Maggie the tenets which she held throughout her life.

McEwan enabled Maggie's confidence so that becoming part of the Marlborough House Set on her marriage and being with royalty was normal for her. At this stage, the loss of Ronnie, was not something McEwan would have countenanced as a lever to damage Maggie's position.

Whatever was happening behind the scenes socially, Maggie was definitely going to remain the Chatelaine of Polesden Lacey and the Mistress of a town house in Charles Street.

Announced in the *Daily Express*, 7th June 1909, the Court Circular, Buckingham Palace, 5th June stated, "The King, attended by Hon. John Ward, left the Palace this afternoon by motor for Polesden Lacey, Dorking, to honour the Hon. Mrs. Ronald Greville with a visit."

Edward VII accepted Maggie's invitation for the weekend of 5th and 6th June 1909. This was a significant moment for Maggie. Ronnie had died more than a year previously. Maggie had already commenced entertaining again after Ronnie's death in 1908, but she required full acceptance at Court, if she was to remain a major player as a single lady in the international aristocratic circle to which she had become accustomed, through her marriage to Ronnie. She was wealthy, because McEwan was really wealthy; her entry into society, supported totally by McEwan, was a positive of no mean measure, but was she still a member of the Marlborough House Set?

This weekend proved that she was. Edward's generosity in staying at Polesden Lacey provided a clear statement that Maggie was "still one of us" in the Royal Court. This was a signal to society that Maggie Greville could not be ignored. More importantly, she was recognised as having an inner position in Edward's personal group. Those aristocrats who wished to be close to Edward did not deviate from accepting this decision.

The guests who spent this weekend with Maggie and William McEwan, in addition to Edward VII and Alice Keppel (the then and last mistress to Edward VII) were: George Keppel, Sonia Keppel, Georgina Countess of Dudley (a previous mistress of Edward VII) and her son Mr John Ward, Lady Sarah Wilson (first woman war reporter in the Boer War), the Marquis de Soveral (Envoy Extraordinary and Minister Plenipotentiary to the Court of St James and Portuguese Minister from 1884 to 1914 in London), Count Albert Mensdorff (Ambassador Extraordinary and Minister Plenipotentiary to the Court of St. James), Lady Violet Savile (neighbour of Maggie in Charles Street),

Lord William and Lady Emily Lurgan, Lord and Lady Innes-Kerr, Sir John Willoughby, and Mrs George Cavendish-Bentinck (although she did not sign the Visitor Book and was also the only person for whom Big Ben was silenced when she was unwell). The missing guest was the Duchess of Manchester, who had been invited but was not present.

Edward VII was in a good mood that particular weekend, as his horse Minoru had won the Derby on 26th May 1909. Edward VII was the first British monarch to own a horse who was a Derby winner.

The *Illustrated Sporting and Dramatic News*, 12th June 1909, stated, "The King week-ended with an old friend of his, the Hon. Mrs. Ronald Greville, widow of Captain the Hon. Ronald Greville, elder of the two sons of Lord Greville. When he was alive, his Majesty went several times to Reigate Priory, which Captain and Mrs. Greville rented from Lady Henry Somerset. He died a year ago last April, and his widow, who is the only child of Mr. William McEwan, a very wealthy Scotsman, has Polesden Lacey, near Dorking, where she had the honour of entertaining his Majesty."

Dinners which were served in Edwardian society were elaborate and were often more than seven courses. After Edward VII became King, the style of service offered in aristocratic circles changed from à la Francaise to à la Russe. This change had already begun in the mid-nineteenth century, though it lingered in France until the late nineteenth century.

Food was now served sequentially à la Russe (so one course after another) in Great Britain. Prior to this, the à la Française method meant that all of the courses were brought to the table together. While it is sometimes stated that Edward VII initiated this method in Great Britain, the change had already begun, but certainly he may have encouraged it. Because of the close position of the kitchen and servery together at Polesden Lacey, with both rooms next to the dining room, Maggie was able to serve "hot food on hot plates". This was not something that was common to all country houses.

I provide a dinner menu, from the 5th and 6th June 1909 weekend at Polesden Lacey:[59] "Consomme Imperiale, Crème Ambassadrice, Darnes de Saumon Sauce Hollandaise et Genevoise, Blanchailles, Boudins de Volaille Princesse, Selles d'Agneau Glace Moscovite, Cailles flanquees d'Ortolans, Salade, Asperges d'Argenteuil Sauce Mousseuse Peches à la Royale, and Barquettes Ecossaises."

The choice of meats provided frequently were: lamb, beef and chicken, with gammon occasionally. Game (in the season) was popular too. Fish was popular, including salmon, dover sole and other white fish. Caviar was often served.

The variety of vegetables, some especially grown "early" and Maggie's early fruits, are detailed in Chapter 8.

Fine wines, champagnes, after-dinner drinks were all served correctly, and if any guests were hungry at midnight, supper was served! The standard and quality of service, food and hospitality was perfect.

As Edward VII said, "Maggie has a genius for hospitality".

Edward liked to be spoiled, given his upbringing, which was devoid of kindness even into adulthood while his mother was alive. Once Edward became King, he ensured that his life was filled with what he wished to do, not what others intended he should do.

Edward's travels in Europe, his visits to relatives abroad, his time spent with his friends, week in and week out, including the weekends, were what he wanted from his court. What Edward wanted; Edward achieved – late in life. Maggie ensured whenever she was entertaining Edward that she provided a fine offer of hospitality combined with luxury.

With Alice Keppel and other guests, Edward enjoyed a weekend (5th and 6th June 1909) with his friends at Polesden Lacey. There were stunning views, magical countryside and sports on offer, which he possibly did not use. He enjoyed relaxing games of cards and billiards, and space away from London without courtiers or anyone else bothering him.

Queen Alexandra cannot have been happy with the scene I describe above, although it was accepted by everyone in Edward's Court. Alexandra's health deteriorated over a period of time, but this does not excuse or change the way Edward VII conducted his personal life. His upbringing no doubt contributed hugely to the "moral code" of the Marlborough House Set that he imposed. Edward's lifestyle regarding ladies was not different to most aristocrats, and as Alice Keppel said (quotation in Chapter 3), discretion among the Set was required for both ladies and gentlemen to fulfil and enjoy their lives.

One small piece of information that affected the postcode for Polesden Lacey crops up at this point in Maggie's life. Edward VII noticed in 1909 when he was staying with Maggie at Polesden Lacey, that the postman delivered letters (on a motorbike with a sidecar) and did not wait for Maggie's replies. He just delivered them and departed. Edward VII said he would have a word with the Postmaster-General when he was back in town, as he thought this arrangement was not adequate. Edward did "have a word".

The Postmaster at Leatherhead was asked if a postman could deliver the mail in the morning, wait until Maggie had written her replies and then return to the Leatherhead Post Office with them. The answer was no! The Postmaster at Dorking was asked the same question, and the answer was yes!

It seems that the reason the postcode at Polesden Lacey is RH (actually RH5 6BD) is because of this agreement. Given its geographical location, one would expect the code to begin with KT. What happened thereafter was that the postman arrived from Dorking and delivered the letters; he was taken to the kitchen, given a breakfast of bacon, eggs, fried bread and tea, and after the best part of an hour, the replies and any new mail were given to the postman, who returned down the hill to Dorking. A number of postmen took turns to deliver post to Maggie (you can understand how they would like to do this), and at Christmas they were each given a small present. The son of one of the postmen, Donald Pirt, recorded in an interview, that his father had received an Edward VII and Queen Alexandra Coronation jug from Maggie at Christmas. This practice continued after Maggie died for a while.

In writing the Maggie Greville story, I note the following regarding Maggie's royal connections.

Edward VII's code of behaviour as an adult, both as Prince and as King, followed a pattern which royalty and aristocrats were conversant with for centuries. Edward's upbringing was, to say the least, extreme. His survival through the difficulties he endured from his mother Queen Victoria was marked, when he "gained some freedom" (possibly from the date of his marriage to Alexandra) by providing a way of life different to that which he had experienced for so long. While his mother remained on the throne, his full expression of enjoyment was held back, but he was able, while not yet King, to begin the process of building his own Court, his own friends and a life not previously available to him.

Maggie was friendly with Princess Beatrice (Queen Victoria's ninth child and fourth daughter). The friendship was lasting. Princess Beatrice dined with Maggie in London and stayed at Polesden Lacey. They met within the circle Maggie had joined, often. When Princess Beatrice was finally allowed to marry Prince Henry of Battenberg (23rd July 1885), it was on the basis that the couple lived with Queen Victoria. They had four children.

Sadly, Prince Henry died in the Asanti War in 1896 from malaria (an unnecessary war for him, except he managed to be away from Queen Victoria's control). Princess Beatrice did not marry again and she remained working as Queen Victoria's unofficial secretary until Queen Victoria died on 22nd January 1901.

Maggie in maintaining this friendship with Princess Beatrice became friends with her four children: a huge enduring friendship with Eugenie (before and after her marriage to Alfonso); another consistent friendship with Alexander Battenberg (Mountbatten/Carisbrooke), who enjoyed his honeymoon with Irene Denison from 19th to 27th July 1917 at Polesden Lacey; Maurice, who died in action in 1914; and Leopold, who died in 1922 during a hip operation. Hence Maggie's long-term commitment was to Eugenie and Alexander.

Maggie becoming acquainted with Edward VII was, as I mention elsewhere, possibly helped by her father's involvement with Edward as Prince and King. By her marriage, Maggie became part of and was accepted into the Marlborough House Set; we understand Edward adored Maggie's genius for hospitality. Not surprising, because Edward really wished to throw over all of the restraint, he had previously experienced. Maggie became a lifelong friend of Alice Keppel, which further enhanced Maggie's position at Court, while Edward was King.

When Ronnie died, the kindness provided by King Edward to Maggie by his visit on 5th and 6th June 1909, ensuring Maggie's continuity in the Marlborough House Set, enabled Maggie to continue her royal thread/connection. This was further managed by Maggie's offer in 1914 to King George and Queen Mary, of the gift of Polesden Lacey to one of their children, when she died. It was decided in 1914, that Bertie would become the recipient of this amazing gift.

Bertie and Elizabeth's honeymoon in 1923, staying at Polesden Lacey for ten days, demonstrated their enduring friendship with Maggie. Coming forward to today, because Maggie's jewellery was gifted to Queen Elizabeth the Queen Mother, then passed on to the Queen, and continuing as it is inherited to Prince Charles and Camilla the Duchess of Cornwall, followed by Prince William and Katherine the Duchess of Cambridge, the jewellery is not just a connection; it is a perpetual link. How many people can achieve such success?

Entertainment was provided by Maggie at Polesden Lacey after dinner throughout her life as a hostess and a key figure in society. Entertainment was also offered at Maggie's London house with the most fashionable entertainers available.

The entertainments changed as with fashion, but they provided a backdrop for some guests to relax, listen to and enjoy, often highly regarded people in showbusiness at the time. Also, those guests who wished could be playing billiards or cards around the corner from the Saloon (at Polesden Lacey) or gossiping, intriguing or flirting with each other while the concert or artists continued to play.

Many of Maggie's guests found that a weekend spent in the country (with such an easy journey from town) enabled them to discuss politics/diplomacy and more away from any public gaze. While news was not, of course, transmitted twenty-four seven in Maggie's day, it was still possible to watch key people moving around London and report on their activities. Being secluded, almost secreted away in Maggie's house as royalty mixed with aristocracy and politicians, was a perfect way of providing a platform for close discussion, among the primary government figures away from town. A look at the Visitor Book at Polesden Lacey, confirms this. The discretion of the servants ensured that this was maintained. Servants did not wish to lose their job, as that would mean losing their home too.

Maggie provided entertainers on Saturday and Sunday evenings (the weekend being Saturday to Monday). Guests deserved the most fashionable artists. Maggie benefited from being approximately one hour from London (as Polesden Lacey still is). Performers and actors working in the theatres and clubs were booked. Many artists would come down from London after their evening show; they were given a meal and performed a late cabaret show before returning to London. On Sunday evenings there was an even better/larger supply of entertainers available. The theatres and clubs closed on Sundays. The artists were happy to earn extra money on such days.

In London at Charles Street, Maggie often required entertainers/artists midweek for the social round. Given that other aristocrats were also employing entertainers, the demand for artists must have been a sound extra source of income for them.

Many of the artists were regular performers at the Embassy Club and the Kit Kat Club. The aristocrats would regularly visit the clubs at the end of an evening out, which consisted of drinks, dinner, a ball or dance (sometimes a theatre) then a late show with dancing at a club.

Maggie used the services of a man named André Charlot (1882-1956), particularly in the 1920s and 1930s, to provide entertainers.[60] He was born in Paris, and was an impresario, known for his highly successful musical revues between 1912 to 1937.

Bert Ambrose and his band (Embassy Club) frequently played for Maggie at both of her houses (not necessarily the whole band, but part of the band). Concerts with classical music were provided, but variety was required, as hostesses had "to keep ahead of the pack" in terms of quality offers.

Charlot provided Noël Coward with his first big break. Artists offered by Maggie included the Dolly Sisters (highly fashionable at the time), other famous artists who "happened to be in town", comedians, jugglers, magicians, ventriloquists, singers, concert musicians, Richard Tauber, Maria Müller (Metropolitan Opera House New York), sometimes almost full orchestras.

In addition, in order to provide real variety, themed parties became desirable. In December 1932 Maggie turned the Charles Street house into a miniature railway station; this turned out to be one of the most spectacular creative parties of not just the season, but for some time after that. Maggie's ivory and gold Ballroom was transformed into a station waiting room, restaurant and bar, and noises including whistling and shunting brought to life "the station atmosphere". The LNER provided posters, and staff from the station helped along the whole of the evening.

EIGHT

Maggie and Her Servants

An "army of servants" was needed at Polesden Lacey to provide this first-class result, and the task was headed by Frank Bole, Maggie's Head Steward. Maggie depended on her staff to provide the best possible standard of service to her guests. I do not believe Maggie Greville exhibited as precise a control mechanism as McEwan, but she did clearly expect to have total success in her entertaining. Much of this burden fell to Francis Bole – Frank, as he was known, and as we shall call him. Without Frank Bole, Maggie's ability to stage manage so much, so well, would have been a little less perfect.

Frank Bole was initially employed as Ronnie's servant (reference Ronnie's statement in his will that Frank was his servant). The exact date for the commencement of Frank's employment is not known. Ronnie died in 1908. Ronnie's Will was written in 1906. Ronnie would not have provided his bequest to Frank, if Frank been on the staff only briefly.

Frank remained with Maggie after Ronnie's death and gradually his importance to Maggie increased.[61] We know that in 1911 Bole was described as a butler (1911 Census). However, Frank's title changed, from the records of travel mostly undertaken with his wife Evelyn. Occasionally Frank travelled with Maggie (but she really needed her head steward, Frank, at home, looking after two houses and a country estate) The occupations Frank provided for his entry to the ship passenger lists were; 1911, butler; 1918, private secretary; 1926, 1928 and 1932, house steward; 1927, secretary; 1927, agent; 1932, steward; and 1939, controller! There are certain variations listed here, but as far as Maggie was concerned, Frank was the managing director or controller of much of her empire.

Frank Bole being Head Steward meant that all of the staff, approximately seventy people at Polesden Lacey, and in excess of one hundred staff when adding in those at Charles Street, all reported to him. Becoming Head Steward made Frank more important than being a head butler. As we know, he worked for Ronnie prior to 1906, followed by Maggie, so Frank was with her for more than thirty-six years. He was with Maggie in the Dorchester Hotel when she died in 1942.

All of the butlers; Adeline Liron, Maggie's personal companion (initially her personal maid) and referred to by Maggie as the Archduchess; Maggie's valet (Herbert Towell); the French chef Monsieur Delachaume for many years; an English lady cook, Eileen Wilson; the maids; the footmen (Charles Street); the chauffeurs and mechanic came under Frank's control. It must be remembered that two houses, two sets of staff, some of whom travelled to both houses as and when necessary, were managed by Frank.

There was, however, a land agent who would care for the estate. A head gardener and a number of gardeners managed the indoor greenhouses and walled gardens; also, the tennis courts, croquet lawn and the golf course. These gardeners were responsible for growing vegetables and fruit, and dressing the flowerbeds to impress guests. The farm workers looked after sheep, pigs, cattle, chickens (the Dorking) and the horses. They also helped to staff the shooting parties when required.

Without a capable staff, Maggie's management of the requirements of royalty, aristocracy and politicians would have been inadequate. Money is more than helpful, but without structural support to continuously provide this vital base, her position in society may have been less secure.

The networking Maggie did, her ability to understand "the system" of what really mattered to so many important people (as they would have regarded themselves), and her intelligence, allowed her to be successful. But the backup of staff, who worked at Polesden Lacey and in London at Charles Street, required someone with more than an average understanding of service to be the Controller.

That person was Frank Crossley Bole (1879–1954), who was born at Somerleyton, Lowestoft, on 8th April.[62] His father James was a gardener and a domestic servant at Somerleyton in 1881. His mother was named Janet, and his parents had moved from Scotland in about 1875.

The owner of Somerleyton was Sir Francis Crossley, a philanthropist, a carpet manufacturer and a Liberal member of Parliament for Halifax.

By 1891 James Bole had moved his family away from Somerleyton to West Ham. They lived at 27 Westbury Road, West Ham.[63] James worked as a nurseryman and florist, so he had taken his wife and family "out of tied service". Frank would have been about twelve years old at the time of the move to West Ham.

Frank may have had one or two previous jobs before he began to work for Ronnie/Maggie, but we have no information to confirm a start date.[64]

We do have the addresses Frank lived at: Frank married his wife Evelyn Mary Wareham (1881–1961) in 1908, and they had three sons, Ronald Francis Crossley Bole (1910–82), Bernard James Bole (1914–2006) and Keith Harry D Bole (1916–98).

We know that Frank and the family lived at 65 Balderton Gardens (just off Oxford Street, London) until 1924. By 1925 the family were living at 42 Stalbridge Flats, 2 Lumley Street (around the corner from the previous address) and the family kept this home until 1939.[65] Latterly, possibly Frank used this more for himself (as a house was purchased in Surrey, as listed below); sometimes he spent nights at 16 Charles Street or at Polesden Lacey, when Maggie had large and important guests to entertain. Frank had rooms in both of Maggie's houses.

By 1933 Frank Bole purchased a house in Ewell Park Gardens (a cul-de-sac off Ewell Park Way), Stoneleigh, Epsom, Surrey. In 1937 Frank moved the family again by purchasing a house in Ewell House Grove, Ewell Village, Epsom, Surrey (again a cul-de-sac). He named the house (a small detached house) Thresons.[66] He had sufficient funds to purchase this property while Maggie was alive. The children attended school/s in London.

Frank Bole managed the London house for Maggie during the week, where everyone who mattered in town came to dine often. Frank also co-ordinated the ordering of meat/fish/fruit and vegetables (other than that provided from the estate). Ordering alcohol and restocking the wine cellars at Polesden Lacey and Charles Street were, realistically, a very important part of Frank Bole's role.

Post for the staff, when received, was distributed by Frank Bole: while this seems a minor duty, it was extremely important to the staff who did not have many days off. Sending and receiving post was really important to Maggie's staff, as it was their communication to "the outside world".

Additionally, Frank Bole supervised the needs and problems of staff working for Maggie, unless or until it was necessary for Frank to advise Maggie that, she needed to address/intervene in a staff situation (family/personal or other problems).

Frank died in 1954 at Epsom and Ewell Cottage Hospital, Epsom, Surrey.[67] From phone records Frank and his family were listed as living at Thresons, Ewell House Grove, until 1953, so we understand that when Frank died, the family remained at this address. It is noted that probate was not granted for Frank until 3rd May 1956, which was unusual. The administration document was issued to the three sons. Frank Bole's probate document stated that His Effects were £11,318.6s.10d, which seems to have been considerable.[68]

One long-standing servant, Arthur Thompson, arrived at Polesden Lacey in 1907 as a groom.[69] His job was to look after the horses and a pony. In an interview conducted in 1988 with Arthur he said, "There was one riding horse, one carriage horse, and a pony for the golf course." His job was to make sure that Mr Ballingore's horse, "the major domo of the estate", was ready for him. Mr Ballingore also took the dogcart to the station to meet people; the gatekeeper Mr Marshall used the pony each day. The animals, the stables, riding boots and riding breeches all had to be cleaned by Arthur each day.

There was also a brougham (a light four-wheeled horse-drawn carriage) used mostly for servants: Arthur used to take some of the maids to the station (and collect them when necessary) if they were going up to Charles Street. Arthur also used the brougham to run errands; for example, bringing the local doctor (Dr Cox at one time) to Polesden Lacey, for anyone who needed some medical help.

Arthur exercised the horses as necessary. He lived next to the riding stables (where the current shop is located). Arthur said he had a bedroom and a bathroom. Len Bates, the golf professional, lived next door to him, and they often played golf in the evening, especially if Maggie was in town or away.

Arthur provided a view of Maggie which showed her harder side (not seen very often, but it was there) and the following incident possibly took place not long after Ronnie died, which may have made Maggie more irritable. Maggie had a German chauffeur (Hemmelkutz) in her early days at Polesden Lacey. Arthur remembers that Maggie wrote a letter to Hemmelkutz, telling him to pick her up at Bookham station, with the Panhard (French manufacturer of early motor cars).

Unfortunately, Hemmelkutz was the only person who could do mechanical repairs, and he had taken the Panhard to pieces to do necessary maintenance, so he arrived at the station in Maggie's Mercedes.

Hemmelkutz returned and told Arthur, "I've got the sack. Yes, I took the Mercedes. She ordered the Panhard, not the Mercedes."

Maggie said to him, "When I order the Panhard, I want the Panhard, not the Mercedes."

Hemmelkutz replied, "Well, I had the Panhard all in pieces. I did not expect you back for another week or two."

His sacking was instant. "So, they had to get two men from the factory to come and put it together. Yes, she sacked him, just like that. And he was a top man, he could get a job anywhere, just like that. They say she was very fair. Very hard though, I believe." So sometimes Maggie displayed her impatient side, but as Arthur admitted, everyone "was well looked after. Well fed, and clothed as well. Always plenty of good food, and three meals a day".

Other male servants were important too. Female servants did not serve in the dining room.

Walter William Bacon, usually known as the drunken butler at Polesden Lacey, had begun work in the late 1920s and was still with Maggie in 1939, but he does disappear from the census listing for Charles Street without us knowing where he disappeared to after this last date.[70] There are a number of stories, some embellished, some possibly true, relating to Bacon while he worked for Maggie.

One famous story relates to the lambs' tongues incident. A rare treat, not attainable very often, certainly a delicacy at that time. Apparently, Bacon was due to serve the tongues. Food was brought from the kitchen into the servery, just next to the Dining Room, and Bacon managed to eat a platter that was meant to offer a small portion to each guest, prior to entering the room.

Maggie enquired of Frank Bole, "What has become of the lambs' tongues?"

Frank Bole, covering for Bacon, said, "There were none to be had in the market this morning."

Unfortunately, Bacon displayed gravy stains down the front of his shirt and suit.

On another occasion Bacon was serving pommes gaufrettes, and he belched heavily and sprayed Maggie, Princess Juliana of the Netherlands and parts of the table!

The third most popular story related to Bacon, was the evening Maggie noticed Bacon was drunk while dinner was being served in the Dining Room. Maggie kept a small notepad with her, and she wrote a note and gave it to Bacon; it read, "You are drunk, leave the room immediately."

Bacon, "up to his tricks", placed the note on a silver salver and presented it to Austen Chamberlain, who was stunned into silence. When everyone was leaving the Dining Room, Maggie enquired as to why Austen had been so quiet during dinner. When Austen explained, she was amused to some extent! Somehow Bacon was humoured and remained working for Maggie for a long time. Osbert Sitwell (one of Maggie's close friends and the Queen Mother's) named Bacon Humpty Dumpty, for certain obvious reasons.

George Henry Moss was a senior butler; he married Emily Baldock in 1916. They had two children.[71] He was employed by Maggie for some time. He sometimes accompanied Maggie on her winter travels in the 1920s and 1930s. He is listed as late as 1933 on the electoral roll for Charles Street and was a beneficiary in Maggie's Will, so she must have regarded him as a capable butler. While Frank Bole was her most important member of staff (and friend), Maggie needed Bole back at home, running her two houses and all that entailed (mostly when she was away), so Moss must have been a good support as a butler when travelling, and remained until 1935.[72] So not for a long period of time in comparison to some servants. Maggie did not need to have a valet, but Towell was possibly employed to help some male guests who did not bring their own man while staying at Polesden Lacey. Maggie took Towell with her on some of her overseas trips.

Usually, a valet looked after a male employer; clothes and all the dressing-room equipment would be maintained by the valet. Maggie may have found his services useful, and he possibly acted as a butler when she was away from home on her trips abroad. He had previously worked for Lord and Lady Howard de Walden, and after leaving Maggie he worked for Anna Dodge, the widow of Horace Dodge, who founded the Dodge Motor Co at Windsor, at least until 1953. An incredibly wealthy employer.

Robert Sydney Nash was Maggie's Maintenance Engineer.[73] He looked after the generator and much more, including running Maggie's fire brigade! He was a capable man who was trusted by Maggie. Robert's son Robert/Bob suffered as a child from rheumatic fever more than once. A local doctor, Dr Warfield, told his parents to send Bob to a convalescent home. The Baptist Sunday school managed a convalescent home at Clacton-on-Sea, and Bob was sent there. His father Robert received a summons from Maggie not long after Bob had gone to Clacton. Someone on the estate had told Maggie that Robert's son Bob was "there on charity".

Maggie said, "I'm surprised that you've got your boy on charity at Clacton-on-Sea."

Bob's father replied, "I'm sorry, Madam, but I am paying twenty-six shillings for four weeks."

Maggie, after appreciating that the gossip she had been told was incorrect, said, "Well, he should stay there five weeks longer, and I'll pay for him."

Maggie went on to arrange for fifty children from the Limehouse district in London to have a week's holiday at this home – Coverdale. Maggie visited the home (getting her chauffeur to take her to see the children). From this time each year, children from the Limehouse District were given a week's holiday, all paid for by Maggie. While this background to the generous side of Maggie could be written about in the charity section of this book, it also serves to demonstrate how much Maggie's servants mattered to her.

Maggie's servants provided the backbone and structure for her successful entertaining, for so many royal guests/maharajahs, politicians and aristocrats. The servants were cared for while they executed their duties to a high standard, and were given free milk every day, and also free firewood. Food remaining from the weekend's entertaining was also given to the servants.

At Christmas, servants with their families living on the estate were given a joint of beef or a turkey. Children on the estate were also given treats at Christmas, and at Easter, an Easter egg hunt was arranged for them in the grounds.

Maggie initiated a servants' ball for her staff from 1909 as an annual event; it is easy to see that entertainment figured highly on her requirements. The annual servants' ball at Christmas gave the servants a first-rate evening, including beer and home-made wine with an excellent dinner; from about 9pm dancing commenced. Maggie took this opportunity to dispense other gifts to the servants.

The Staff Social Club (the current Polesden Lacey shop) offered billiards, darts, cards and dominoes, as well as beer and other drinks. The club opened at 6pm and closed officially at 10pm. Friendly competitions with other similar clubs within a ten-mile radius took place. Additionally, there was a library in the social club for servants, and books could be borrowed and signed for as they were taken out.

Individual examples of Maggie's generosity to the servants were numerous; an example being when Gertie Hulton (second lady's maid) was married in October 1931. Gertie appears for the first time on the electoral roll in 1928, living at Charles Street.

Maggie was fond of Gertie and really did not want Gertie to marry; Maggie advised Gertie that if she married "she would not like to wash her own floors, something she did not have to do as a lady's maid" (Gertie did marry Frederick Palmer Jessup). Also, Maggie promised that if Gertie stayed with her, she would see that she was looked after for the rest of her life. On Gertie's wedding day, Maggie gave Gertie the use of her Rolls-Royce for the wedding.

Gertie was married from Charles Street, which shows Maggie's affection for Gertie. Maggie attended the wedding by arriving in a taxicab! Gertie's husband Frederick Jessup was in service for some years and later worked in a bank. Gertie continued to work for Maggie and often accompanied Maggie on trips abroad, including times when Adeline accompanied Maggie. It does seem that Maggie really cared for Gertie, whom she regarded as a lady with style. Gertie played the piano, sang and made a great addition to parties when Maggie travelled. Maggie had wanted Gertie to remain with her, because Maggie regarded Gertie as "a lady, who was gracious, always beautifully dressed and behaved". By 1933 Gertie and Frederick lived in Acton, and one child, Susan, was born in 1938.

Gladys Yealland worked for Maggie as Maggie's personal lady's maid, from 1933 to 1942. Gladys was based mostly at Charles Street. She travelled with Maggie overseas and was close to Maggie. Gladys was named in Maggie's Will as a beneficiary, and bequeathed £500. If at any time after Maggie's death Adeline Liron was unable to look after Maggie's dogs, Gladys was to be given an additional £100 per annum to do this.

A letter in the archives at Polesden Lacey confirms that when the Queen (Mother) visited Maggie at Charles Street, Gladys said she would curtsy to the Queen but not to the children. Maggie seemed to find this acceptable! After Maggie died, Gladys worked on ocean liners, Cunard, followed by Union-Castle, and met her husband (a hairdresser), Alexander Tait, on board a ship.

Diana Davidson was Maggie's housekeeper from 1932 to 1937. She was a capable lady and liked by Maggie. While Diana was at Polesden Lacey she met Jesse Hewins, a gardener. They married in July 1937. Maggie was sent a piece of the wedding cake. A letter thanking Diana for the cake is on file at Polesden Lacey. After their marriage they moved away and lived in Uxbridge.

Monsieur Delachaume was a French chef based at Charles Street. He came to Polesden Lacey for the weekends, when important guests were being entertained. Maggie always used coal to fire/heat the ovens, both at Charles Street and Polesden Lacey. Limited information exists about Monsieur Delachaume. He lived in Pimlico and he is described as a cook on the 1911 Census; his wife was named Eugenie. Having a French chef was considered to be prestigious and added to your social position.

Maggie's English cook at Polesden Lacey was Eileen Beal (née Wilson). Eileen travelled up to Scotland with Maggie when Maggie spent time there in the summer months. Eileen took provisions with her, to help to provide what she knew Maggie would wish her to cook.

Nellie Duncan looked after Maggie's dogs when Maggie was travelling. Nellie used to send Maggie postcards (as though the dogs had drawn/written the postcards themselves) when she was on one of her long winter trips. Maggie's fondness for Nellie is demonstrated by what Maggie did for Nellie, when Maggie visited New Zealand and Australia in 1927. Maggie took Nellie to Australia, because Nellie had a sister and family there, and clearly loved being able to see them. Maggie did not have to do this, but Maggie's fondness shows through in correspondence from Maggie to Nellie. Nellie departed before Maggie to return to England. After Nellie departed, Maggie stayed at Admiralty House in Sydney to welcome the arrival of Bertie and Elizabeth on the *Renown* in March 1927.

Megan Hill, one of Maggie's kitchen maids, was originally hired to work at Charles Street and worked in town during the week, and at Polesden Lacey at the weekend. Megan made a visit with her granddaughter Wendy in 1999, to Polesden Lacey for the first time since she departed in 1929 (seventy years later).[74]

Megan recalled being driven to and from these properties by Rolls-Royce by an under-chauffeur, Jimmy. She said the senior chauffeurs who drove Maggie and her guests had a different uniform to the chauffeurs who drove the servants; Maggie's personal chauffeurs wore gold braid!

As a kitchen maid, Megan never walked through the jib door which led from the servery to the dining room! When she entered the kitchen on this return visit, she commented on the kitchen floor: "This was my floor, this was the wooden floor that we scrubbed every morning, when I was here." Although the cooking equipment, ovens and more have been removed from the old kitchen, the large old dresser remains from which she used to hang the copper pots and pans that she cleaned. Meghan made the comment that she used salt and sand to clean these pots. Meghan confirmed that there were six ovens in the kitchen in her time. When she came into the dining room, she remembered that "the food all the staff had enjoyed had been exceptional, the same as that enjoyed in this room".

Meghan met Roland Hill at Polesden Lacey; he was in charge of the glasshouses. There were plenty of other offers of interest from the young men who worked at Polesden Lacey, but Meghan did not care for them too much. When she met Roland, she thought he was different. Meghan actually asked

Roland to take her to the Friday night "hop" dance at the social club which Maggie had created for her staff.

The location of the club was where the current retail shop is now situated at Polesden Lacey, but at the time of Meghan's visit in 1999, this area was the restaurant. Meghan said, Maggie had changed the old stable block into the social club, and ensured it was done to a high standard. The dance started at 9/10pm depending on when staff duties finished (if Maggie was not entertaining on a Friday night, they would "get away early"). The dance finished at midnight.

Roland, who was second to the head gardener (Meghan said), had the job of arranging fresh flowers in the house prior to Maggie's weekend entertaining. On one particular occasion, he was summoned back to the house, having spent the morning arranging the flowers, "to do something about the dead flowers in the dining room". Meghan recalled "that the house was in panic", as an important function that evening "could be ruined by his failure". Roland had spent a long time arranging the flowers, including the anemones in the dining room. "As the afternoon light faded all the buds had closed tight shut. It was electric light that saved the day, and probably his job; all available lamps were positioned around the flowers and at the eleventh hour they thankfully reopened."

The needs of lady guests who required buttonholes to match their dresses for Royal Ascot had to be addressed successfully; the male guests would line up and walk to the greenhouse, where they were given their buttonholes.

Maggie's guests were offered early strawberries and pineapples (from the pineapple pit) and other exotic fruits. These were just some of the "essentials" required for Maggie to impress at her dining table. Flowers in the house had to be spectacular. Second rate for anything Maggie did or wanted was not acceptable.

Maggie employed a secretary/controller to maintain and oversee her accounts. From 1930 to 1932, Miss H Lysaght Griffin worked for Maggie, who required that her accounts should be well managed.[75] I consider that Maggie had to run what amounted to a large business. While Frank Bole was the visible face of her business as the "on-the-spot managing director", his services were practical on the whole.

Miss Griffin had previously worked for Lord Beaverbrook as one of his secretaries, and she followed Maggie's employment by becoming secretary to the headmaster of Eton College. She had a varied pattern of work, but her principal responsibility concerned the household accounts for Polesden Lacey and Charles Street, which were approximately £10,000 annually, which today would translate into more than £600,000.

Miss Griffin approved payments to traders, suppliers and to staff. This was not a small task, to keep two houses and an estate running smoothly. She was able to authorise payments without referring to Maggie prior to paying them, so she was really trusted. Miss Lysaght's salary during these years was £550 per year. Maggie clearly liked Miss Griffin and remained friends with her after she departed in 1932. Several years later (1938) Maggie was in correspondence with her, while Maggie was staying at the Hotel de Paris in Monte Carlo, from where she wrote to Miss Griffin.

Yes, Maggie had more than enough money from McEwan, but this had to be translated into an outstanding service to guests. McEwan was included with Maggie's guests when she entertained. He was the benefactor, and without him, none of this could have taken place. Maggie could not have become so successful within society, without William McEwan's money and support initially. While he was alive, until 1913, McEwan did everything he could to support and advise Maggie.

In the late nineteenth and early twentieth centuries, domestic service in private homes made up a high proportion of women's employment. Domestic work remained a large employer, with forty-one per cent of the female workforce employed as servants in 1891. This dropped to twenty-four per cent by 1931 (post-war changes were well underway), but domestic service remained the largest single female employment sector, with around 1.6 million servants.

The mistress of a country house (or a London house) was meant to provide one month's notice, or wages in lieu of the notice period, but they were not legally compelled to provide a reference.

By the interwar years around one third of these servants were non-residential. But their employment conditions remained similar to those of Victorian servants, with very limited time off, and low rates of pay. National Insurance benefits had been available to some workers from 1911, but domestic servants were one of the last groups to be included in 1938.

Slowly, more commercial work began to be available, for people who had previously been servants in houses owned by aristocrats. Engineers working in industry from 1890, were able to finish work at midday Saturday and return to work on Monday morning. Workers in the textile industry worked a five-and-a-half-day week from 1901. But for people in service in households, time off was scarce. Hence the importance of post (letters and parcels). After World War II, many women did not return to their domestic service roles. The numbers of servants continued to dwindle in the twentieth century.

How Was Maggie Affected?

We know Maggie held on to her staff (on the whole) for many years. Maggie was a generous employer, if staff gave her their full commitment. When staff were in trouble or needed health treatment (unaffordable to most of them), Maggie located a doctor, sorted out what treatment was needed (including operations) and paid the costs, as the National Health Service was not introduced until 1948. Domestic staff lost their home if they lost their job. It is understandable that numbers declined and people began to work away from such employment.

Maggie entertained at Polesden Lacey from 1907 after purchasing the house, even though building work was being carried out. Initially there was a day visit in May 1907 by Edward VII with Alice Keppel and members of the Marlborough House Set, who were staying with Maggie and Ronnie for the weekend at Reigate Priory (a house they were renting).[76] By the autumn of 1907, guests were staying at Polesden Lacey for the weekend.

The visit of Edward VII to Polesden Lacey for the weekend of 5th and 6th June 1909, signalled emphatically that Maggie was back in society. She also began to be included in visits to other country houses.[77] On 7th, 8th and 9th September 1909 (midweek), Maggie was in the house party at Rufford Abbey which included Edward VII, Alice Keppel, Lady Londonderry, Lady Sarah Wilson and other members of the Set. Edward VII was present to attend the St Leger, where his horse Minoru was running in the race. The winning horse was Bayardo, ridden by Danny Maher. Edward's horse, Minoru, was fourth in the race. By Saturday 11th September 1909 (weekend) Maggie was in Edward's party which travelled to Duntreath Castle, Stirlingshire, to be guests of Lord and Lady Edmonstone (Alice Keppel's brother Archibald and sister-in-law Ida). Life had "picked up" for Maggie, and while she was still wearing mourning clothes, albeit with a few small changes to her apparel, she was beginning to commence her elevation back into the best society could offer.

Maggie began again to spend her time entertaining at Charles Street from Monday to Thursday. She participated in Court events, and was entertained and participated in the calendar, society offered. She began to be involved more in charity work.

Adeline Liron was originally Maggie's personal maid.[78] Maggie called her "the Archduchess" when talking of her to anyone. Adeline became a companion to Maggie and was dressed in clothes which reflected the relationship; Adeline dressed more and more similarly to Maggie as their relationship grew. Adeline accompanied Maggie on some of her long-distance travels (during the winter months) and Adeline travelled first-class. This can be seen from the ship embarkation information. There would have been no point in Adeline, having accommodation away from Maggie when travelling. Maggie required Adeline for every possible need, and she needed Adeline to be close by. Had Adeline been placed in the lower decks, Maggie's conveniences would have suffered.

Adeline seems to have joined Maggie from around 1908. Who was Adeline? Adeline was born on 28th June 1873 at Cuncy-lès-Varzy. Her father was Philip Liron, a carpenter, and her mother was (possibly) Jeanneton Nigolais. When Adeline travelled with Maggie, she offered two different birth places, hence one hundred per cent certain proof is not available.

As we know, Maggie travelled extensively in the winter months. We know Adeline travelled on the following ships and places with Maggie:[79] to New York on the *Mauretania* (25th January 1920); from Havana to Florida on the *Miami* (7th April 1920), including Frank Bole (Maggie's Head Steward); India in 1921–22; from Southampton to Buenos Aires on board the *Andes* (12th December 1924); on the *Olympic* (24th April 1925), including George Moss (Maggie's butler); New Zealand and Australia, 1927; on the *Empress of France* (7th January 1928), from Southampton to Jamaica, including George Moss; on the *New Northland* (21st February 1928), including George Moss; on the *Empress of India* (29th April 1931), from Yokohama to San Francisco, including Herbert Towell (Maggie's valet); on the *Bremen* (2nd February 1935), from Southampton to New York, including George Moss; on the *Lurline* (22nd February 1935), from Los Angeles to Honolulu, including George Moss; on the *Malolo* (14th March 1935), from Honolulu to San Francisco, including George Moss; on the *Bremen* (25th April 1935), from New York to Southampton; on the *Empress of Britain* (15th April 1936) from Yokohama to San Francisco, including Herbert Towell; on the *Bremen* (15th May 1936), from New York to Southampton, including Herbert Towell. Quite a list, which shows how close and important this relationship was.

Initially, Adeline helped Maggie with her hair (never forget the need for ladies to have their hair "put up" to hold their tiaras), her clothes and all her personal requirements. Also, some of Maggie's correspondence would have been dealt with by Adeline, although Maggie did employ secretaries too. Maggie relied on Adeline, and any gossip about Adeline being poached by someone else in society was met with abrupt rebuttals, as I explain below.

On one of Maggie's foreign trips, Maggie and Adeline were photographed on board a ship; they were both dressed almost identically in wool coats with fur collars. Later, Maggie was spotted with Adeline dining at the Café Royal in London, just as two friends might. Beverley Nichols said of Maggie on this occasion, "And though she loved power, she was not really a snob. One day I walked into the ground floor of the Café Royal and saw Maggie, in a plain black dress, sitting in a corner dining with the Archduchess, there was nothing incongruous or embarrassing about it. Why should there be? The two women were not only mistress and maid, they were friends."

Beverley Nichols also described in his book, *The Sweet and Twenties*, the following: "Once when I was staying at Polesden, Maggie took me aside and led me down the long corridor towards the drawing room. Halfway down she paused in front of a dubious Ruysdael (her taste in pictures was by no means impeccable). She put her finger to her lips. 'My dear,' she said in a stage whisper, 'do you know what I have just been told? I have been told that Gracie Vanderbilt has an extraordinary notion she might be able to entice away the Archduchess! And I don't believe she has ever spoken to her. It's simply jealousy.' I expressed astonishment. 'She may be very rich,' continued Maggie, with a snort of indignation, 'but she is not as rich as that!' Then a softer note came into her voice. 'And in any case, it is not a question of money. I don't believe the Archduchess would ever leave me even if Gracie were to offer a million dollars. Poor Gracie! Such a snob. And like all Americans, no sense of proportion.'"[80]

Maggie gave Adeline many presents over the years. In her Will, Maggie bequeathed to Adeline "£50 per month, plus £100 per annum", as long as she cared for Maggie's dogs. Adeline also received "Two rows of pearls, all my wearing apparel and my trinkets and other articles of personal use and any pieces of jewellery which do not exceed £100 each in value". Some of these trinkets were Faberge and Cartier. Adeline was able to continue to live at Polesden Lacey for the rest of her life and was given the use of the whole of Maggie's apartment.

Adeline received over ninety items for her personal use, which were valued at no more than £100 each.[81] Some of these items were: a blue Faberge enamel cigarette case with an X set in diamonds and a blue enamel cigarette lighter. Many of the items were made of gold and had diamonds or other jewels dressing them, such as evening bags, boxes, a paper knife, cigarette holders or boxes, pens and lorgnettes. Most of the items were small but valuable!

Adeline remained at Polesden Lacey for a long time. Later she became ill and she died at Wyke House, Isleworth, on 13th February 1959 (a private hospital specialising in the care of mentally ill patients). Adeline bequeathed an estate valued at £19,083. Probate was granted to Robin Fedden (General Manager of Polesden Lacey at that time). Adeline's sister was the beneficiary of her will.

She was recorded as being eighty-five years old, with the cause of death being "terminal bronchopneumonia and general physical and mental decline". A sad finale for a lady who had enjoyed a fascinating life with her "best friend" Maggie.

One of Maggie's valued members of staff was Sydney William Henry Smith, Head Chauffeur (1883–1961). Smith was born in Paddington, London; his father was a coachman. He married Louisa Maud Parker in 1904. They had two children, Dora (born 1904) and Arthur (born 1906), both born before Smith joined Maggie as a chauffeur in 1906. Smith remained with Maggie for thirty-six years until she died.

After becoming Head Chauffeur; Smith and his family lived at Polesden Lacey and also at 11 Hays Mews (behind 16 Charles Street, which was also owned by Maggie). Smith enjoyed working conditions which were not too onerous. When Maggie required Smith to drive her, Smith "would summon the under-chauffeur, Jefferies, to prepare the car and deliver it to him in pristine condition". When Smith returned the car, the under-chauffeur took "the car to wash and polish it ready for the next outing".

Maggie frequently demonstrated her generosity to her staff. When Louisa needed an operation, Maggie organised and paid for it, including aftercare (Maggie chose the King's surgeon).

The Smith family remember that Maggie was a very generous lady. Sydney Smith's grandson (Edward Colling) has said that in addition to the Servants' Ball held at Polesden Lacey at Christmas each year to say thank you to the staff, and the presents they were all given, the staff in London were able to attend a servants' ball at the Albert Hall each year.

Tickets were expensive for the staff. Maggie paid for their tickets, and she would turn up briefly to wish them an enjoyable evening at the Albert Hall.

One unusual piece of information also offered by Sidney Smith's grandson was that, Smith smuggled into England a small dog for Maggie (it was believed it was a Pekinese) inside his sleeve! No doubt he drove the car carefully.

Smith was the last person to drive Maggie; he drove her to and from the Dorchester Hotel, which was where she resided when she wanted to be "in town" as the war proceeded, and it was where she died.

Frederick Henry Hart was a coachman/chauffeur who began working for William McEwan, and his address was originally listed at 14 Hayes Mewes, behind 16 Charles Street. He married Alice (a cook) in 1910. They had six children. After McEwan died in 1913, he worked for Maggie. He lived with his family, firstly at Tanners Hatch until 1915, which the family named as the Three Bears Cottage (now a YHA hostel). Frederick, with the family, moved to Polesden Stables in 1916, followed by either Tower House or Bailiffs House. Maggie used to bring back presents for the children when she returned home from travelling.

The children have a memory of their father driving to Brighton to pick up the Dolly Sisters (an exciting theatrical act at the time), who were booked as entertainment for Maggie's guests, who included King Farouk while he was staying at Polesden Lacey.[82] Alice would help out when Maggie had large house parties at Polesden Lacey. Maggie paid for medical treatment for Frederick when he suffered from arthritis in his later years, and after he died in 1932, Alice and the family remained at Polesden Lacey, and moved to Goldstone Cottage. Maggie made provision in her Will for Alice and the children to continue to live at Goldstone Cottage, but Alice did not receive any money; as "an occasional helper" at Polesden Lacey in the house Alice was not officially a paid member of staff.

When two of the Harts' children began to work as maids for Maggie at Charles Street, Marie settled down as a maid and worked well, but her sister Lorna objected to some of the work, including cleaning the inside and outside of a coal bucket! Lorna did not last long as a maid and obtained a job working for Sainsbury's the grocers.

There was a third chauffeur, Alfred William Wesley, who arrived at Polesden Lacey in 1929. He lived variously at the following properties: Yew Tree Farm; 1932, at North Lodge; 1933, at Dairy Cottage; 1934, at Tanners Hatch and 1935, back at Yew Tree Farm. He married Dorothy Wales in 1935, and it is recorded that they were given a clock as a wedding present. Alfred was a member of the fire team, and also did some golf caddying for some of the guests. The family lived in Bookham after Maggie died. Alfred is buried in the graveyard at St Nicholas Church, Bookham.

"The Hon Mrs Ronald Greville unusually bought two Rolls-Royces at a time, 1915, when virtually all Rolls-Royce car production was being sold to the War office or being converted to armoured cars, so she must have been a woman of considerable influence!"[83] The style of coachwork that Maggie preferred was a landaulette, with a folding rear section to the body allowing the owners to take fresh air but also to be seen.

The two cars were: Rolls-Royce Silver Ghost Chassis 29 AD, first delivered 2nd March 1915, registration LM 8119, with a landaulette body by the famous coach builders Barker of London; Rolls-Royce Silver Ghost Chassis 29 RD, first delivered 13th July 1915, registration LO 6311 with a landaulette body again by Barker of London. This car was delivered to Maggie's London residence, 16 Charles Street. This car appears to have been retained by her until her death in 1942.

Maggie bought another Silver Ghost Chassis 20 YG, registration XN 3825, which was probably delivered in late 1922 or early 1923 when the body had been fitted by Hooper, the coach builders much favoured by the King. Then Maggie sold her oldest Silver Ghost 29 AD.

We know from Maggie's Will, that she bequeathed all of her motor cars and all of the garage furniture to her chauffeur Sidney Smith. Sadly, he seems to have been overwhelmed by the bequest, and a letter from the family in recent years stated that Sydney Smith set about selling the cars, not long after Maggie died.

NINE
Managing Polesden Lacey

Head Gardeners

1911–15, R Davidson
1916–26, Harry Prince
1926–38, George Twinn
1938–64, Henry Smith
1964–73, AG Ellis
1973–2000, Robert Hall
2000–10, Stephen Torode
2010, Tim Parker until Chris Gaskin took over temporarily
2015–20, Jamie Harris

Garden and Outdoor Managers

Simon Akeroyd (during Tim Parker's time)
Tony Gregory (during Jamie Harris' time)
2017–22, Alex Wigley[84]

Some of the above dates (up to 1938) are sometimes quoted with a one-year variation. A single start date and a single finish date have been chosen by reviewing several references.

It becomes evident that Maggie wanted the gardens to showcase her house in the way her paintings, porcelain, and the art and other artefacts did. Maggie wanted to offer to her guests not just a weekend place to stay, but a house which was significant and had relevance to society (foreign visitors, including royalty, politicians and ambassadors). Having the gardens reflect back to the house, a manicured, stunning and comprehensive offer of flowers, fruit, and vegetables, was a win for Maggie. Add in the interest caused by the success of some of her poultry at competitions, and a picture of a lady emerges who was involved in more than a surface acceptance of having "nice gardens". Maggie employed enough of the right people to ensure first-class results.

Maggie's gardens at Polesden Lacey were designed to receive guests. The variety and lavishness of horticultural displays, were the most important elements of garden design in Edwardian society.

The golf course (nine holes) at Polesden Lacey may have been established by Sir Clinton Dawkins. There are a number of publications stating that he arranged for a golf course to be created. Sir Dawkins died in 1905, and there is no actual proof of this work being executed. In the 2011 Garden Conservation Plan for Polesden Lacey, undertaken by Acta for the National Trust, doubt is expressed as to whether Maggie or Dawkins organised the golf course.[85]

Maggie wanted a golf course and would have ensured that the course was of a high standard, whether she initiated the layout or improved it. Two of Maggie's gardeners maintained the course. Maggie did employ Harry Vardon as a golf professional.

By the 1920s, the garden staff and some of the estate children were "employed" as caddies by Maggie's guests. The tips they received were pooled, although in the early days, guests carried their own clubs. Early on Saturday morning the greens were "caned" to remove the dew, so Maggie's guests could have an early start. The estate staff were allowed to play golf in the evenings, when there were no guests staying at the house. By 1923 we know that a rustic wooden shelter was in place on the golf course, presumably offering the halfway house refreshments.

The layout of the golf course began by turning left by the current archway to Polesden Lacey (this archway was constructed after Maggie died, but in order to pinpoint the direction of the golf course, I use this modern addition) at the front of the driveway, continuing left into a field which is now used for dog walkers to exercise their dogs. Eight holes were in place in this field, and the ninth hole was in place on the ground beyond the east front of the house.

Frank Boyd was the Greenkeeper for the golf course at Polesden Lacey, from the early 1930s. He married Violet, who had been a maid for Maggie at Charles Street and at Polesden Lacey. They lived with their two children in a bungalow which still exists (recently this house became a small pre-school for nursery children). One of their children, Christine, was born at St Thomas' Hospital, London. Maggie discovered that Violet had an ovarian cyst, which at the time could have killed her. Maggie made arrangements for Violet to remain in hospital for five months before she gave birth to Christine. This was one of many kindnesses Maggie provided during her life to her staff and their families.

During World War II, Frank Boyd and the family departed from Polesden Lacey. Some of the flowerbeds and the golf course were required at this time, for crop growing and for whatever was needed in World War II.

Maggie also employed bailiffs and estate/poultry managers.[86] By 1911 George Stevens was Poultry Manager/farmer. The family lived at Yew Tree Farm. He was married and had three children. By 1922, his name does not appear on the electoral rolls, so he had moved on.

James Stirling Hepburn was Estate Manager from 1927 until 1932. He was an expert in poultry. He was married firstly to Elsie. They had three children, James, John and David. The boys attended Ardingly College, Sussex. Elsie died in 1931 from Graves' disease (hyperthyroidism). At that time there was no treatment, whereas today this illness is managed medically. James departed from Polesden Lacey in 1932. He went on to partner without marrying Annie Mason (the children's nanny originally), after Elsie's death. Seemingly another seven children were born to James and Annie. In 1941 James married Christina Annie Mackinnon (another lady) in Norfolk, which is where James died in 1957.

James's expertise in managing poultry was recognised. The 2nd Annual Poultry Sale at Polesden Lacey in 1930 stated that "Mr. J. S. Hepburn, who has been responsible for the breeding of the poultry, will be pleased to give buyers any possible assistance". It has been confirmed that a photograph of Polesden Farm Barn, was the back cover for the catalogue. A letter is on file requesting if James could judge the geese at the Royal Association of British Dairy Farmers, which suggests his knowledge was well known in this aspect of farm management.

What Did Maggie Do with the Gardens?

After Maggie bought Polesden Lacey in 1907, "Grandiose plans/ambitious plans by Frank Stuart Murray of Durand, Murray and Seddon were outlined, for the south garden and other areas – but mostly these plans were not implemented. A large number of design proposals survive from this period." The actual schemes which were implemented were, semi-circular and rectangular bays/bastions along the terrace (Long Walk) in place today, and a new scheme for the forecourt east of the house.

"Mrs Greville's evolved gardening philosophy concentrated on roses, herbaceous plants and lawns, typically English specialities which her foreign guests could not grow in their own countries."

In the 2011 Garden Survey of Polesden Lacey by Acta, Sarah Rutherford described the following areas of varying significance:[87]

Exceptional Significance

North drive; ha-ha; south lawn, including the terrace and parterre; the long walk, known as Sheridan's Walk (not built by Sheridan).

Considerable Significance

Forecourt and sunken approach; walnut tree lawn/surrounding avenues; iris garden; herbaceous borders; rose garden, including walls and tower; sunken lane; herb/lavender garden; gardener's cottage; glasshouses; winter garden; old kitchen garden; thatched bridge; the ladies' garden; sunken garden; croquet lawn; lower sunken garden; peristyle at end of Sheridan's Walk; Nun's Walk; Bagden Drive; Preserve Copse; Admiral's Walk.

Some Significance

Dog's Graveyard; lower bridge; Roman Bath lawn; stable yard environs and cottages; the new tennis courts (now staff car park); new kitchen garden.

Cheals of Crawley worked at Polesden Lacey in 1908 and for some time later. John/Ernest Cheal recalled in some notes (dated 1908), which have been supplied to the National Trust by Alison Benton in 2001, that the firm "carried out a lot of work in this garden including a lot of alterations to the drive, and the new forecourt, and later we altered and replanted the rose garden and other planting about the place".

Henry Smith (head gardener from 1938 for twenty-six years, so mostly for the National Trust, as Maggie died in 1942) said the old kitchen gardens had been remodelled by 1910, when the wall south of the rose garden and the iris and lavender gardens was created. As this is confirmed by Cheals (above) this can be accepted as accurate.

Plans for a sunken garden were discarded by 1912. By 1917/18 the garden ledger for the walled garden, shows wall planting pockets constructed by Cheals. The rustic summerhouses were in place in 1938, at each corner of the Rose Garden (photographs exist at Polesden Lacey showing these).

Some plans were simplified prior to being executed, as stated above. The pergola (always stunning during the rose-flowering season) was created with rough wooden poles as support for the climbing roses, and these were in place by 1908–09, as erected by Cheals. These poles were replaced about four years ago, and while the contractor thought that providing smooth poles would be better, and arrived with smooth new poles to replace the old poles, the contractor had to take them back and replace them, with identical rough poles, which are in position now.

Between 1908–12 a large new kitchen garden was created by linking a thatched bridge across Yew Tree Lane.[88] Nearly six acres of vegetables were required to supply both Polesden Lacey in the season, and the town house in Charles Street. Mr Davidson (Head Gardener) suggested this in 1910: "Because the men had to walk all the way round to get to the vegetables."

The iris and herb gardens were laid out to the west of the rose garden and the glasshouses. From circa 1910 a large rock and water garden was designed for the area south of the tennis (later croquet) lawn, apparently by Pulham & Co using Westmorland stone. It is said that a disagreement with the contractors meant that only a small was part executed. The only signed known plan, which remains by Pulham, is for alterations which were not executed to the south terraces.

Between 1912 and 1916 Maggie's dog cemetery was created. Maggie owned seventeen dogs during her adult life, and they are buried in this cemetery with their own gravestones.

In 1914 the tennis lawn was created by terracing the south side of the old walled gardens. This area became the croquet lawn, once the new hard tennis courts were constructed circa 1915 for the use of wounded officers whilst they were recuperating at Polesden Lacey (if they were well enough to use them).

In 1918, £40 was spent on the tennis courts, including £9 hauling material for them, and £31 was paid to Slocock, for a yew hedge to enclose them.

Clock golf was established at the south-east corner of the croquet lawn by a blue spruce. In 1914 an icehouse was visible/shown for the first time in the Preserve Copse. The 1917/18 garden ledger for the walled garden describes wall-planting pockets that remain in use today.

The estate ledgers for 1915–18 provide some detail as to the type of horticultural activity after Mrs Greville's main alterations to the garden. The labour ranged from £1,116 for the year 1915–16 to £850 for 1916–17 and nearly £900 in 1917–18.

A labouring man's wages was £1 a week; this would suggest up to twenty staff in 1915–16, reducing to around fifteen to sixteen staff the following two years, probably because of the war. Items bought included fifty-seven tons of peat manure in 1915, with a further fifty yards manure in 1916. Fewer plants were bought in 1915–16 compared with the following two years: nearly £62 of which £43 was spent on bulbs, and £14 went to Paul's nurseries for roses.

On the golf course, one man and an assistant were paid £146 for the year's labour to maintain it in comparison with the cost of a dozen golf balls, which was £1.10.6d. About the same amount was spent in the following two years employing a man and his assistant to maintain the course.

In 1916–17, £164 or so was spent on seeds, plants and bulbs, including £3 on lily of the valley roots. Well-known nurseries were patronised, including Suttons, Carters, Russell, Waterer, Slocock, Perry, Carter, Bunyard, Jackman for clematis, Rivers, Paul and Allgrove.

Cheals and Sons were arranging more pockets for plants in the new garden wall (on the south side of the walled garden). Water was laid on in the kitchen garden; a new barbed-wire fence was put up around the kitchen garden.

A Ransomes motor mower was used, and in 1917–18, £24 or so was spent on fuel.

The statuary collection set out in garden was possibly supplied by White Allom, but we do not have confirmation of this. I met with White Allom, as discussed earlier, but they have no records existing of their early work.

Roderick Davidson was at Polesden Lacey by 1911 as Head Gardener.[89]

He married Mary Scott in 1895 in Selkirk. They had three children: Violet, born 1896; Jessamine, born 1901 and Donald, born 1906. They all lived in the gardener's cottage. It has been recorded that in May 1913, Mr. Davidson showed the Headley Gardeners Mutual Improvement Society around the grounds. Maggie entertained this group, and they were given "a bountiful meal in the dining room". Mr Davidson departed from Polesden Lacey in 1915 and went on to other employment. His work was praised; a reference from Maggie and another employer confirms his ability.

Harry Prince's father had been Head Gardener at Dartrey Castle, Ireland (demolished in 1946); Harry worked there for one year, then he moved to the Botanic Gardens at Glasnevin, north-west of Dublin. Harry worked at a number of properties before coming to Polesden Lacey: Bear Wood Gardens, Wokingham; Hillingdon Court Gardens, Hillingdon; Messrs Veitch's Chelsea Nursery (a famous plant nursery – the Chelsea business closed in 1914, though the Exeter business continued); and Downside Gardens Leatherhead (at the time these gardens provided roses and chrysanthemums of a very high standard, which were displayed in many exhibitions in various parts of Great Britain). At Polesden Lacey, Harry regularly took flowers in the pony and trap to the station, to be placed on the train and taken up to Charles Street.

Harry was responsible for Maggie winning the RHS show 22nd May 1917 Silver Bankside Medal of the society for a remarkable vegetable collection. Harry Prince said to a gardening correspondent that "the potatoes, lettuce, peas, turnips, carrots, radishes and mustard and cress were grown in cold frames with hot beds". He also said "the potatoes, which were particularly fine (especially the Sharps Victors), were planted in the second week of February and were grown with the aid of a hot bed of leaves with two foot of soil on top. There was no earthing up". He added that "the vegetables grown outside included asparagus, onions, spinach, rhubarb and a very useful green, but little grown in this country – spinach beet. French beans, cucumbers and tomatoes were all house grown with heat".

Harry married in September 1922 in London. Their son Eric was born in 1923 at Polesden Lacey. In 1925 Harry moved to Reading, joining Suttons Seeds. He worked extensively in design, and was responsible for many gardens in the area. He was a member and judge for the RHS for over thirty years, and contributed to articles/committees, and was a lecturer, being given the Association of Honour by the RHS. He retired in 1954 but continued to be associated with a number of gardening organisations.

George Twinn is listed as living at the gardeners' house from 1926–38.

During his time as Head Gardener, George listed a careful gardening calendar, including all of the vegetable- and flower-planting times and schemes. His details show precision, and from this long list, we can see how Maggie required an extensive variety of food to service both of her houses. To make a detailed list here would not necessarily be fascinating reading. The use of frames and greenhouses enabled this incredible variety to be produced.

George's list is comprehensive from January through to December. His comments in his list include: "hardening off", keeping some plants dry, others well-watered but with good air circulation in frames, careful forward management and maintenance of frames and greenhouses, the raising of annuals, pot planting, renewal of "hot beds" in addition to the prime requirements of the vegetable garden and the flower garden.

A letter George sent to Jessie Hewins, dated 3rd November 1932 (who was employed a while later) at Polesden Lacey, shows his thoroughness and possibly his seriousness:[90]

"I have before me your application for post as inside foreman here and am giving the matter my consideration.

As you may see I have an advert coming out tomorrow in the *Gardeners Chronicle* (which should have been out last week) and as no doubt I shall have replies to this I am deferring my decision till next week, and I will notify you.

In the meantime, I can give you these particulars. We grow large batch of hydrangeas and various annuals in pots, lorraines and mums for winter." Referring to flowers, he said, "In the summer there is a good deal of decorating and sometimes some to do in the London house. My foreman Hill, who is leaving, came from Shugborough and has been most satisfactory.

I will write you later. Yours faithfully, GE Twinn."

Henry Smith, Head Gardener from 1938, produced out-of-season flowers and fruit and vegetables for Maggie. He knew she wanted "lots of flowers". The Charles Street house, was always decked out with flowers profusely, when Maggie entertained her star guests.

Maggie's favourite flowers were violets, which were in flower from early November to March, and in abundance because they were grown in a whole row of cold frames in the frame yard.

The particular violet Maggie favoured was Princess of Wales odorata.[91]

The violets were raised "from where they were grown in in the garden with as much earth as possible". The violets were lifted in August from the garden into the cold frames, because Maggie required them from November to March.

"They were either planted straight into the bed, or into six-inch pots. The pots had to be well drained, preferably with broken bones instead of crocks.

The roots took hold of the bones and this fed the plants and made them produce flowers. The best compost was four parts turfy loam to one part each of rotted manure, leaf mould and sand with a sprinkling of soot. The pots were plunged up to their rims in rows and well-watered to settle the soil. The frames were kept closed for three or four days after they were planted, and shaded if the sun was strong. Lights were used to help maintain temperature, day and night, with adjustments as necessary."

The violets were grown in pots for the house, but also were used as cut flowers. Maggie also liked lily of the valley. See my note re the violets Maggie organised for Ronnie's coffin, for his funeral in Chapter 6.

Begonias are frequently mentioned dressing Charles Street. Begonia Gloire de Lorraine was grown under glass. Poinsettias also were in great demand for autumn and Christmas. Sweet peas were grown, which had to have five flowers to a stem (for judging standards, as Maggie enjoyed exhibiting them at shows).

Maggie liked orchids too, so they were produced in the greenhouse. Henry Smith grew carnations and chrysanthemums from cuttings. Maggie required carnations, and Henry Smith recorded that. one thousand carnations were grown each year in six-inch pots. While Maggie liked and used chrysanthemums, they may not have been her most favourite flower, but they fitted/complemented the rose damask paper on the dining-room walls at Polesden Lacey. She used these flowers in the Charles Street house too.

We must not forget Maggie loved roses. Her attention to the Rose Garden was shown in her emphasis to her head gardeners, as to how important this garden was. During Henry Smith's time, the roses (heavily perfumed varieties) were grown with peach and greengage trees trained on the walls.

Henry Smith said he had fourteen gardeners, plus himself as head gardener, when he became head gardener and that he "had the right to hire and fire".

Maggie had checked with Henry's previous employer that he "was good at growing roses". Henry said that his interview with Maggie for the job was conducted by Maggie, who was in bed (unwell). Maggie said to Henry, "Smith, I want you to speak to me as if I were a man." Maggie asked Henry "to concentrate growing things suitable for the English climate", as her foreign friends "were used to exotic plants and couldn't grow lawns and roses".

The working day at that time was: 6am to 8am, work; 8am to 9am, breakfast; 9am to 1pm, work; 1pm to 2pm, lunch; 2pm to 6pm, work.

Pineapples were grown in pits, forced strawberries were taken to the heated vinery (strawberries had to be identical in size to bring to the table for guests) and mushrooms were forced. Maggie required that grapes grown in the greenhouses for her guests, "must have the bloom undisturbed on each fruit".

In addition to the main frames in the frame yard, there were also some extra cold frames "for herbs, vegetable seedlings and salad". Peas, dwarf beans, potatoes and tomatoes were all produced to order. Maggie liked to have fresh English peas, new potatoes and asparagus as soon as they could be available. The greenhouses were heated by coke. Thirty tons of coke were used annually for heating.

The Bailiff at this time was Mr Watson, who managed the estate and the forestry. There was a staff/estate cricket team at Polesden Lacey from the 1920s. Matches were played on Saturday afternoon. Visiting teams were given tea, which was made by the wives of the players and the children. When Polesden Lacey "was playing away", the team travelled by a lorry; some of the children accompanied them, as they usually did the scoring.

There were two locations for cricket matches at Polesden Lacey; one was where the camping site is now situated, and the other was in a field not far from stable courtyard. Unfortunately, fifteen Jersey cows also shared this field.

The Head Cowman "supplied enough milk for the main house and all of the staff". The Head Cowman made butter every day, "4lbs of which was delivered to the house every morning along with the milk and cream". In the evening more milk and cream were delivered to the house. The staff also received milk twice a day. When Maggie was not entertaining and was away on her travels, a local farmer from Effingham collected any surplus milk to sell.

Prior to World War II, Maggie's staff enjoyed the Staff Social Club, which was where the present Polesden Lacey's shop is now situated. The club had: billiards, darts, dominoes, hoopla rings and cards, a small library and a licensed bar. The bar opened in the evenings at 6pm and closed at 10pm (officially). In the 1930s Mr J Kelley (Maggie's House Carpenter and a resident), earned £1 per week to look after the club. Staff could borrow books (Maggie supplied them) singly by signing a register for them. The gardeners finished work at 1pm on Saturdays, and the club was often visited after work.

There was also a Polesden Lacey Fire Crew. The role of fire officer was added to the estate maintenance engineer's job (he received three shillings for each occasion he was required/called out). The crew each earned two shillings "when they were called out" and also for regular drills which Maggie "called" on summer weekends "to show off the crew to her guests". A hooter was sounded, and the fire truck/cart which was stored in an archway under the water tower (stable courtyard) was brought out, with its ladder, hosepipes and a hand pump. Gossip says that if the men were short of money, they would ask the fire officer for an extra drill/practice, to earn some cash.

This, of course, changed when World War II began.

In 1939 life changed. Henry Smith found he had only two full-time under gardeners, Fred Lambert and George Butcher.[92] Two land girls came to work at Polesden Lacey, and they helped produce vegetables and flowers for Maggie while she was in London. At this time, some herbaceous beds and cultivated areas of the garden were just grassed over.

The south side of the herbaceous border did not become a vegetable plot, but it was grassed over. This southern flowerbed was completely replanted three years ago. It is stunning in the summer already, and recreates the borders with the arrangement Maggie maintained until World War II.

In World War II Maggie agreed to extend vegetable growing, in addition to what was grown in the kitchen garden, by the use of land north of the kitchen garden. The croquet lawn was not used for vegetable growing. It was cut for hay for use by animals. The Rose Garden was not turned into a vegetable plot. Roses continued to be grown there.

Petrol was rationed, but there was enough to take the produce which Maggie wanted, to Charles Street (or to the Dorchester Hotel), but there was not enough petrol available to mow the lawns. Mr Wren drove the van (Maggie's red Ford van) up to town, and milk, cream, butter and eggs were also included in the daily trip. Manual scything was carried out and a horse-drawn hay cutter was used to keep the lawns respectable.

Henry Smith's son, David H Smith recorded his memories of living at Polesden Lacey as a child; as his father was Head Gardener. David grew up at Polesden Lacey, with the troops being present for about two years of his life. David's record is valuable, and provides clarity, on so much help Maggie made available to troops in World War II.[93]

This information is followed and added to, by an unknown army officer's report from the Archives at Polesden Lacey, regarding the time he was stationed at Polesden Lacey in World War II. Entitled "Memoranda", this report provides additional insight into Maggie's contribution in World War II at Polesden Lacey.

David Smith said that by the second half of 1939, Polesden Lacey had become an HQ for ammunition depots, because once it was understood World

War II was proceeding badly for Great Britain, Maggie agreed that some British troops could be billeted on the estate. By the Dunkirk evacuation of 1940, (codenamed Operation Dynamo), the evacuation of Allied soldiers during World War II from the beaches and harbour of Dunkirk in the north of France, between 26th May and 4th June 1940, took place. This was an unbelievable effort to bring back so many troops who would otherwise have died.

On 10th May 1940 Churchill took over as Prime Minister. Great Britain was facing a dire situation, with insufficient tanks, equipment, lack of planes, lack of planning and lack of most of the accoutrements for war. Prior to the commencement of World War II, appeasement had failed (understandably, as it was purposeless).

Other authors have provided detailed knowledge of the build-up to World War II. I offer a limited amount of background to emphasise how badly prepared Britain was, and how dire the situation was for Britain, even after World War II had commenced, and to clarify the need for Churchill, when he took over, to act immediately to change the country's inability to fight effectively against Nazism, into a country with the means to do so.

I establish how much Maggie did to enable our troops to be helped, while such incredibly difficult circumstances prevailed.

Prior to World War II, Neville Chamberlain had adopted the policy of appeasement, ignoring his Foreign Secretary, Anthony Eden, a number of times, including rebuffing Roosevelt's offer in January 1938 to hold an international conference, which Eden was in favour of, as he believed that having America involved would be extremely beneficial to the international situation.[94]

This was followed by Chamberlain's policy of allowing Mussolini to conquer Abyssinia (Ethiopia), again against Eden's agreement, and by keeping Eden out of discussions as much as possible. Eden decided he had to resign on 20th February 1938. He was replaced as Foreign Secretary by Lord Halifax, another appeaser.

Chamberlain continued with his own attempts to deal with Hitler.[95] It took until a meeting on 9th May 1940 for Chamberlain to accept that he had to resign as Prime Minister (Halifax was at the meeting and it was to be either Halifax or Churchill to take over as Prime Minister), and it was agreed that Churchill would become Prime Minister. Clement Attlee and Arthur Greenwood stated that the Labour Party would not join a coalition government under Chamberlain (subsequently confirmed on 10th May from the Labour conference in Bournemouth). There was a hesitation the following morning 10th May by Chamberlain, after the invasion of Holland and Belgium, as he thought he might stay on as Prime Minister. After a full statement by the Labour Party that it would only serve in a new government under a new Prime Minister, Churchill met with the King shortly after 6pm. Churchill began his work as Prime Minister on the evening of 10th May.

Lord Beaverbrook spent the next three days "helping" Churchill appoint his Cabinet and his War Cabinet.

On 14th May Lord Beaverbrook was appointed Minister of Aircraft Production. On 17th May Lord Beaverbrook began the task of getting planes built, after assessing the aircraft production companies' ability to produce them. Beaverbrook's management of aircraft production made a real difference to World War II.[96]

In May 1940, the situation of troops on the ground offered an enormous problem in the theatre of war. Great Britain faced an unprecedented and almost impossible situation. Churchill said on 28th May, after nine War Cabinet meetings and additional Cabinet meetings in May (since he became PM), that, "It was idle to think that, if we tried to make peace now, we should get better terms from Germany than if we went on and fought it out." This was the War Cabinet's decision and was endorsed by the full Cabinet. Maggie wholeheartedly supported the government in the herculean task, which had finally reared fully into place.

The question of rescuing the Allied troops from France needed instant action. At the Cabinet meeting on 31st May 1940 (at 11.30am), it was noted that 224,000 British troops and 34,000 Allied troops had been evacuated by more than eight hundred vessels. Belgium had ceased fire on the morning of 28th May. On 14th June the German forces entered Paris. France signed an armistice with Germany on 22nd June (effective from 25th June). Italy declared war on Great Britain and France on 10th June (evening).

The troops returning from France were brought back by the Allied forces, and needed housing and training until they were sent back to war. We do not as yet have precise numbers of troops being stationed at Polesden Lacey, but many were billeted in huts in the Orchard, and by the tennis court.

"Mrs Greville agreed to house many of these men and gave the military free reign to train over the estate until their return to France. Dunkirk veterans soon appeared."

"A Bren gun sandbagged emplacement appeared near the Head Gardener's cottage, and it was manned. Officers were billeted in what had been the Bothy and what is now the restaurant, then there was a recreation room complete with a stage where ENSA (a division of the NAAFI) came to entertain the troops. A space was always reserved for Mrs Greville and Madame Liron, her companion, if they were in residence at the time."[97]

The space David described as now being the "restaurant" has in turn been changed to the large Polesden Lacey Shop. Smith confirmed that Maggie was at this time in a wheelchair, so a space was kept for Maggie with a seat next to her for Madam Liron. These troops stayed for about two years; they moved out when the army was reorganised, and training bases were in action in preparation for D-Day.

David Smith's record is sound, but we now also know that some officers were staying in Polesden Lacey House, not only in the bothy, as well the troops who were billeted in the grounds.

Additionally, Maggie agreed that Canadian troops could be billeted in the woods "bordering the road to Bookham, and they were also based in the grounds of Southey Hall". Maggie only wanted British troops on her estate.

During the Battle of Britain, July to October 1940, Maggie helped in another, smaller way. A good number of men in the RAF who had suffered disfiguring injuries as aircrew and were badly burnt, were treated at Headley Court in Ashtead. Maggie arranged for these men to be invited to Polesden Lacey for a day out, and given afternoon tea.

Over 330,000 Allied troops were brought back between 26th May and June 4th 1940 in Operation Dynamo, the evacuation of Dunkirk. Some of the officers who stayed in the house as Maggie's guests enjoyed lunch and dinner, often with some of Maggie's fascinating friends. Some officers billeted in the grounds were also invited to dine in the house.

One (unnamed) officer wrote in his memoranda, about his time at Polesden Lacey.[98] He said, "In 1939 Middle of July my section went to Polesden Lacey Nr. D S 'y to establish an AMN Dp. [*Ammunition Depot*] and be the advance party for the rest of the company."

He also said, "Had numerous invites to dine and lunch in the house and in that way met many illustrious people such as Baron de Cartier de Marchienne, Belgian Ambassador. A most charming and lovable old man."

Baron Ernest-Emile de Cartier de Marchienne's career was outstanding. The details of his international roles, and his time in Great Britain (1927–46) as Envoy Extraordinary and Minister Plenipotentiary (this title was later renamed/ and became known as ambassador, when gradually legations became embassies, after World War II), proves how much he mattered.

Maggie trusted the Baron to be her host to the officers staying at Polesden Lacey, in the house, when frequently she was unwell. The officers dined in the house on both Christmas Eve and on New Year's Eve, even though Maggie herself was particularly unwell on this last date; Baron Cartier de Marchienne again acted as host, on New Year's Eve (forty-one guests dined).

This same unnamed officer also commented about chatting to the Marquess of Crewe and Lady Crewe. The Marquess was a huge landowner, so the conversation was all about agriculture.

Other interesting people whom the officer met were Sir Horace Rumbold, ex-British Ambassador to Berlin, who said he warned the British government in the early 1930s that Germany wanted revenge for the Treaty of Versailles; Herschel Johnston (at that time counsellor at the US Embassy in Great Britain, later ambassador to Sweden, the UN and Brazil); Sir Eric Phipps (a retired ambassador to Germany and France), who also had warned the British government of Germany's military strength and ambitions in 1934 and '35; in addition to many diplomats, politicians and friends of Maggie. I have more to say of some of Maggie's political friends in Chapter 20.[99] Dining in the house, meeting influential and often political guests, must have been fascinating for those officers, who enjoyed fine wine and food at the same time. A short break from the unbelievable reality of World War II.

Maggie provided tennis courts (lawn) for her guests from the beginning of her ownership, located where the current croquet lawn is situated. In World War I, the hard courts were built for the use of those men who were able to play tennis.

Photographs of the 1923 honeymoon of Bertie and Elizabeth, show both of them on the same hard tennis courts; the Duchess of York is sitting down on a bench during a match, and there is a photograph of Bertie playing tennis. In 1981 these hard tennis courts were made into the staff car park. Today they are used by staff and volunteers for parking. Archery was sometimes offered to guests as a distraction also.

Polesden Lacey was hit by bombs in 1942: "A string of four bombs fell on the estate, one landing among the glasshouses, at the back of what was then the garden office. A second bomb landed at the back of bungalow no 2, a third outside Mrs Greville's quarters, on the east side of the house, by the cedar of Lebanon, and the fourth into the hill below the Long Walk where today a tree grows, on the pile of chalk where the soil was displaced when the bomb exploded."

The outlines of the two greenhouses which were bombed in World War II remain visible in the Rose Garden. From 1961, the planting of the outside of the rose garden with ground-covering shrubs and herbaceous plants began to save labour, and provide colour before roses flowered. The maintenance of the Rose

Garden today continues to demonstrate the original high standard Maggie offered, now executed by the head of the outdoor estate and a brilliant team of gardeners.

The Farms, Bagden, Yew Tree and Goldstone (and Polesden Farm in the Park)

Poultry, sheep, pigs, horses, award-winning turkeys, the Dorking chicken (five digits, instead of the usual four on each foot) were raised at Polesden Lacey. Maintaining flowerbeds, fruit, vegetables, the golf course, tennis courts and caring for horses were all part of farming and gardening at Polesden Lacey. Impressing the guests was the most important point of all of this activity.

In addition to the formal gardens, the farms at Polesden Lacey provide so much space; there are approximately 1,400 acres. In addition to the gardens, which were required to show off/present the best of horticulture, with the flowerbeds providing almost perfect specimens of flowers/roses and more, when the guests were present, both houses required fresh picked flowers for all of the key rooms. Vegetables and fruit (many grown out of season inside the greenhouses and pineapple pit) were essential, to showcase Maggie's superb dinner parties. Flowers were vitally important too.

Sometimes, during Royal Ascot week, the Gold Cup was displayed on the table at dinner at Polesden Lacey, as the winner would be a guest of Mrs Greville's. Certainly, the Aga Khan stayed seventeen times for Royal Ascot prior to World War II. Male guests staying at Polesden for Royal Ascot collected their buttonholes from the greenhouse. The ladies were provided with their flower sprays; by their maids collecting them, or by the Head Greenhouse Keeper bringing them to the house.

In 1942 Maggie was buried in the Memorial Garden (also known as the Seasons or Ladies' Garden). Details are discussed in Chapter 19.

The open-air theatre was constructed in 1951 and is situated east of the house. This area continues to be used every year. The arch which Maggie requested should be built (in her will) in memory of her father was not constructed until 1958, just above the North Lodge (house).

By 1972 some fruit and vegetables were again grown in the kitchen garden.

The 1987 storm in Great Britain resulted in damage to so much of the landscape everywhere; a quarter to half of the mature trees were lost at Polesden Lacey, including many avenue trees.

I provide a list of trees which were planted by royalty over the years.[100] King Edward VII planted two trees: a black mulberry in 1907 and a copper beech in 1909. These have all gone. The following list is in order of position, moving south from the house:

1. Black mulberry, King Edward VII, 19th May 1907.
2. Blue spruce (picea pungens "Glauca"), King Fuad of Egypt, 27th July 1929.
3. Purple beech, King Edward VII, 6th June 1909.
4. Blue spruce, Queen Mary, 7th August 1915.
5. Blue spruce, King George V, 7th August 1915.
6. Blue spruce, Princess Henry of Battenberg, 13th July 1914.
7. Blue spruce, Queen Victoria Eugenie of Spain, 12th July 1920.
8. Blue spruce, King Alphonso XIII of Spain, 12th July 1920.
9. Blue spruce, Duchess of York on honeymoon, 6th May 1923.
10. Blue spruce, Duke of York on honeymoon, 6th May 1923.
11. Queen Elizabeth the Queen Mother planted another tree for the Silver Jubilee, 24th June 1977.
12. Black mulberry, Prince Charles, 1988, planted to replace the tree planted by Edward VII blown down in the storm.

Maggie wanted the gardens to be first-class. No doubt about this. In showcasing the gardens, and in offering absolute first-class standards, the staff were able to provide this as with everything else she chose to do,

Graham Stuart Thomas advised on the garden at Polesden Lacey from 1955–85, advising the agent Robin Fedden, who had been overseeing the garden until then. Thomas' reports cover the whole garden and provide detail on most aspects. Thomas advised throughout the National Trust's gardens during this period and was one of the country's most renowned plantsmen and garden authors. From 1979 to 1989, Tony Lord was the adviser to National Trust Gardens.

The car park in Orchard Field next to the Preserve Copse was moved in 2010, to north of stable block and enlarged. Today, even this area is often inadequate for parking for huge numbers of visitors to Polesden Lacey, and fields are frequently used as car parks (weather permitting).

TEN

Maggie the Collector

First, Maggie was a collector of people. She became friends with royalty, maharajahs, politicians and people from many different backgrounds. Because she "collected people", she needed to showcase a collection of art, artefacts, furniture, porcelain, silver and more in her country house Polesden Lacey, and her town house in Charles Street, London, which was commensurate with the guests' own interests and expectations.

For Maggie, showing off her paintings was an essential part of a demonstration of her ability to have made it through becoming "nouveau riche", and being able to present to respected eminent guests that she understood and knew which artists mattered (Dutch, for example). Many of her guests were richer than she was. But to guests and friends, how much did this matter? The Visitor Book at Polesden Lacey has an incredible array of names, through royals, aristocrats and politicians.

That Maggie may have suffered from some criticisms from guests (who may have possessed envy of her position) because she was less educated than they were, is not the point. Maggie displayed her knowledge, having been tutored by William McEwan, and after receiving advice from experts as to her buying choices, and from appreciating what her new friends displayed in their properties. Additionally, Maggie bought what she liked. Of course, not all of Maggie's buying choices were perfect. Many were!

Maggie's guests while staying for the weekend were able to enjoy a first-class collection.[101] As an astute lady interested in people, she wanted her wide circle of friends to enjoy the paintings. When royal friends provided stunning masterpieces in their properties, it was not always possible to compete. Yet there was always scope for new money to be turned into "old" by the provision of sometimes centuries-old exhibits. Showcasing her paintings was important to Maggie. Maggie made "safe" choices. There are no Pre-Raphaelite paintings in the collection. Too avant-garde, too risky. Maggie followed sound advice for recommended purchases, although at times some of her critics would suggest otherwise.

McEwan was advised to collect Dutch art (he asked advice when he became wealthy) and Maggie continued to collect Dutch art, although she branched out to other international artists. The paintings at Polesden Lacey are visited, by so many people who have travelled thousands of miles for holidays, and in particular to visit museums and art galleries, because the paintings possess both quality and rarity, and some are outstanding.

I offer some information about the Dutch art and some fine paintings, but there are so many more paintings to appreciate on a visit to Polesden Lacey.[102] Not all can be discussed in this book.

One outstanding example of Dutch art is "The Introduction" by Gerard ter Borch the Younger (1617–81). A woman in a dazzling white gown delicately accepts the gallant address of a smiling officer in a richly appointed Dutch interior. Behind them, several more figures congregate around a table, one of whom plays the lute. For all the fine manners on display in this scene, all may not be quite as respectable as it first seems. This painting may, however, be showing an improper rendezvous?

The next (and for me the most outstanding of all of the paintings at Polesden Lacey, but visitors will have their own preferences), is "The Colf Players" by Pieter de Hooch (1629–84) The painting is circa 1660. This painting is now known as the "Colf Players", as the original word for golf was "colf". The painting is known to be one of the "earliest pictorial representations of the game of golf" and was loaned for exhibition by Maggie; it has been exhibited many times by the National Trust and is always in demand for exhibitions. The artist was a master of perspective and detail, and "a wizard with light".

Continuing with Dutch art, there are three paintings by David Teniers at Polesden Lacey. David Teniers the Younger (1610–90): "The Card Players", circa 1645; "The Tric-Trac Players", circa 1640; "The Alchemist", 1640s. Two are tavern scenes; this Flemish artist often presents centrally, people gambling on games of chance. The third painting of "The Alchemist" suggests that the man has not realised the futility of his work, although others have. These paintings are fascinating and important. There are more fine Dutch paintings in the collection.

There are a number of religious paintings at the west end of the south corridor. Maggie was not religious. They are fourteenth- and fifteenth-century and are significant and relevant to the history of art. Some of Maggie's religious pictures include Francescuccio Ghissi, "The Madonna of Humility"; Bartolo de Fredi, "The Adoration of the Magi"; and "The Miracle of the Founding Santa Maria Maggiore", attributed to Pietro Perugino.

Some of the key paintings I list below, but unless I write a book about the art at Polesden Lacey, it is impossible to discuss all of the paintings.

Bernardo Strozzi (1581–1644), "A Venetian Gentleman", 1630s, is the earliest recorded acquisition of an old master for the collection by Maggie, who romantically referred to its subject as a "cavalier".

The painting by Jacob Levecq (1634–75), "An Unknown Man", aged nineteen, dated 1654, was by a pupil of Rembrandt who was trained in Rembrandt's studio. It is recognised that this painting "is in the style of Rembrandt".

The painting of Eva Marie Veigel, Mrs. Garrick, (1724–1822) by Johann Zoffany (1733–1810) has been displayed in the Portico bedroom – her husband David Garrick was actor manager of the Drury Lane Theatre. Zoffany was a stunning portraitist who executed until the latest stages of his life, the most meticulous and detailed portraits.

Sir Joshua Reynolds (1723–92), "Nymph and Piping Boy", circa 1785–86, is in place over the fireplace in the Dining Room.[103] Experimental techniques were offered by Reynolds, and this painting has severe cracking in the black areas which Maggie was alerted to; as this is bitumen, the painting cannot be restored. Maggie understood this disfigurement and her desire for a Reynolds enabled her to overlook the problem. It was purchased for £7,410 in 1917. Bitumen is a naturally occurring, non-drying, tarry substance used in paint mixtures, especially to enrich the appearance of dark tones. Bitumen became very popular as a paint additive in the late eighteenth century and early nineteenth. However, because it does not dry, it eventually causes often severe darkening and cracking of the paint.

Another important painting owned by Maggie is from the studio of Sir Peter Lely (1618–80), a painting of Frances Teresa Stuart, Duchess of Richmond (1647–1702), painted circa 1670. There is the suggestion that the head may have been painted by Lely and the rest of the painting executed by his students. This is possibly copied from the original in situ at Goodwood House, Sussex.

The painting by Sir Thomas Lawrence entitled "The Masters Pattinson" is of huge importance at Polesden Lacey. Maggie purchased this painting for £12,000 from Agnews in 1918. It is stunning and is in place in the Dining Room.

Items Bequeathed from McEwan

It can be noted that some of the most important paintings were inherited from her father and include David Teniers, "The Tric-Trac Players"; Gerard Ter Borch, "An Officer Making His Bow to a Lady"; Pieter De Hooch, "The Colf Players"; and paintings by Salomon van Ruysdael, Jacob van Ruisdael, Isaack van Ostade and Adriaen van Ostade. Additionally, Frans van Mieris' minutely painted self-portrait; Aelbert Cuyp, "A Landscape with a Herdsman and Bull"; Jan van Goyen, "The Beach at Scheveningen" and his delicate landscape drawing, "The Ramparts at Dordecht", remain on show today.

William McEwan favoured Scottish artists in addition to Dutch. There are at least eleven paintings by Scottish artists at Polesden Lacey. With reference to Henry Raeburn (1756–1823), McEwan purchased two paintings by the artist: Isabella Simpson in 1896 for £2,500 via Agnews, and Sir William Macleod Bannatyne for £367 in 1897. The sellers were never named.

Maggie purchased two paintings by Raeburn: George and Maria Stewart in 1919 for £5,500 via Colnaghi; the Paterson Children in 1918 for £23,000 via Agnews); this last price was far in excess of its value and was valued at half this amount for probate.

Maggie inherited a total of seventeen paintings from her father (including the two portraits of him). The first portrait of her father is situated in the Dining Room. When Maggie was entertaining, this portrait was placed (as it is now) behind her chair at the head of the table. But when (for example) Maggie entertained Edward VII and Alice Keppel, and other members of the Marlborough House Set, there was no point in being isolated from such an incredibly important guest such as the King, by placing him at the other end of the table. The King was seated in the middle of one long side (of a narrow Edwardian table), Maggie was positioned on one side of the King and Alice on the other side. The painting was always visible.

According to Maggie, this "striking likeness" of her beloved father was painted by Benjamin Constant (1845–1902) and was the result of six sittings at the Savoy hotel; it cost £1,200. It was painted in 1900. Maggie claimed her father did not like the painting. Possibly he looked a little serious. Although Maggie said it was one of Constant's finest paintings.

Benjamin Constant was a successful artist who was celebrated in London, Paris and America. Constant studied at the Ecole des Beaux Arts and was a pupil of Alexandre Cabanel (1823–89). Constant travelled in 1872 to Morocco and his work thereafter was influenced by Orientalism. By 1880 Constant decided to change direction with his work and produced murals and portraits. In 1896 he became a Commander of the Legion of Honour. Constant became highly popular with the British aristocracy. He painted Queen Victoria, Pope Leo XIII and Queen Alexandra, and a number of aristocrats. Constant worked in America and was one of the first French artists to work professionally there. Constant himself said, "America made me a portrait painter. Until I went there, I was almost solely a painter of subject pictures."

The second painting of McEwan is in the Billiard Room and was painted by Walter William Ouless (1901). Ouless was an artist from Jersey and was considered "a safe pair of hands". McEwan perhaps looks more relaxed. When you have sufficient funds, if the first result is not quite to your liking, having another version created can be more satisfactory.

There are two paintings of Maggie at Polesden Lacey.

The most important portrait (of two) of Maggie is situated at top of the main stairs (as it was in place when Maggie lived at Polesden Lacey), and was painted by Charles Auguste Émile Durand, known as Carolus-Duran (1837–1917) while on her honeymoon in Paris in 1891. The great sense of confidence caught by Carolus-Duran, painter of Parisian society ladies and demi-mondaines, provided a perfect result. Maggie appears to be relaxed and in charge of her life in this portrait. Carolus-Duran was known for a technique known as "au premier coup", which was painting, stroke by stroke, without reworking. He painted members of high society and from 1870 concentrated on portrait paintings. He became a Knight of the Legion d'Honneur in 1872, becoming a Grand Officer by 1890. He had an illustrious career and was a member, among other institutions, of the Academie des Beaux-Arts by 1904. His studio was in the Boulevard du Montparnasse, from where he also provided painting lessons. One of his students was the American artist John Singer Sargent.

The second portrait of Maggie at Polesden Lacey is placed in the Saloon (Gold Room) and was painted by Hermann Schmiechen (1855–1925). This German artist was working in London as a fashionable portrait painter, when he created Maggie's portrait as a sweet and modest unmarried lady. Previously, we understand that this portrait was hung in the morning room, at Charles Street. Hermann Schmiechen was born in Neumarkt, Prussian Silesia. By 1872 he was a student in Breslau to Albrecht Brauer; by 1873 he was studying at the Dusseldorf Academy under the direction of Karl Muller and Eduard von Gebhardt, followed by training at the Julian Academie in Paris, then became a sought-after portrait painter in Dusseldorf. He worked at Queen Victoria's invitation in London between 1883–1901. He painted Queen Victoria's granddaughters, Princess Victoria of Hesse and Princess Elizabeth of Hesse, in 1880, and Mary Adelaide, Duchess of Teck (the mother of George V's wife Queen Mary), in 1882.

He was popular at this time as a portraitist of the English aristocracy. He exhibited in exhibitions in London, Liverpool and Manchester, which were held between 1884–95.

From 1901 he worked back in Germany in Berlin. While he was in England, he became a theosophist under the influence of Helena Blavastky, and he continued to participate in the theosophical society on his return to Berlin. We believe this painting of Maggie was created when Maggie was twenty-four years old. Neumarkt, Silesia, became part of unified Germany in 1871.

Polesden Lacey is worth visiting for many reasons, but the art is fine, honest and totally enthralling, particularly for anyone interested in Dutch art.

The Collection

The font and the sarcophagus are both recognised as two "top" items of significance in the National Trust.[104]

The tapestries in the Central Hall consist of: a sixteenth-century tapestry made in Brussels which has been attributed to Leo van den Hecke (one from a set of eight); two circa 1700, "Dido and Aeneas", and "A Scene from the Story of Aeneas"; and "The Kermesse" or "Village Fete", dated in the second half of the seventeenth century.

The marble sarcophagus (or coffin) shows carvings of a Bacchic procession of men, women, elephants, lions and leopards, and winged lions at the sides. It is Roman, third century AD. The lid is missing. Originally the deceased's coffin would have been in place inside the sarcophagus.

The font (or Holy Water Stoup), thirteenth-century, is in place in the entrance lobby to Polesden Lacey. It was made in Lombardy, Italy, and is made of Veronese marble. There is a presumption that Maggie acquired this important item via White Allom, who were responsible as interior decorators and antique reclamation specialists for providing Maggie with much of the interior fixtures and fittings, during 1907 to 1908 at Polesden Lacey?

Carpets

One carpet which for a long time was displayed on the hall table is from Persia (Kiran) and was made in the second half of the nineteenth century. This carpet is not currently on display. There are a number of carpets which are important and are of significant historic interest.[105] The carpet which is in place in front of the Finnish cabinet at the west end of the south corridor is extremely rare.

Most Indian carpets from this period are believed to be from Agra, Amritsar or Lahore in the north, but some were produced in the south of the country. Indian prisoners have been making carpets in jails ever since the sixteenth-century Mughal Emperor Akbar introduced Persian skilled carpet weavers, to teach the prisoners a trade and keep them occupied. There is a long tradition and years of skill and knowledge found in those prisons.

The carpet in the Tea Room is Indian and is a late nineteenth-century jail carpet, which was made in Jaipur or Agra. The carpet measures 3.63 metres in length. The carpet was believed to have been gifted to Maggie by the Maharajah of Agra and Jaipur, Sahib Bahdoor, when he stayed at Polesden Lacey. A visually stunning piece of textile, the carpet's beautifully designed abstract white central motif is dotted with small red petals. The navy-blue background is showered with a multitude of interchangeable shapes linked with red or white lines. Three borders are covered with a detailed geometric design and filled with the primary colours of red, white and blue. The carpet sits comfortably with the room's feminine pastoral colours of soft pinks, creamy whites and yellows, refreshing hues of blues, greens and sparkling gold. This carpet was situated in the study, but the National Trust moved it to the Tea Room to preserve its delicate condition.

The carpet in the Study is circa 1850, seemingly Persian, possibly from Herez.

In the Dining Room, the pelmets are eighteenth-century, and it is believed that White Allom reclaimed them from elsewhere. There are no notes currently available to provide evidence.

Silver

Maggie enjoyed owning silver. Being nouveau riche, she apparently liked to have a number of pieces on the dining table when entertaining. She bought (or had someone bidding for her) many of her silver items at auctions. In the Tea Room at Polesden Lacey, there are a number of pieces on show. Beverley Nichols described this room when afternoon tea was served in one of his books.

I do not provide a full listing of the silver at Polesden Lacey. I offer some highlights as I hope I offer enough information to suggest that a visit to Polesden Lacey to look at the silver is worthwhile.

Maggie's silver items are dated seventeenth, eighteenth and nineteenth century.[106] Maggie collected throughout her life, and one piece of silver – a tankard dated 1681 with the mark RN – was acquired as late as 1937 by Maggie after it had come to auction in 1932, via the Dunn Gardner Sale. Its decoration consists of birds, fruit, foliage and a fountain. It joined another tankard by David Willaume dated 1701 which had belonged to Sir JT Firbank MP, and was sold for the first time by Christie's in 1904, then resold in 1916 to Maggie.

Some of the items in the Dining Room and Tea Room are really lovely. Their dates, because they were purchased on separate occasions, vary hugely. They form a collection made to impress. Old silver added to the gravitas of Maggie's art; early porcelain, maiolica, furniture and tapestries helped to reinforce her position solidly, at least in her eyes.

In the Tea Room there is a teapot on a stand, which belonged to Maggie's father with his initials on it, and it was made by Marshall & Sons (87 George Street, Edinburgh). Tea caddies are dated 1770 by Samuel Taylor (a boxed set) and there is a sugar vase dated 1763, inside a silver-mounted rosewood box by Reily and Storer, dated 1840. There is an additional tea caddy dated 1726. This room was used for tea by everyone staying at Polesden Lacey and at other times of the day too. Dishes which held cakes, scones and sandwiches are stunning, as Maggie needed them to be; the oval cake basket with pierced sides was made by John Luff and dated 1741; one large salver is hallmarked London 1770 and has the coat of arms Richard and Elizabeth Day, who were married in that year.

There are two more teapots in this room, the smaller thought to be produced by John Fawdery, London, in 1729, the other was made by Gabriel Sleath in 1717 in London. A cake basket (designed to look like a scallop shell) is dated 1750 by Philip Garden, London.

In the Dining Room a good number of pieces are displayed, some in cabinets, some on the table, the way Maggie liked to display her silver. There are three sugar casters; these are remnants from two sets of caster sugar holders, one by Charles Adam, dated 1709; two by Anthony Nelme, both dated 1721. The other three pieces were sold in 1943 at Christie's by the National Trust. There are two pieces of silver made by John Timbrell, dated 1699 and 1704. Candlesticks mattered to Maggie (she had electricity in the house, but dining required the subtlety of candles). There are candlesticks by John Horsley, London, dated 1762.

Silver tankards, mugs, salvers, candlesticks and more, reflect back a safe recognisable offering to say that the owner is comfortable about her position and her metier. McEwan's money provided "the backing". The silver is fine, and while it has sometimes been altered in its history, it is safe.

Fabergé and Edward VII's Massive Commission to Fabergé

Maggie had in her possession some stunning miniatures and gifts made by Fabergé, Cartier, Collingwood and other established companies. They are on show at Polesden Lacey at times (not permanently), and they are a superb addition to the collection.

Most of the pieces were gifts to her from her friends and guests. The British Royal family, following on from the Russian Royals, collected Fabergé. Edward VII and Queen Alexandra were fascinated by Fabergé.[107] The British Royal collection has one of the largest (known) collections in the world (other than the collection owned by the Russian Royal family). The Queen and the Prince of Wales have continued to add to the Fabergé collection.

HC Bainbridge was manager of the London Fabergé branch which opened in 1903 (Dover Street first, followed by Bond Street, London). Bainbridge often received requests from Edward VII and Queen Alexandra, for Fabergé pieces they could purchase, to give to their family and friends. Edward and Alexandra had separate collections; they liked to compete with each other.

The House of Fabergé was founded in 1842 in St Petersburg by Gustave Fabergé, who was born in Estonia. He established himself in a humble basement shop, in a fashionable district in St Petersburg and his success was rapid. Gustave retired to Dresden in 1860. His son Carl was only fourteen years old, so he completed his education, toured Europe and studied the art of the goldsmith while managers ran the company.

From 1872, Carl (aged twenty-six) was mentored by Hiskias Pendin (Gustave's work master) at Fabergé, while he learnt how to run the company and create the most perfect pieces of Fabergé. When Pendin died in 1882, Carl took charge of the company. Fabergé was purchased/collected by Tsar Alexander III and Nicholas II. The House of Fabergé completed fifty Imperial Eggs for the Russian Royal Family: for Alexander III to present to his wife, the Dowager Empress Maria Feodorovna; for Nicholas II to present to his mother, the Dowager Empress Maria Feodorovna, and for his wife, the Empress Alexandra Feodorovna. Of these, forty-three are known to have survived.

In 1907 Bainbridge claimed that the Sandringham commission "had come to him as a way of meeting the King's and Queen's desire for Fabergé work, and moreover, to satisfy the constant demand from their family and friends, who wished to purchase presents from Fabergé for them".

Bainbridge himself was in a difficult position, trying to exhibit a full range of Fabergé, providing pieces not only for his royal clients but also for the rest of his aristocratic clients. Because Bainbridge struggled to find new ideas for Fabergé, he said, he had the idea that if all of the animals at Sandringham could be modelled in wax, then produced by Fabergé in Moscow, there would be a large new range to offer.

Once Carl Fabergé agreed to this idea, the proposal was put to Edward VII. Bainbridge said that it was Alice Keppel who made the suggestion to Edward, who agreed immediately. The idea that Alice Keppel was the "go-between" to present this idea to Edward, is stated in the Fabergé book *Fabergé Animals* written by Caroline de Guitaut, sold by Buckingham Palace in their shop. It seems that Alice discussed this with Maggie, who was naturally delighted that there could be an increase in choices of Fabergé available.

Bainbridge visited Sandringham; he met with Edward's land agent, Frank Beck, and was provided with a list of animals, which was huge! This turned out to be the largest commission Bainbridge ever received for the London branch. Every piece commissioned was to be unique, so no duplicates to Queen Alexandra's collection should ever appear. Edward suggested his racehorse

Persimmon, all of Queen Alexandra's dogs, Edward's dog Caesar, and all of the farm animals at Sandringham could be made into models by Fabergé.

A number of sculptors were sent to Sandringham, and among them were Frank Lutiger and Boris Frodman-Cluzel. By the late autumn 1907, the sculptors were busy at Sandringham. On 8th December 1907, the wax models were viewed by Edward VII, who suggested one or two minor changes but otherwise said, "I think the work splendid." Previously, it has been stated that the animals created by Fabergé for the British market were produced haphazardly. This is not correct. Fabergé sent some of his finest sculptors from St Petersburg to Sandringham, "where they stayed several weeks making portraits in wax".

The wax models were sent/taken to St Petersburg. From 1908 the use of stone became more important to Fabergé, and it is from this timing that the commission from Sandringham slotted into the ever-increasing production of figures, animals and flowers. Once the stonework was completed, the jewels or gold were added as required.

Some of Maggie's Fabergé pieces (there are seven items in her collection) are exquisite but do not include any of Edward's farm animals. However, Maggie did possess other animals. Edward's presents to Maggie included a blue lapis lazuli seal with his crest, a broach with diamonds and rubies, and a shagreen box with tortoise shell (not Fabergé).

King Edward VII's initial idea for the Sandringham commission of hardstone animals was, for Fabergé to immortalise his favourite dogs and racehorses. The actual commission extended to all the animals on the Sandringham estate. As King Edward doted on Caesar, he was arguably the most important subject of the commission. Indeed, when His Majesty unveiled the wax models Fabergé's team had prepared on the Norfolk estate, Caesar was at his side.

The actual carved stone model was not delivered to England until several months after the King's death. Carved from chalcedony and embellished with gold, enamel and rubies, it was purchased from the London branch of Fabergé by Maggie, a close friend of Queen Mary, for £35. Maggie gave the model to Queen Alexandra. As with the actual Caesar, the dog's collar reads "I belong to the King". After Edward VII's death in May 1910, Caesar wandered the corridors of Buckingham Palace looking for his master. His last duty was to walk behind the King's coffin, led by a Highlander. Caesar died in 1914, and he is buried in the grounds of Marlborough House, which was the London residence of Edward, Prince of Wales and Princess Alexandra, prior to them becoming King and Queen.

Miniatures – Tessiers

Miniatures were collected originally as love tokens or friendship or even as an expression of loyalty. They were popular gifts prior to photography becoming a more modern way of presenting special tokens to loved ones. As they were small, they were popular up until the beginning of the twentieth century.

Maggie's possessed a miniature collection, which was acquired mainly between 1891 and 1910, and includes English and Continental seventeenth-, eighteenth- and nineteenth-century portraits by or attributed to Peter Cross, Christian Richter, John Smart, William Grimaldi and Andrew Plimer.

Many of the miniatures were reframed by Tessiers, a London specialist jeweller/dealer.[108] In 1740, two French Huguenot merchants named Henry (Henri) and James (Jacques) Tessier (who had come from France or Switzerland), were in partnership with John Anthony Loubier at Basinghall Street, London. In 1794, the firm of Charles Loubier, Tessier & Co were listed as "merchants" at 27 Austin Friars, London. The Tessier family/company continued to evolve as the family grew; they owned shops in central London through the nineteenth century, at South Audley Street and New Bond Street. They were fashionable and successful, selling jewellery.

Family miniatures, including portraits of William McEwan, Maggie's mother Helen Anderson and her husband Ronnie Greville, are also on show at Polesden Lacey. They are, of course, more modern and were created in the early twentieth century by Eunice Pattinson.

Furniture

Some of Maggie's furniture is considered to be first-class, some less so. Buying furniture through advisers brought benefits. Some pieces experienced changes before Maggie purchased them. The National Trust kept the pieces they believed were of first order, and sold at the sales at Christies, Manson & Woods (Christies's today) in 1943, those they considered to be of secondary importance. A number of pieces are outstanding; I highlight only a few of them. A visit to the house is the way to appreciate them.

The commode beneath the portrait of Maggie in the Saloon is considered to be of national importance. This French Louis XV commode is circa 1750 and is stamped by Jacques-Philippe Carel (active between 1723–60).[109] The commode also has the stamp of Dennis Gentry, an ébéniste (cabinet maker) who was also a dealer. Hence it is possible that he designed, repaired or maybe only handled the furniture as a dealer. Additionally, one of the ormolu mounts has the signature of Jacques Caffieri (1675–1735), one of the most famous practitioners of such Rococo style.

There two more commodes in the Saloon: French, Louis XV, circa 1775, with a Rouge Royale marble-top; the other is circa 1770–05, French, with a Breccia marble top, with high-quality ormolu mounts, but this is unstamped and may be the work of the German Parisian ébéniste Christophe Wolff (1720–95)?

In the Tea Room there are a number of Louis XV and Louis XVI pieces of furniture. They are small but beautiful, and some of them would have been situated elsewhere in the house (possibly in bedrooms) in Maggie's day.

The commode underneath the portrait of William McEwan in the Dining Room displays panels of Chinese lacquer bordered with English japanning and mounted in ormolu (circa 1760–65). This style was associated with Pierre Langlois (active 1759–81), a Parisian ébéniste who worked in London by 1759.

Of interest in the Dining Room is the secretaire, which has veneered black and gold Chinese lacquer mounted in ormolu (made in 1745), and has been stamped eight times by the ébéniste Jean-Baptiste Tuart (1700–67), and also by the retailer Leonard Boudin (1735–1807).

It should not be forgotten that Maggie created a house to impress, and also for her guests to relax. The Billiard Room has a billiard table by Burroughs & Watts (this particular table was in the staff social club when Maggie was alive, and it was brought down to the house from the club house and has round country-style legs). The original table in the Billiard Room was the same make as the current table (but it had Regency-style legs); it was removed by the National Trust. Whether it was in poor condition or due to another reason, is not known.

The clocks at Polesden Lacey are worth looking at;[110] in the east corridor there is a black and gold japanned wall clock, with a painted dial – R Hardy, Newark (circa 1750–60). There is a longcase clock, walnut and marquetry, circa 1695; inscribed on the dial is Rob Halstead, London His workshop was in Fleet Street.

On the staircase landing there is a clock by Robert Mawley, circa 1750. It chimes or offers "as St Mary's, Cambridge".

There is a longcase clock with a silver dial in the lobby, inscribed by John Payne (1731–95), London, circa 1760.

In the Study there is a longcase clock by John Ellicott (London, 1706–72), who became a mathematician as well as an influential clockmaker (he spent time working on complex pendulums) and he was admitted to the Royal Society in 1738. The family were amongst the finest of clockmakers of the eighteenth century in Great Britain. This clock was signed Ellicott (different generations had different ways of signing, and therefore this dates the clock to 1760–69). The clock is made of mahogany, silver, brass, steel and glass.

The Billiard Room has a French ormolu clock which is nineteenth-century but is in the style of Jean Corrier, who was active late eighteenth and nineteenth century.

There are three clocks in the Saloon: two are French ormolu, Louis XV, both eighteenth-century (on the mantelpieces) but with a modern movement in one of them. There is also a third clock here, which is a carved giltwood wall clock, French, Louis XV. The thermometer is dated circa 1750, and the barometer (both by Cappy & Mossy, French), in a parcel gilt circular case, is dated 1776.

There is a clock in the Tea Room on the mantelpiece, ormolu, signed by Jean-Baptiste du Tertre, a Parisian clockmaker (1715–72). The movement has been replaced. Just a small taste of what can be seen in the house.

Porcelain

In the Study there are collections of both Meissen and Furstenberg porcelain.[111] Some early pieces of both these companies are rare. The Meissen tea, coffee and chocolate services are 1725–35, painted with wharf and chinoiserie scenes in the style of JG Herold (1696–1775), who was the most important artist at the Meissen factory, from 1720. There is also a Meissen yellow-ground cream jug, circa 1735 with military scenes. Meissen was producing porcelain from 1710 in Dresden.

There is rare Furstenberg tea and coffee service, circa 1770, which has paintings of monkeys carrying out human activities, which is possibly by CG Albert. Furstenberg was established in 1747.

The Sevres Tea Set dated 1921/23 (in the tea room) was given to Maggie by Baron Blanesburgh – Robert Younger (the son of William McEwan's sister Janet and her husband James Younger) – her cousin. Maggie chose to give this tea set away to Elsie Grant (one of her maids) in May 1940. This tea service seems to be unique. No more created? But clearly Maggie, at the time of receiving the gift, was not much enamoured.

This tea service in the Tea Room at Polesden Lacey was designed by Eric Bagge, who was an architect and an interior decorator who designed furniture, fabrics, wallpapers, accessories and silver. Eric Bagge also supplied designs for the Sevres factory to Maurice Genoli (Head of Faience from 1924 and then Head of the Design Studio from 1928).

At the 1925 "Paris Exposition des Arts Decoratifs et Industriel Modernes" Eric Bagge designed the "Hall of Jewelry" among other exhibits. He was a member of the Groupes des Architect Modernes.

He became artistic director of the modern store "Palais du Marbre", and in 1930 he opened his own retail shop in Paris. Bagge favoured the clean, streamlined style influenced by the Cubist movement. This tea set appeared in an auction a few years ago, and Polesden Lacey was fortunate to be able to buy back this important porcelain. Some restoration work was required, and it is now back on show.

Maggie collected Maiolica (1515–50 approximately);[112] Polesden Lacey showcases one of the largest Collection known, outside national museums. Tancred Borenius (1885–1948) gave Maggie advice on some of her paintings (seventeenth-century), and significantly on some of the fifteenth-century Italian paintings and Maiolica. When Maggie was collecting, there was available professional advice from art historians. Being nouveau riche, Maggie availed herself (as did many other collectors) of this knowledge.

There are a number of suggestions that names such as Bernard Berenson, Charles Langton Douglas (joint editor of the Burlington Magazine in 1903) and Borenius were profiting from their advice. The art historians were knowledgeable and important as serious influencers and were monetarised, possibly, with the result that some of their attributions were overvalued. This has been discussed by a number of experts.

But Maggie wanted advice and she got it. By 1919 Maggie's Maiolica was very special. There are twenty-three pieces of Maiolica on display at Polesden Lacey (School of Urbino). One of the most famous artists was Francesco Xante Avelli de Rovigo, and four pieces signed by him are in the collection.

Maggie collected this tin-glazed earthenware (lead with tin for opacity) no doubt because she liked it, but also one of her good friends Henry Harris was an even larger/more fastidious collector than she was. Henry is listed in the Visitor Book at Polesden Lacey many times, and the first date is 1908 (25th January), so their friendship was long-lasting. Henry said of Maggie "one can live without everyone really; everyone but Maggie; she's like dram drinking".

A suggested date for Maggie getting to know Borenius is 1919, but that is because his name appears in the Visitor Book (14th June 1919), staying at

Polesden Lacey. However, it is likely he had known Maggie for much longer, and she met with him in London much earlier.

Tancred Borenius (1885–1948) was an expert dealer and was the first Professor of Art at London University (editor of the *Burlington* magazine, 1940–44).[113] Borenius made money by selling Maiolica to Maggie. Possibly he made large amounts of money selling to Henry Harris too. While Borenius was respected for his knowledge, it was known that he sometimes traded some certificates of authentication for payment.

In 1925 at a sale at Christie's of Sir Francis Cook Collection, Tancred bought eight pieces of Maiolica that he sold to Maggie. These particular items include three extremely rare parrots or hawks, which are considered to be particularly significant (cost at the time was £110.5 shillings for all three).

There was an element of competition between Maggie and Henry, although Henry Harris's collection was, in Maggie's lifetime, even more important than Maggie's. Borenius published privately a catalogue of Henry's Maiolica collection in 1930. The book was named "Catalogue Collection of Italian Maiolica belonging to Henry Harris by Tancred Borenius".

Borenius cultivated social contacts; he became the art advisor to the Earl of Harewood; he "helped" Queen Mary with some of her collection when she was staying with her daughter Mary at Harewood. In 1924 he began to advise Sotheby's Auction House. Interestingly, Borenius began to play a part as a part-time MI6 agent. There are a number of suggestions that Borenius was involved in negotiations to bring Rudolf Hess back to Great Britain. Borenius was "away" from January to March 1941, and had been briefed or at least introduced by Claude Dansey (Deputy Director of MI6) to this project. This story is sometimes refuted and sometimes advanced. Some further investigations have provided an outline of how Borenius was involved in 1941, and if anyone wishes to discover more, there are some new sources available. Borenius had a sad ending to his life in 1948, but from Maggie's viewpoint he had been the supplier and adviser she needed – reference her Maiolica purchases.

Kangxi 1662–1722

There are 180 pieces of Asian art (porcelain, books and paintings) at Polesden Lacey; there was an exhibition in 2014 entitled "Beyond the Dragon" which highlighted some selected pieces in the house. However, more pieces are on display permanently; they are quite dramatic. The words "Kangxi porcelain" evoke images of two distinct palettes – blue and white and famille-verte. The blue and white porcelain displayed in the south east corridor and the library is of the Kangxi period, and is extensive. The variety and size of some of the pieces at Polesden Lacey furnish the house in an overstated, overlaid manner – something to like or dislike. Certainly, some of today's Chinese visitors appreciate the collection.

Why did Maggie collect so much of the Chinese art? She was certainly attracted to it. The history of the success of the Chinese people selling to Europeans is long. There is evidence from the seventh century to the tenth century that porcelain was exported to the West (Tang Dynasty). From the tenth to the thirteenth century the Song Dynasty chose Jingdezhen as the centre of porcelain production because of the availability of kaolin. The thirteenth to fourteenth century saw the Yuan Dynasty continue the work, but it was the Ming Dynasty, fourteenth to seventeenth century, that produced what is regarded as first-class work by the introduction of manganese to prevent cobalt from burning in the furnaces and bleeding. Much of this porcelain was produced at Jingdezhen, south-west of Shanghai. Porcelain from the Kangxi period (1662–1722) is one of the most recognisable areas of Chinese ceramics.

The Kangxi emperor (lived 1654–1722, reigned 1662–1722) was the second emperor of China during the newly established Manchu Qing Dynasty. He was given the name Xuanye and was the fourth Emperor of the Qing Dynasty, and the second Qing emperor to rule over China. The Kangxi Emperor is seen as one of the greatest Emperors of China for his educated rule: suppression of rebellions; patronage of literary, scientific and artistic developments. He ushered in the "High Qing" period of prosperity and peace.

An important milestone in the timeline of Chinese ceramics is the reopening of the imperial kilns in Jingdezhen, which were largely neglected during the decline of the preceding Ming Dynasty. These kilns, in addition to the new technologies gained by the Kangxi Emperor's welcoming relationship with the Jesuits, resulted in an imperial and commercial porcelain industry, which refined traditional techniques and encouraged the development of new designs and palettes, which allowed this period to be one of the most supremely successful production periods for China in porcelain. It is also evident that "the Kangxi Emperor managed to raise the capacity and ability of manufactories overall. This fits in with a man who was more passionately interested in progress than in extravagancies for his own person".

The Kangxi Emperor selected his fourth son as the Yongzheng Emperor (13th December 1678–8th October 1735), born Yinzhen, and he was the fifth Emperor of the Qing Dynasty and the third Qing emperor to rule over China proper. He reigned from 1722 to 1735.

Qianlong 1736–95

The Qianlong Emperor (25th September 1711–7th February 1799) was the sixth Emperor of the Qing Dynasty and the fourth Qing emperor to rule over China proper. He reigned from 1735 to 1796. Born Hongli, the fourth son of the Yongzheng Emperor, he reigned officially from 11th October 1735 to 8th February 1796.[114]

Good solid pieces, including a few which are outstanding, are on display at Polesden Lacey. There a large number of Qianlong jars, jugs, plates, vases and objects in the house. There are two spectacular geese (permanently on show in the dining room) which are Qianlong (circa 1780). A porcelain Qianlong teapot in the form of a Mandarin duck is colourful and painted in enamel colours. Also, a figure of a cat has been returned from Trerice in Cornwall to Polesden Lacey, and is now on show. There is a large Chinese lacquer folding screen (date unknown) in store.

The dogs of Fo (there are eighteen in the house) are fascinating for their details. These dogs are actually Chinese lions. Some of the dogs hold the ball (world) in different positions on their head, foot or paw. These animals were guardians in their larger forms, and were often positioned outside the entrance to places of worship in Chinese Buddhism. Used in Imperial Chinese palaces and tombs, the lions subsequently spread to other parts of Asia, including Japan, Korea, Tibet, Thailand, Burma, Vietnam, Sri Lanka, Nepal, Cambodia, Laos, Taiwan and Singapore. Usually, the lions were presented in pairs, as a manifestation of yin and yang, the female representing yin and the male yang.

Japanese Porcelain

There are also Japanese items: woodblock prints, bound in three red cloth books – all beautiful. There are also some large Japanese bowls. Porcelain production in Japan started later than that in China. It was not until the seventeenth century that Japanese made porcelain. Japanese artists developed their own style of porcelain emphasising aesthetic qualities of a natural "organic earthy" feeling, simplicity and austerity.

Most of Maggie's collection was created, as I have said, by buying at auction, and from Bond Street dealers. When aristocrats travelled, they made some purchases. Maggie collected Chinese glass paintings on her travels. These paintings were not considered to be of museum quality, and were sold by the National Trust in 1943.

Did Maggie's paintings make a difference to Polesden Lacey? Yes, as they were fashionable. They also provide in the long south corridor a fusion of art with porcelain, in a setting micromanaged as a stage set for artefacts. If other aristocrats had more or finer paintings or porcelain, how much did this matter? Maggie enjoyed showcasing her artefacts; they were vital (especially being nouveau riche); they were the essential background to enable her social position, to appear to be at the top of most aristocrats' expectations of members of society.

Maggie brought to Polesden Lacey, above all else, friends. People mattered to her more than objects. Rich, poor, educated, intelligent, considerate, influential (political), hardworking and often royal. Maggie had a fascination for intrigue (at times), endeavouring to influence and manage the leading lights in international society and government (as much as she could).

Maggie enjoyed the company of less well-known people who possessed abilities, which were still at their nascent stages. As the Chatelaine of Polesden Lacey she was enabled by the backing of almost infinite money, to indulge her friends, some of whom had yet to make their way in life.

ELEVEN

Maggie's Travels

Maggie's travel arrangements during the winter followed an established pattern for English aristocrats. Going abroad until the beginning of the season was "de rigeur". The London social scene was defined by the timing of the Royal family's residence in London, from April to July, and again from October until Christmas. It is argued that Parliament affected the dates for the season, as members from both the House of Lords and the House of Commons were participants in the season. The shooting season began, as it still does, on 12th August each year.

The Queen today continues the tradition of partitioning up the year, but without the rigidity of some of the customs of George III/Queen Charlotte's reign. Queen Charlotte's Ball still exists/existed up to the 241st Ball, which took place on 17th May 2019, in London, in aid of the Smile Train (the Ball supports a different charity each year).

Until 1958 (when the Queen terminated this custom) debutantes were presented at Court. Once married, the ladies were again presented at Court by their mothers-in-law.

It was essential to be dressed for such occasions correctly, and it was always necessary to visit a successful fashion house. In Maggie's day, a visit to the couturiers situated in or near Hanover Square and Bond Street, was an immediate requirement on arriving home from winter journeys.

Norman Hartnell, favoured by Queen Elizabeth the Queen Mother;

Handley-Seymour in New Bond Street; Miss Gray (court dressmaker) in Brook Street; Victor Stiebel and other English couturiers were available to provide high-quality dresses for aristocrats at such receptions, unless a trip to Paris for a Worth/Coco Chanel original, was deemed necessary. Yes, some people did make the journey to Paris.

Maggie began to regularly host guests at Polesden Lacey, and with new additions from her star-studded list of international friends, guests were offered a high standard of both cuisine and service; Maggie entertained at Christmas at Polesden Lacey most years. Increasingly, Maggie Greville travelled during most winters to countries, far away from the cold climate of Great Britain. Rarely, but occasionally, Maggie stayed at the houses of her friends at Christmas. At Christmas 1927, Maggie stayed with the Londonderry family at Wynard Hall, and did not entertain at Polesden Lacey, but this was not her usual way of celebrating Christmas.

There were exceptions to her usual pattern:[115] she sometimes departed on her travels, prior to Christmas, to places including India, 1921–22, and arrived home in March 1922. In the spring of 1923, Maggie was in South Africa. Maggie arrived home in time for Bertie and Elizabeth's wedding (26th April), on board the Balmoral Castle on 23rd April, at Southampton – just in time.

Maggie travelled to Ceylon and the East, 1923–24; she was away in Burma, Siam, Penang, Bangkok, Singapore and Java from December 1923, and departed on 27th March 1924 on board the SS *Naldera* to return home in April. She was in South America, 1924–25; Maggie departed on 12th December 1924 for South America on board the SS *Andes* and returned in April 1925. Maggie visited Brazil, Argentina, Chile, Bolivia, Uruguay, Peru and, travelling via the Panama Canal, Cuba. After this trip, Maggie planned to go to China.

However, Lord George Curzon advised Maggie not to go to China on this occasion, as there was much "unrest and unease", and he did not believe such a journey would ensure her safety and comfort. However, Maggie did visit both China and Japan in her travelling years.

Maggie was fortunate to have the company of Agustin Edwards Mac-Clure (Chilean Plenipotentiary to Great Britain and President of the General Assembly of the League of Nations, 1922/23) and his wife Olga for much of her time in South America.[116] Maggie was adventurous, and her journeys, while taken in the best possible way, were often dangerous at times as well as exciting. She travelled by train frequently. The train crossed flimsy wooden bridges and reached Lake Titicaca, 12,600 feet above sea level (possibly the highest navigable lake in the world?), and she reached Agna Caliester, Peru, 14,000 feet above sea level. She stayed in Santiago for several weeks (Agustin Edwards' hometown).

Maggie, the lady adventurer, travelled across the world in excellent circumstances but sometimes with risks. Some of the photographs taken of Maggie on her trip to South America (1924–25) show the risks she took. On her homeward journey in 1925, she boarded the SS *Esquibo* at the Port of Mollendo, Peru, by being winched aboard the ship by a crane, sitting in an armchair! Quite a dramatic photograph.

Maggie returned to the UK from New York aboard the *Olympic* (White Star Line), the sister ship to the *Titanic*, and arrived back at Southampton.

Maggie was received abroad almost as if she were the government's representative. Maggie had letters of introduction to key people; kings/queens/maharajahs/prime ministers/governors of regions. Additionally, messages were sent ahead of her visits to countries, to the embassies or foreign offices.

Maggie's ability to entertain kings, queens, maharajahs, politicians and aristocrats was demonstrated by her international Visitor Book guest list. King Fuad of Egypt dined with Maggie on his first visit to England for seventeen years in July 1927, and stayed with her at Polesden Lacey, 27–28th July 1929.

Maggie visited New Zealand and Australia in 1927.[117] While in New Zealand, she visited Rotorua. She arrived in Australia by 24th February. She stayed from 26th February at the Carrington, the oldest hotel in Katoomba, New South Wales. The hotel occupies the highest point in the town, and was established in 1883 as the Great Western, renamed as the Carrington in 1886. By March 1927 Maggie was in Canberra and travelled in a special car in Victoria, followed by travelling in the Chief Commissioner of Railways' own railway carriage (James Fraser). Maggie arrived in Sydney and stayed at Admiralty House from 23rd to 27th March. There is a photograph of the *Renown* arriving in Sydney harbour on 26th March; on board were Bertie and Elizabeth. Maggie was able "to meet and greet Bertie and Elizabeth on their arrival". Rather special to be so involved with the royal couple, Maggie's friends.

King Fuad offered Maggie spectacular hospitality when she was staying in Egypt in 1932.[118] On Tuesday 22nd March 1932, "King Fuad, accompanied by Kaimakain Mahmud Shukri Bey, aide de camp, motored from Koubbeh Palace to Abdin Palace, where His Majesty gave an audience to Mrs Ronald Greville, and at 1pm a luncheon party was given in her honour, to which Yussef Aslan Cattani Pasha and Mme Cattani Pasha, lady in waiting to the Queen, and the high officials of the Palace were invited." The lunch party was in return for

Maggie's hospitality to King Fuad in England. Maggie stayed at Shepheard's Hotel in Cairo, which was known for its grandeur and famous guest list, which included the Aga Khan, Winston Churchill and the Maharajah of Jodhpur. The hotel was established in 1841 by Samuel Shepheard and Mr Hill.

Adeline Liron, Maggie's personal maid and later her companion, usually travelled with her; Adeline travelled first-class. Maggie did not want Adeline occupying a second/lower cabin. Maggie required Adeline to look after all of her needs and also wanted her companionship. Adeline's cabin had to be as near as possible to Maggie's (discussed in Chapter 7). George Moss (senior butler) and his wife Hilda often accompanied Maggie. Sometimes Herbert Towell (valet) travelled with her.

Frank Bole was, for the most part, required to remain in England to look after both Polesden Lacey and the Charles Street house, and one hundred-plus staff (about seventy staff at Polesden Lacey and the larger total made up from staff at Charles Street) with all of their attending needs. He was given a holiday abroad at a different time of the year and travelled by ship with his wife Evelyn, usually second class, between the years 1926 to 1939.

Only rarely did Frank Bole, Head Steward, accompany Maggie on her travels. He was on a ship named *Miami* returning from Havana (April 1920) with Maggie and Adeline Liron. In February 1927 Frank Bole accompanied Maggie on the ship *Jan Pieterszoon Coen* to Genoa.[119]

In Egypt, Maggie was received and entertained with dignity and style by the King. The British High Commissioner in Cairo at the time of her visit was Sir Percy Loraine, who succeeded George Lloyd (whom Maggie disliked).

Maggie visited America a number of times, the first date being November 1909. Subsequently, she travelled to or through America a number of times. Listing all of Maggie's travels would be lengthy. Until her health failed in her later years, she had an enthusiasm for travel in comfort, which she sustained for many, many years.

Maggie's journeys in Europe were also extensive; Cannes/Monte Carlo, Baden-Baden for the health cures. France, particularly, as so many of the international royals established themselves in Cannes/Monte Carlo, in addition to many politicians holidaying abroad. The South of France provided everyone (royalty, aristocrats and politicians mixed with businessmen) the opportunity to entertain rather as though they were back at home in London.

Aristocrats/royalty gathered in Paris for the couture and the jewellery (Maggie's fondness for Boucheron cannot be exaggerated). They also enjoyed the most fashionable areas of Italy and Spain. From the late nineteenth century to the early twentieth century, a number of travel companies were established in London; Thomas Cook & Company moved their office from Ludgate Circus in 1924 to Berkeley Square, specifically to catch the aristocrats' business.

Thomas Cook provided for the first time, hotel coupons (established from 1868 for payment of meals and rooms, instead of money) at the hotels of choice for travellers. Thomas Cook also established the circular note (first issued in 1878, and the forerunner of travellers' cheques). Thomas Cook's main competitor was Henry Gaze and Son, copying Cook's provision of hotel coupons. From the 1890s other travel companies were established: Dean & Dawson (1871), John Frames Tours (1881), Quintin Hogg's Polytechnic Tours (1886), Sir Henry Lunn's (1895).[120]

In Great Britain, passports were standardised in 1855 and issued solely to British nationals and were a single-sheet paper document; by 1914 a photograph was required. In 1915, after the British Nationality and the Status of Aliens Act was passed, a new format was established – the single sheet of paper folded into eight with a cardboard cover. A description of the holder was required with a photograph; the document had to be renewed every two years. Examples of shipping lines Maggie used for her travel were: *Olympic*, White Star Line; *Balmoral*, Union Castle Line; *Mauretania*, Cunard; *Empress of India*, Canadian Pacific Steamship; *Lurline* and *Malolo*, the Matson line.

In May 1933 Maggie travelled on an aeroplane.[121] This was the first time she had flown. She returned from Paris (Le Bourget) to London (Croydon) in order to attend the Foreign Office reception which was being held in honour of Aime-Benjamin Fleuriau – Comte de Bellevue (the French ambassador and his wife). The ambassador served from 1924 to 1933 in London. The reception was for his retirement, and Maggie did not want to miss out on such an important social occasion.

Maggie's Head Chauffeur, Sidney Smith, met her at the airport, and her return to London was made in time for the Foreign Office reception in honour of Monsieur de Fleuriau. Both Fleuriau and his wife lunched with George V and Queen Mary at Windsor on 3rd May.

Travel by plane was becoming more fashionable and recognised for its speed. The Paris, Le Bourget, to Croydon, London, route was initially the busiest "in the world", and it was at Croydon that international air services began. Air traffic control was initiated at Croydon. The distress call "mayday, mayday,

mayday" was established at Croydon airport. The new terminal was completed on 28th January 1928 and was officially opened on 2nd May.

Imperial Airways operated from Croydon, and from 1924 the London–Paris route was served initially by a de Havilland DH 34. Planes flew at a low level and were noisy. Imperial Airways Silver Wings Service offered cocktails, three-course meals, afternoon tea with pastries and a chauffeur service to central London.

The background to some of Maggie's foreign travel sometimes had underlying situations/experiences, which would not normally be part of such journeys. Maggie's first trip to India provides an example. The closeness of the relationship between all of the people involved, endured throughout their lives.

Rufus Daniel Isaacs, 1st Marquess of Reading GCB, GCSI, GCIE, GCVO, PC, KC (1860-1935) by Fred Bremner (photographer) India

© National Trust Images, Collections-Public / Fred Bremner (India)

The first time Maggie visited India was in 1921–22, when her close friend Lord Reading was Viceroy.[122] Maggie was sometimes cunning. She did not have a small-town outlook on life. The highlight of this particular trip was spending time in Delhi at Viceroy House with Lord and Lady Reading. Maggie adored Lord Reading. The Prince of Wales also was on a very similar date/s to Maggie's schedule travelling in India. He too was at Viceroy House. Louis Mountbatten (1900–79) was with Edward as his aide de camp.

Edwina Ashley (1900–60) followed everyone out to "join the party". She arrived in Delhi at Viceroy House on Sunday 12th February 1922. Maggie was, for the most part, Edwina's chaperone while she was there.

Maggie claimed that she introduced Edwina to Louis. However, Philip Ziegler in his book *Mountbatten*, the official biography, stated that they had met earlier at Claridge's in October 1920, at a ball given by Mrs Cornelia Vanderbilt.[123] They were, after all, in the same aristocratic circle. Edwina did stay at Polesden Lacey in July 1920, but this was not at the same time as Mountbatten. Philip Ziegler believed that they began to notice each other in a more interested way from August 1921, when they were both in the same party at Cowes. They did both stay with Maggie 14th to 17th October 1921 at Polesden Lacey, so it seems that Philp Ziegler was correct.

Maggie was quite keen on the idea of them becoming acquainted, but because Edwina was so rich, she thought that Edwina should think first rather than rush to marry Mountbatten. Edwina had inherited from her grandfather Sir Ernest Cassel a fortune on 21st September 1921.

Sir Ernest Cassel's wife (Annette Mary Maud Maxwell) died in 1881. Their only daughter, Amalia Mary Maud, married Wilfred Ashley, but she died in 1911.

Edwina's father, Wilfred Ashley, married again in 1914, after which Edwina spent some time at boarding schools, which was not acceptable to her. Her grandfather Sir Ernest invited Edwina to stay with him at Brook House, Park Lane, and they grew closer, which is why Edwina inherited from Sir Ernest Cassel more of a fortune than her sister Mary.[124]

Edwina's initial bequest from Sir Ernest was £2.3 million. Sir Ernest's sister (Wilhelmina) was bequeathed Brook House in Park Lane and £30,000 annually for the rest of her life. When Wilhelmina died in 1925, Edwina received Brook House and more money.

Edwina and Louis were clearly smitten with each other at this stage of their lives. Louis's salary at this time was £310 a year, and his income from dividends was an additional amount of £300. While such money differences may not matter, as Edwina was in mourning for her grandfather and Louis was in mourning for his father, who died on 11th September 1921, it was not at the time considered to be acceptable in society to become engaged. This did not prevent Louis from expressing to Edwina his real feelings, in a letter he sent to her the night prior to his departure for India, with Edward Prince of Wales.

Edwina seemed pleased to understand Louis' commitment to her, prior to his departure for India. When Edwina arrived at Viceroy House, Louis was absolutely thrilled. The couple really badgered Maggie in her suite at Viceroy House, telling her they wished to become engaged. Maggie at this stage had reservations. Maggie, while staying at Viceroy House, sent a handwritten to Lord Reading on 20th February 1922 (morning), talking about Edwina and Louis.[125]

She wrote on Viceroy House, Delhi letterhead:

"My dear Viceroy,

I am absolutely wretched about that child – I couldn't sleep a wink, I have grave misgivings. They were both at me last night – and she will not be reasonable, all I begged for was that no engagement should take place now, in a year she would be sick of him.

She has promised me that she will not write home until she has seen you, but she promised me she would do nothing here – I want time – this is absolutely confidential only I feel she is being thrown to the wolves so although it is mean of one to betray a confidence I feel you are the only pillar of strength and if only that mother of his is told, she will be bound round – and there will be no escape – his tone too last night upset me. He said he would talk his mother round but she would not be too difficult. I said she [*Edwina*] was the one prize and there was not a mother in England who would not want her. I don't dislike him but he is wily and I am really wretched and very sore at her breaking her word to me. And she looked so white-faced and motherless last night. Dear Viceroy please insist on no engagement – I have failed ignominiously but you are so strong. Bless you and forgive me, Maggie Greville."

Maggie and Lord Reading failed. Edwina and Louis announced their engagement while in Delhi. Edwina's father (Wilfred Ashley) found out by hearing of the engagement by this announcement, before a letter arrived at home for him, telling him about the engagement.

Later, Maggie was very supportive of both of them, and attended their wedding and continued the friendship. Naturally she wished to be included, not excluded from the lives of the couple. Edwina married Mountbatten on 18th July 1922 at St Margaret's, Westminster. Louis was a British Royal Navy Officer and Statesman. He was an uncle of Prince Philip, Duke of Edinburgh, and was second cousin once removed of Queen Elizabeth II.

In 1932 Edwina was involved in a court case.[126] The *People* newspaper published a thinly disguised report that she was having an affair with a West Indian night club singer. Edwina Mountbatten sued and won, because the newspaper was unable to prove which singer it was.

Edwina was thought to be "having an affair with Paul Robeson"; Edwina was actually having an affair with Leslie "Hutch" Hutchinson. It was easy for her to stand up in court, as the newspaper had not got the correct information.

Maggie maintained her friendship with Edwina and Louis throughout her life. When Maggie was not well, but was still doing some entertaining while she was living at the Dorchester Hotel, London, in 1942, she held a dinner party which included Louis and others.

Later, Louis Mountbatten became Viceroy of India in February 1947. Edwina was the last Vicereine. Louis became Governor-General of India after the partition of India and Pakistan on 15th August 1947 until June 1948. They had two children, Patricia (1924–2017) and Pamela (1929–).

In 1947 rumours were spread about Edwina having an affair with Nehru, when Louis was Viceroy of India. Edwina said to Louis that the relationship was "mostly spiritual".

At the age of fifty-nine Edwina died on 21st February 1960 (unknown causes) in British North Borneo (now Sabah), on an inspection tour for St John's Ambulance Brigade. Nehru sent the Indian navy frigate INS *Trishul* (an Indian destroyer) to escort the *Wakeful*, when the wreath was cast into the water to honour Edwina's burial at sea.

In August 1979, Mountbatten was assassinated by a bomb that was hidden aboard his fishing boat in Mullaghmore, County Sligo, Ireland, by members of the Provisional Irish Republican Army.

Near the beginning of Maggie's trip to India (1921–22), when Maggie was in Calcutta (December 1921), she met Conrad Corfield (1893–1980) – knighted in 1945, who was, at that time, assistant private secretary to Lord Reading.[127] Conrad Corfield commented that he met Maggie several times, and he said, "At one vice-regal dinner party she wore emeralds, which I find it hard to describe except that they seemed to cover her from forehead to fingers. At a subsequent party she wore diamonds of equal magnificence and extent."

When Corfield congratulated Maggie on the beauty of the jewels, Maggie asked Corfield whether he "thought they were real". He replied, "I was no expert but they looked real enough to me." Maggie told Corfield that "one set was real and the other false". Maggie also said she had never met anyone who could tell which jewels were false. Maggie had copies of her important jewels made, and travelled with both the real and a false copy of each set, on her travels.

Maggie had arranged with the insurance company that, she would swap from real to false jewels on different journeys, without allowing anyone to know. Maggie obtained a reduction in her insurance costs by doing this. Shrewd, rich and certainly prudent. Corfield added, "Maggie was also very good company."

TWELVE

Third Death

In 1913, William McEwan died at 16 Charles Street, London, on Monday 12th May at midday. The funeral took place at St Nicholas Church, Bookham, on Thursday 15th May.[128] "The Rev Bernard Shaw [*Vicar of the Church of Annunciation, Brianstone Street, London*] and the Rector of Great Bookham the Rev GS Bird were the officiating clergy."

There was a very long list of mourners, and I name only a few: the Hon Mrs Greville (daughter), Lord Greville, Mr William Younger and Mr Robert Younger (nephews), and among those present were Prince Victor Duleep Singh, the Earl and Countess of Granard, the Earl of Ilchester, the Hon Mrs G Keppel, General Sir Arthur Paget and representatives from the brewery and the Edinburgh Constituency. Valet to late King Edward VII, Mr Wrightson, and the body servant/valet to late King Edward VII, Mr H Vine, were also present. Mr F Samuels (steward to William McEwan) and Frank Bole (Maggie's Head Steward) were in attendance.

"The coffin was of polished oak with brass furniture and bore the inscription William McEwan, born 14th July 1827, died 12th May 1913."

A memorial service was held in Edinburgh at precisely the same time at Greyfriars, by the Rev Dr Wallace Williamson, Moderator Designate of the General Assembly of the Church of Scotland, assisted by the Rev AB Grant, minister of Old Greyfriars. The service commenced at 3.30pm.

It had been known by everyone close to McEwan, that he had become frail.

His death to Maggie could not have come as a huge surprise, but because she really had depended on him (forever) her loss was huge.

When McEwan died there many newspaper articles about him which were complimentary. There was a recognition for his achievements as a self-made businessman, brewer, politician and philanthropist. His death certificate includes arteriosclerosis and cardiac failure as reasons for death on 12th May 1913.[129] McEwan's Will was dated 13th July 1910.[130]

William McEwan gave bequests to his relatives. Shares to: Maggie, his one and only daughter; William Younger of Ravenswood (Roxburgh) – nephew; Robert Younger of South Audley Street – nephew; Giles Stephen Holland (Earl of Ilchester) Holland House; and Captain, the Hon Edward Dawson. Many of the staff who worked in McEwan's brewery, including agencies in Glasgow, Newcastle upon Tyne and Dundee, received £500 each. His servants: Frederick Samuels (McEwan's butler) received £4,000 and Henry Vine (valet) £200. Other staff were given one year's wages. Other bequests included the Royal Infirmary Edinburgh (£15,000) and the Convalescent Home connected to the Royal Infirmary (£1,000).

McEwan bequeathed his parents' home in Alloa: "To dispone and convey to the said Robert Younger the dwelling house and pertinents in Forth Street, Alloa belonging to me with the whole household furniture and plenishing therein including bed and table linen, china plate, pictures, books… at the date of my death".

The bequest of McEwan's ordinary shares in the brewery were given to Maggie, including any dividends due and not paid to McEwan. In his Will he stated that: "I direct my trustees to deliver and to pay and convey and make over to the said the Honourable Mrs Margaret Helen Greville (and her heirs and assignees) the whole rest residue and remainder of my means and estate. And I declare (first) that the bequests of ordinary shares of William McEwan and Company Limited herein shall carry right to the dividends (as far as not actually paid over to me) on said shares for the financial year of/the company at my death."

One very interesting clause appeared on page 95 of McEwan's Will, which stated clearly, referring to his bequests to Maggie, that "the whole bequests made to or which should devolve upon females shall belong to themselves alone and as their own sole and separate estate exclusive of the jus mariti, right of administration and all other rights of any husbands whom they may marry [*and inserted by hand – "may have married"*]" and "that where in these presents more than one legacy or bequest is made in favour of the same person such legacies or bequests should be held to be cumulative and not substitutionary".

Wow! Had this been challenged by a future husband by Maggie marrying again, would McEwan's bequest to Maggie have been upheld?

Jus mariti was the (now obsolete) right of a husband to his wife's estate. What McEwan was saying was that he wanted Maggie to keep his bequest to her and her alone. He also stated in his Will that "I Do hereby Give, Grant, Assign, Dispose, Devise, Legate and Bequeath to and in favour of The Honourable Margaret Greville of Eleven Charles Street, Berkeley Square in the County of London, lawful daughter of me and Mrs Helen McEwan, my late wife".

He went on to say that he was "a domiciled Scotchman and that these presents shall be construed according to the Law of Scotland".

I located William McEwan's Will in Scotland, as you would expect. We did not have a copy of it at Polesden Lacey. However, I did try the English Probate Office first, as he had died in England. I was informed that although they had once had a copy, they had destroyed it. Fortunately, the Scottish Office kept his Will intact, including the Eik ("additional confirmation of an item which allows the executor to administer an item of estate that had previously been overlooked or has just materialised after the original confirmation has been obtained").

McEwan made clear that Maggie was his daughter and he wanted her to inherit his fortune, without any interference from any man! A continuing and significant approach to the management of his daughter and her assets, even after McEwan had died.

The *Financial Times* on 4th May 1913 said: "The death of Mr McEwan brings to a close a long and in many respects a singularly remarkable career, and marks the passing away of a sound businessman of extraordinary energy and vitality and striking personality... Few men have laboured so hard for success as did Mr McEwan, and few have accomplished so much... Self-help, a determined nature, and inexhaustible energy were the secret of his success."

William McEwan's Bequests to His Daughter

Maggie inherited most of her father's fortune (1.5 million pounds). In 1889 McEwan banked half a million pounds when he incorporated his company; he invested this sum in worldwide stocks and shares. At the time of his death, McEwan owned shares in twelve railway companies.[131] His investments in these companies included the Caledonian Railway, which he used regularly to transport his beer (£88,400 probate). He invested in four more British railway companies: the Great Western, the North Eastern, the London and Western Railway (£133,125 probate, largest of rail share holdings), and the Midland Railway.

Additionally, he invested in foreign railway companies, which were the Pennsylvania Railroad Company, the Nashville Florence & Sheffield Railway, the Northern Pacific Railway Company, the Baltimore & Ohio Railroad Company, and the Atcheson, Topeka & Sante Fe Railway, the Great Northern Railway (USA), and the Union Pacific Railway (£122,300 probate).

In addition to shares in his own company valued at £326,250 (probate) the rest of his investments were in chemical and industrial companies, with his largest shareholding in other shares, in the Hudson's Bay Company (£246,250 probate). His shrewdness brought success, but with the majority of his shares in railway stocks, had he been mistaken in backing the industrial revolution, Polesden Lacey would be a different place today. Maggie's inheritance from McEwan included more than money: paintings (seventeen at Polesden Lacey) and other artefacts.

In June 1913, it was announced that Maggie had gifted to Edinburgh University 25 Palmerston Place; as "one of the largest and most handsomely appointed houses in Edinburgh" there was a suggestion that "the house may be utilised as a residence for the Principal, or as a hostel for lady students". As William McEwan had been one of the most important benefactors to Edinburgh, as outlined in Chapter 1, this gift was an added bonus to the city.

THIRTEEN

Maggie the Hostess

A description provided by Anne de Courcy of Maggie's dining room at Polesden Lacey, and referring to Maggie (written in 1989 and reissued in 2009), offers the following:[132] "At Polesden Lacey, a huge building of golden stone overlooking the surrounding Surrey countryside, she had had the long dining table specially made so that people could talk to those opposite as well as their neighbours on each side. Against the prevailing trend, she seldom decorated it with flowers, instead preferring the simplicity of superb damask linen, old silver and plain white candles with parchment shades. The tablecloth, like the napkins which bore her monogram, was woven in Ireland, the glass and china were plain and unadorned save for a narrow border of gold round the edges of the plates, goblets and finger bowls, but the sixteen silver candlesticks, set in pairs down the table, were heavily chased. Between them stood tankards, goblets and porringers from her collection of Georgian and Carolingian silver."

It is impossible to exaggerate the importance of Maggie's guest list (Visitor Book).[133] Maggie's connections from her early days of marrying into the Marlborough House Set, and entertaining Edward VII, George V and Queen Mary, and the future King George VI and Queen Elizabeth, were extended and maintained. Key royal friendships were important, British and international royals, including maharajahs, were her network. Maggie was always active in managing her incredible contacts.

Maggie never gossiped about her royal friends. Maggie did gossip about other members of society, such as Emerald Cunard. Also, Alice Keppel (a great friend) of whom Maggie critically said "to hear Alice talk, you would think she had to swim the Channel with her maid between her teeth" (1940).

Maggie managed to be involved, included and played an important part in the royal circle in Britain, and on her travels in Europe and across the world. In 1924 when Princess Beatrice (Queen Victoria's daughter) departed for South Africa, to stay with Princess Alice and the Earl of Athlone (Governor General), Maggie was at Waterloo Station to say goodbye to Beatrice, with a number of Beatrice's close friends.

Maggie met royalty, made friends with royalty, entertained at her two homes, and met and entertained them in Europe. Royal connections were maintained!

In the summer months, Maggie entertained the Duke and Duchess of York (usually the weekend after Royal Ascot), so they could both relax after so much entertaining. Additionally, the third weekend of July, was another summer favourite time for Bertie and Elizabeth to stay at Polesden Lacey.

The gardens, the flowers and the produce, provided a spectacular backdrop for all of Maggie's guests to enjoy themselves. Roses, crimson, pink, white and the American Pillar roses, and bowls of sweet peas filled many rooms with their fragrance at this time. Hydrangeas were often used to fill the fireplaces in summer. The flowerbeds were at their best and easily accessed without too much walking.

The fruit and vegetables offered from cold frames were potatoes, lettuce, peas, turnips, carrots, radishes, mustard and cress. Vegetables grown outside included asparagus, onions, spinach, rhubarb and spinach beet (uncommon in Great Britain at this time). French beans, cucumbers and tomatoes were grown in the heated greenhouses (bombed in World War II). Peaches, strawberries, cherries and sometimes mangoes were also offered to complete the feeling of wellbeing when being entertained by Maggie.

With the bonus of the farms' produce, and any delicacies acquired in the open market, the standard of dining was always of the highest. Maggie's staff helped to stage manage perfect weekends for international guests.

The bonus of golf, tennis, croquet and the grounds, created a magical retreat from town. The evening entertainers provided the amusement. The conversation and social intrigues would surpass everything else.

Maggie enjoyed the company of politicians; she believed she could influence and enable political change/s. In Cannes in March 1913, she met up with Bonar Law, Lloyd George, Sir Rufus and Lady Isaacs, Mr and Mrs Winston Churchill, Lord and Lady Charles Beresford, Mr Balfour and Joseph Chamberlain.[134]

A formidable group of politicians, if they can be labelled a group. Maggie entertained both royalty and politicians in Cannes, as they all enjoyed having the court abroad, and discussing the latest international events.

Many politicians came to Polesden Lacey on a regular basis. Some repeatedly, others more occasionally. Many of Maggie's guests were rich; being rich was not a requirement to be a guest at Charles Street or Polesden Lacey. Maggie entertained up-and-coming young people who had not necessarily made any money, and whom she wished to encourage.

How rich was Maggie? She inherited 1.5 million pounds (valued possibly at eighty to one hundred million pounds today), and two sets of brewery shares (30,000 preference and 30,000 non-preference), from her father in 1913.[135] Were some of Maggie's guests richer than she was?

Maggie was surrounded by wealthy guests. Examples of wealthy guests are clear from the Visitor Book. Lord and Lady Granard enjoyed Maggie's hospitality from 1926 to 1938. Lady Granard (American by birth) inherited just under 2.5 million pounds from her father Mr Ogden Mills, in 1929. With her inheritance came a stable of thoroughbred horses in France.

Maggie was pretty rich. Not as rich as some aristocrats. In September 1921 Edwina Ashley (Mountbatten) inherited more than Maggie (£2.3 million from her grandfather Sir Ernest Cassel), and later (1925) Brook House after Sr Ernest's sister Wilhelmina/Edwina's aunt died, and when her father died (Wilfred Ashley) Broadlands. Other people Maggie mixed with, had fortunes too. But Maggie had more than enough to enjoy life.

Other guests, such as the Rothschild family (guests 1930 to 1938), were incredibly wealthy. Maharajahs, international royalty and aristocratic families, such as Devonshire, Curzon, Londonderry, Westminster (Grosvenor), and Harold and Anastasia (de Torby) Wernher (guests 1926 to 1938), were extremely rich and were richer than Maggie. But, as Edward VII said, "Maggie had a genius for hospitality."

Maggie's social life was a continuing story of being involved with many Royals, not just wealthy people or aristocrats. In June 1937, Maggie was in a party held by Edwina and Louis Mountbatten, in their new apartment at the top of Brook House, to celebrate their new home. Edwina sold Brook House to the builders Gee, Walker & Slater in/by 1933. High taxation and running costs caused her to sell, with an agreement that the Mountbattens would be provided with an apartment in the new building.

The builders demolished Brook House and most flats were completed by

1935, but it was not until 1937 that Edwina and Louis' large penthouse was ready. The apartment was two storeys high and access was by a lift only.

The party of just under twenty people included Bertie and Elizabeth, along with Edwina's sister (Mrs Cunningham Reid), Countess Spencer, the Duchess of Sutherland and Maggie Greville.[136] This was a relaxed occasion and two films were shown after dinner, one being a Mickey Mouse film and the other *A Star Is Born*. Edwina wore a dress which was aquamarine in colour, and her tiara was made of aquamarines and diamonds. Maggie wore a pink sequinned dress, and with it a large brooch of diamonds and rubies.

The party was intended to give Bertie and Elizabeth a relaxing evening, amongst close friends. Maggie must have loved being included in such a special dinner party. She certainly enjoyed being friendly with royalty. Let us not underestimate Maggie's method of mixing politicians into her social sphere too.

Maggie had become a star in an international circle at the top of society. This allowed Maggie to appear as first-class. While this had become normal for Maggie through her extensive networking and entertaining, did she ever reflect on her early life while growing up? Maggie was looked after by McEwan throughout her childhood, but she could not have presumed that the doors which had subsequently opened for her, would bring her to the pinnacle of society.

In November 1928, Maggie entertained at 16 Charles Street many royal members of society and other notable guests to a dinner, which was followed by a dance for an additional hundred guests.[137] Notable royals who were present included the Queen of Spain and her daughters Beatriz and Maria Christina, the Duke of Sutherland, Lady Louis Mountbatten (Edwina), the Marchioness of Curzon and Princess Sybille of Saxe-Coburg-Gotha, and the Marquess of Londonderry.

Diana Churchill was accompanied by her father Winston. The Marquess Merry del Val (Spanish ambassador) escorted Maggie into dinner. Two tables were set out for dinner, with the young people sharing the smaller table. Both tables were decorated with pink chrysanthemums. The ballroom was decorated with pink begonias.

Maggie had arranged for a cocktail bar to be installed, which was quite an innovation. It was not until 1936 that Maggie actually held a cocktail party (the modern rage). But offering cocktails was now fashionable. Maggie wore a lemon-coloured dress, with her magnificent diamond and emerald necklace.

The Savoy Hotel had spearheaded the fashionable ideas of having cocktails mixed, led by "Kitty & Coley" (Ada Coleman and Ruth Burgess), followed by Harry Craddock, who ran the Savoy Cocktail Bar from 1920. Harry produced *The Savoy Cocktail Book* in 1930, containing 750 recipes.[138]

Mrs Jacques (Consuelo) Balsan was a guest with her husband at Polesden Lacey in 1928 (she was previously married to the Duke of Marlborough) and she had inherited from her Vanderbilt family a fortune, and possessed a fine jewellery collection.

Maggie's links with so many international royals, can be recognised from their return visits so often, to both Polesden Lacey and Charles Street. In 1927 King Fuad of Egypt made his first visit to England for seventeen years. He arrived in London on 4th July and watched the Harrow-Eton match at Lords on 8th July, with the Prime Minister Stanley Baldwin also present.

King Fuad dined with Maggie on 12th July at Charles Street. In July 1929 King Fuad stayed at Polesden Lacey for the weekend (27th–28th), and the guest list included, in addition to Mohammed Mahmoud Pasha (Prime Minister of Egypt), Ahmed Pasha Hassanein, the Prince and Princess of Connaught, Viscountess Churchill, the Marchioness of Carisbrooke and other important guests. During dinner on Sunday 28th July, four musicians played Eastern music in the central hall outside the dining room. After dinner (from about 11pm) on the same evening, the entertainment at Polesden Lacey was provided by André Charlot in the saloon.[139] The guests were able to enjoy a number of variety acts, including Jean Barry and Dave Fitzgibbon, Marie Burke and Ivor Weir.

Maggie entertained her friends in Charles Street during the week (Monday to Thursday); the guest list can be described as spectacular. Anyone in town who mattered appeared at her house, usually for dinner and sometimes also for lunch. Most aristocrats and royal families lived in or near the village of Mayfair. This meant that their ability to partake of each other's hospitality was easy, comfortable and reflected well, with their own desires for mixing with key members of society.

Maggie often hosted thirty to forty guests to dinner at Charles Street. Sometimes sixty to seventy and more guests were given dinner. If a cabaret entertainment was offered, then supper too was served, with additional guests dropping in for this. The guest list in Maggie's case included royalty (kings, queens, maharajahs), aristocrats, politicians, ambassadors, prime ministers, inventors, scientists and people she had got to know for the first time. Maggie maintained her friendships, while adding in new people in town. Being rich was not a requirement; being of interest was.

The Maharajahs!

It is impossible to underestimate the wealth of the maharajahs. The jewellery they wore was astounding, magnificent, rare and valuable. When they were dressed in their own country, they looked spectacular, because the jewellery raised their image and helped to manifest their omnipotence.

During the day in Great Britain, they wore normal clothes. In the evening, or when attending Court or society (day or evening) events of the season, their clothes and their jewels expressed their nobility, indicated their monarchy and eminence.

Maggie, with her love of jewels and her interest intellectually in people who mattered, clearly enjoyed her association and friendship with her Indian friends. As I stated earlier, the maharajahs and the aristocrats were impressing each other and themselves. Not a normal life to most people, but it was to these powerful leaders, who were fabulously rich, and were world travellers who owned so much.

I visited the Al Thani Exhibition (Jewellery, November 2015 to April 2016) when it was at the V&A Museum in London.[140] It was incredible. To see some of the jewels I had studied, which belonged to some of these maharajahs, showcased in such style, provided a visit which was and is unforgettable. It would be an understatement to say that the jewellery on show was astounding.

Maggie's first and successful trip to India (1921–22) provided her with friendships with a number of maharajahs. In July 1923 Maggie gave an "at home" at 16 Charles Street to meet with the members of the newly formed British Indian Union.[141] Two hundred guests attended this reception, including the Maharajah of Nawanagar (Jam Shri Ranjitsinhji, the cricketer) – the first of two maharajahs from Nawanagar Maggie knew; and the Maharajah of Kapurthala (Jagatjit Singh).

Distinguished guests who were statesmen and diplomats and aristocrats, and clever and interesting Indian ladies and gentlemen, were included in the guest list. The Duke and Duchess of Marlborough, the Duke and Duchess of Abercorn, the Earl and Countess of Shaftesbury, Colonel and Mrs Wilfred Ashley, Mrs and Miss Vanderbilt, Muriel Countess de la Warr, to name only a few.

All of the guests were members and friends of the British Indian Union (President Duke of Connaught). "The Indian ladies in gorgeous saris, and the Indian gentlemen in native and European dress, who glided out into the rain to find their motor cars or taxis, looked really like actors in some Eastern play set in the West."

Maggie met the maharajahs in India and in London when they were in town. She clearly enjoyed their company and possibly the prestige they brought. Her close friendship with them allowed her to have another entrée in society, in addition to those she already managed. The maharajahs added, embellished and created another level to Maggie's style, which was dramatic and extravagant. Entertaining them in the setting of Polesden Lacey's Gold Room, was a dream come true for Maggie.

Six Maharajahs (some with their wives), and Indira Maharani of Cooch Behar who stayed at Polesden Lacey on her own (her husband Jitendra had died of alcoholism aged thirty-six in 1922), were guests at Polesden Lacey from 1927 until 1937.[142] Maggie got to know the six maharajahs who stayed often really well. She certainly enjoyed their company and enjoyed staying with them and being entertained by them, on her two trips to India. Maggie was given the use of royal trains and Rolls-Royce cars, when she was travelling in India by her hosts. Her hospitality at Viceroy House too was superb. There were also some additional relatives of the maharajahs, who came to stay.

Maggie's second trip to India proved to be less successful. She was welcomed by her friends, arrived in Bombay in January and stayed in India until May 1934, but she was very unwell when she departed from Bombay.

I provide a brief background below of some of Maggie's favourite maharajahs.

The Maharajah of Mysore (1884–1940) was photographed in the rose garden at Polesden Lacey in December 1930. He "arrived and stayed December 1930". He was the twenty-fourth ruler of Wodiyar/Wodeyar Dynasty of Mysore, which ruled from 1399 to 1950. His mother had ruled as Regent from 1894 to February 1902. Lord George Curzon invested him with full powers on 8th August 1902. He enlarged a democratic forum and established the Legislative Council in 1907; he strived to improve social conditions for the poorest people and to improve public health. Mysore was the first Indian state to generate hydroelectricity and the first city to have street lights. He had a number of interests, including education and the fine arts, and music. Maggie enjoyed the friendship of the man who created, possibly, "the best administered state in the world".

The Maharajah of Kapurthala (1872–1949) was a great friend of Maggie's. There is usually a photograph of him on display at Polesden Lacey. He spent a lot of time in London. He ascended the throne of Kapurthala in 1877. He took over full power in 1890, and officially became Maharajah in 1911. He built a number of palaces and gardens in Kapurthala; the largest palace was modelled on the Palace of Versailles. He was a worldwide traveller and a Francophile. He served as the Representative of the League of Nations in 1926, '27 and '29. He continued as the Leader of the PEPSU (combined eight princely states in India) until his death in 1946. He stayed at Polesden Lacey in 1930, '34, '35, '36, '37 and '38. He had six wives and several children, and some of his family accompanied him to Polesden Lacey. He was known to enjoy the London nightlife.

The Maharajah of Jaipur (1912–70) Man Singh II was adopted by Madho Singh II in 1921, and his name was changed at that time. Man Singh II was born Mor Mukut Singh, and his real father was Sawai Singh. He became Maharajah of Jaipur on 18th September 1922 (aged eleven years) after the death of Madho Singh on 7th September. In 1947 he consented to Jaipur becoming part of the Dominion of India. In 1949 he merged Jaipur with Rajasthan, thereby surrendering his sovereignty, and becoming Rajpramukh (Governor) until 1956. When additional reorganisation of the India states took place, he retained his titles, privileges and income until he died in 1970.

He was interested in promoting tourism (he changed Rambagh Palace into a luxury hotel). He was interested in new technology and weaponry for the Indian Army. In 1965 he became ambassador to Spain and spent time in Europe. He was a very successful polo player and won a number of trophies, including the World Cup. He owned a house Saint Hill Manor in East Sussex during the 1950s. He had three wives simultaneously. His third wife was Gayatri Devi, a stunning beauty who was the daughter of Maharajah Jitendra Narayan of Cooch Behar and his wife Indira. He died after an accident playing polo at Cirencester.

He stayed at Polesden Lacey in 1935 and 1936 on his own, and with his second wife in 1937 (Maharani Kishore Kanwar).

The Maharani of Cooch Behar, Indira (1892–1968), stayed with Maggie from 16th to 18th July 1927. She was an interesting lady whom Maggie appreciated. She was also very beautiful. Indira had broken off the engagement to the intended husband, her father the Maharajah of Baroda had chosen for her (the ruler of Gwalior). She came to London and married Jitendra (1911) without any of her family being present. She was a strong lady. After her husband Jitendra died in 1922 from alcoholism, Indira managed as Regent, until their elder son Jagaddipendra Narayan became Maharajah of Cooch Behar in 1936.

Maggie and Indira met in both London and India. They both attended the wedding of Edwina Ashley to Louis Mountbatten, on 18th July 1922. Maggie arrived with Indira, who looked splendid in a beautiful sari. They would both have enjoyed being together, and being dressed in stunning jewels at such a special event.

The Maharajah of Nawanagar Jam Shri Ranjitsinhji (1872–1933) stayed at Polesden Lacey in 1931. He also dined at Charles Street. He was the cricketer! Ranjitsinhji was adopted by Vibhaji II Ranmalji (the Jam Sahib), who disinherited his own son and adopted first Jhalamsinji, who died in 1878 (possibly by being poisoned), although this adoption was not completed, because one of Vibhaji's wives produced a son.

However, when the chosen heir to Nawanagar died in 1906, although it was a controversial decision, Jam Shri Ranjitsinhji became the Maharajah of Nawanagar, created as such by the British administrators in India.

Ranjitsinhji's interest in cricket began in the 1880s. He was educated at Rajkumar College, then at Trinity College, Cambridge (departing in 1904 without graduating). He played for Cambridgeshire County, MCC, Sussex and England. His style of playing was controversial, due to his leg glance and cut shot strokes.

His interests were cricket, tennis, billiards, photography and jewellery. His finances were erratic. He did not pay loans back. In Nawanagar he made some bad decisions (trying to claim back land given or sold long ago): charging new taxes and accumulating possessions. His interest in jewellery was of paramount importance to him. One of his most famous necklaces contained 277 carats of first-class emeralds (created by Cartier in 1926).

His knowledge of pearls was outstanding. He went on adding to his jewellery collection after he was installed as Maharajah of Nawanagar. He served as an honorary major and colonel in World War I. Maggie entertained him at Charles Street in December 1930. He stayed at Polesden Lacey in 1924 (June 14th to 16th) and in 1932.

His nephew, the Maharajah of Nawanagar Digvijaysinhji (1895–1966) succeeded Ranjitsinhji in 1933. Digvijaysinhji was an officer in the British Army from 1919–31. He represented India at the League of Nations in 1920. During World War II he established a camp for Polish children fleeing from Russia in Jamnagar Balachadi, and the camp remained open until 1945. He was a strong supporter of Indian Independence and among the first to sign the Instrument for Accession. He too played cricket and was President of the Board of Control for Cricket in India (1937–38). He played one first-class cricket match captaining Western India against the MCC (1933–34). In 1935 he married Maharajakumari Baiji Raj Shrikanchan Kunverba Sahiba (1910–94); together they had three sons and a daughter.

His interest in jewellery proved to be spectacular. He owned a 61.50 carat whiskey-coloured diamond named "The Eye of the Tiger" which was mounted on a turban aigrette in 1934. I saw this on show at the V&A, Al Thani Exhibition (Jewellery). Absolutely amazing! He and his wife dined at Polesden Lacey in June and July 1937, and they also stayed for the weekend of 31st July 1937. How Maggie would have enjoyed entertaining, being with such incredibly well-dressed guests in terms of jewellery.

The Saloon would have been a dazzling place on such an occasion (also when his uncle stayed at Polesden Lacey in 1924 and 1932). Maggie (in particular) would have loved all of this spectacle.

The Maharajah of Baroda (1863–1939) Sayajirao Gaekwad III reigned from 1875 to 1939. He succeeded to the throne after the British government removed his uncle Malharro of Baroda as ruler, because his uncle had attempted to poison the Maharani of Baroda Jamnabai (her husband had died). Sayajirao's uncle was imprisoned.

Savajirao was chosen from a list of successors within the Gaekwad dynasty and adopted by the Maharani. When he was nineteen years old, he took on full powers (December 1881). He was passionate about social mobility, judicial and agricultural reform, and education. He opened new schools and libraries in Baroda. He banned child marriage, legalised divorce and removed the stigma of the untouchable class.

He also developed Sanskrit and the textile industry and improved religious education and the promotion of the arts. His own collection of books became the basis for the Central Library of Baroda.

Unfortunately, he upset the British monarchy unintentionally. He was a teetotaller and drank the Queen's health in water! He attended the Delhi Durbars, and when George V and Queen Mary were both present in 1911, he dressed in a plain tunic (instead of being dressed in his finest jewels) and bowed only once instead of three times!

However, he was an Anglophile. He purchased Lord Tennyson's former home in Surrey (Aldworth House, near Haslemere in Lurgashall, but actually in Sussex). He had two wives; his first wife died of tuberculosis when she was twenty, having given birth to three children. He married secondly Shrimant Akhand Soubhagyvati Maharani Chimna Bai II (1871–1958) in 1884, and they were married for fifty-three years until he died in December 1939 (she died in 1958 in Bombay). His second wife Shrimant was responsible for promoting women's rights for Indian women, and he adopted and accepted these ideas.

They had three sons and one daughter, Indira Devi, who married the Maharajah of Cooch Behar in 1911, as discussed above.

The Maharajah and Maharani stayed at Polesden Lacey for Christmas 1930. Additionally, they dined in London at Charles Street in 1930, and also in 1934, '36 and '37.

There were three Round Table Conferences (India) in London (1930, '31 and '32) organised by the British government to discuss constitutional reforms in India.[143] The conferences followed the Simon Commission (which had been unpopular in India, with protests), because there were no Indian representatives included in this Commission. Deciding the future of India was unlikely to succeed from the results of this report, so the government instituted a series of Round Table Conferences. In 1930, the First Round Table Conference (India) took place in London from November 1930 to January 1931. The Indian National Congress did not attend and progress was limited.

The Second Round Table Conference took place from September to December 1931, and the Indian National Congress and Gandhi attended. This conference was well attended, with a large number of maharajahs present. Once again progress for constitutional reform was limited.

The third and final Round Table Conference took place in November to December 1932, without the Indian National Congress and Gandhi. This was even less successful as most of the important Indian representatives did not attend, and the total number of attendees was only forty-six. Later the India Act of 1935 was set up by the British government, to initiate significant changes to the colonial administration to India, which was the basis for the Indian Independence Act of 1947, when British India became India and Pakistan.

Lord Reading (one of Maggie's dearest friends) gave a reception for the Indian princes on 16th December 1930 (he was Viceroy of India from April 1921–April 1926). Lord Reading wore the Star of India. His daughter-in-law Lady Erleigh acted as hostess, as his first wife Alice had died in January. Everyone who mattered attended this reception. The Prince of Wales arrived and also wore the Star of India, and the Prime Minister Ramsay MacDonald.

Maggie looked stunning in a black dress, with three rows of solitaire diamonds as her necklace.[144] She was seen talking to her Indian friends; they really were her friends and not acquaintances.

How much did the maharajahs matter to Maggie? She arranged for the Curry Kitchen to be built to service their requirements. Not many aristocrats would have contemplated such a generous move. The chefs who accompanied the maharajahs were accommodated at Polesden Lacey. It would have been fascinating to have observed a dinner party at Polesden Lacey, when some of Maggie's guests enjoyed French food, and the maharajahs enjoyed their chosen dishes!

The Saloon (just under twenty-four carat gold leaf on the walls) must have shimmered, with the combination of the décor and royalty, including maharajahs showing their wealth. What fun! Being nouveau riche, Maggie and some of her guests demonstrated their inherited wealth. Traditionally, a show of wealth and opulence have always been visible in royal palaces.

Some friendships mattered to Maggie on a very personal level.[145] There is a story which I have found dubious/questionable over the years, but Robert Boothby (not liked by everyone) wrote and confirmed that this story was accurate in his book, *Recollections of a Rebel*, Chapter 5, "The Social Scene Between the Wars". When he was with Maggie in the Saloon/Gold Room, Maggie pointed to the carpet and said, "This is the spot John Simon fell on his knees to ask me to marry him; I refused." Then she added with a wink, "I think I was right, don't you?"

Boothby added Maggie "was capable of some pretty caustic things, but I found, in the course of time, that she always told the truth".

Another comment that Maggie made to Boothby was, "I don't think you will ever get high office." Boothby asked Maggie why she said this to him, and her reply was, "Because I don't think you really want it. But make whatever life you choose within Parliament, because you have the making of a good parliamentarian."

FOURTEEN
Maggie's Charity Work

M aggie was incredibly generous throughout her life. Her inheritance enabled her to be generous, but not everyone who is wealthy becomes a benefactor to other people.

Maggie's generosity combined with her shrewdness was demonstrated on many occasions. She was known to recycle some of her unwanted gifts, such as the paper knife she "gifted" to Beverley Nichols one Christmas Eve after dinner. Lady Chamberlain confirmed to Beverley that she had given this knife to Maggie "three years earlier".[146] Yes, this side of Maggie's character did exist.

However, Maggie's generosity was often boundless: the support she gave to many charities; the children from the Limehouse district in the East End of London being given a week's holiday at Coverdale (Clacton) every year; her kindness when she discovered Robert Sidney Nash's son Bob was at Clacton-on-Sea recovering from rheumatic fever and needed longer to recover, by paying for five more weeks. I mention this above in discussing servants in Chapter 8.

Maggie gave 25 Palmerston Place to Edinburgh University for their use, as discussed in Chapter 2.

Maggie's support to hospitals included medical research.

For many years, Maggie held a number of fundraising events to provide significant sums of money for charities. She wanted to help the war effort in World War I.[147] She provided Polesden Lacey as a Convalescent Home in 1915–

16, and she gave the use of 11 Charles Street to the Maple Leaf Club.[148] Maggie gave the P8643 Spitfire to the government in World War II.

Maggie also provided Polesden Lacey in World War II as an HQ for the army (ammunition depot) and offered space for troops to stay in the grounds.[149] Maggie provided accommodation for officers to stay in the house and invited them to dine in the house, mixing with her guests.

A continuing offer of hospitality for troops, with performances given by ENSA, was established. More details of Maggie's contributions in World War II are in Chapter 17.

Maggie's kindness to staff who had problems was not always known. Sometimes she was known to sack a member of staff because they did not work well. But she had a strong caring connection to her staff, many of whom stayed for a long time.

The McEwan Pretsell Scheme in Edinburgh, for students at Herriot Watt College and the Edinburgh Art College, was set up in the 1880s by William McEwan and a businessman, James Pretsell.[150] The scheme was established for the benefit of apprentices and young people who wished to study at evening classes, to improve their knowledge and skills, but were unable to afford educational fees. The courses offered were in engineering, building, plumbing, mining, printing or commerce. After her father died, Maggie continued to fund the scheme. Students applying for help had to possess suitable educational qualifications for the courses, and they had to prove their requirement for financial help with the fees.

In 1937 Maggie was still involved with the scheme; she visited the college to present the admission cards for the evening classes to two hundred students in that particular year.

The principal of the college, Mr Cameron Smaile, welcomed Maggie and told the students, that many previous students had been extremely successful in industry and commerce.

Maggie made lots of gifts to staff at Christmas and paid for and organised the staff party. She loaned paintings for charities' exhibitions and gave money or help where and when it was needed. None of this was compulsory. Maggie chose kindness and practical help, as a way of making a difference to people who were sometimes in trouble. Hosting innumerable fundraising events based at Charles Street, was another way she demonstrated her commitment to such situations.

Yes, she was a gossip (but not about her royal friends), but she possessed, as Osbert Sitwell said, "an ability to sum anyone up in an instant". Her strong character, combined with her intelligence, guided her spectacularly through her life.

Maggie's always had long list of charitable work; one example is the Red Cross Pearl Necklace Sale at Christie's, London on 19th December 1918, at which Maggie contributed a pearl as requested and which has been verified. The sale was held to raise money for returning wounded troops in 1918.[151]

Lady Mary Northcliffe asked ladies to donate one pearl from their necklaces, to be made into new necklaces and auctioned.

The women of the empire donated 3,716 pearls and fifty rubies (for the clasps). Forty-one necklaces were sold on this day. "The sale at Christie's totalled £82,492.10 shillings. Viewing on Day 1 was charged at 5 shillings per person, which increased the total to £83,290.12 shillings. Pearl necklaces each conveyed a message more tender and more personal than all the other gifts to the Red Cross" (Hannen).

Additional cash donations were received from India, the Colonies and Egypt, of £8,553. The most expensive necklace donated on this day was the Carrington Pearl Necklace, with a Canary Yellow (rare) diamond clasp which was sold for 35,000 guineas. Carrington bought this necklace back.

Maggie had donated a fine pearl, and she also donated a ruby and brilliant (diamond) pendant to this same charity. The ruby and brilliant pendant was sold earlier in 1918 (10th April) by Christie's. The design was a pendant designed as flower ribands attached to wings (Lot 429) and sold for £315 to Drayson (jeweller).

Additional items of jewellery were also sold on 19th December 1918: scarf pins/studs and rings. In total the Red Cross raised £149,616 in 1918 from various auctions.

Polesden Lacey became a World War I Convalescent Home in June 1915; it was closed at the end of 1915 and reopened again in 1916; it remained open until the end of 1916.

Maggie agreed to provide part of Polesden Lacey as a Convalescent Home for officers who had been injured and had been sent back to Great Britain, after they had been patched up in hospital. Many of the men arrived at Polesden Lacey, after surgery/medical treatment at King Edward VII Hospital (originally named King Edward's VII Sister Agnes Hospital, after the founder Agnes Keyser – one of Edward's mistresses). Polesden Lacey was never a hospital, but Maggie's DBE awarded in 1922 states that Polesden Lacey was a hospital. Hence this label is sometimes incorrectly attached to the house. Clandon Park (nearby) was a hospital in World War I, and had an operating theatre. Polesden Lacey gave the men the chance to recuperate and heal (to some extent) from their injuries, after their incredibly difficult experiences in World War I.

The nurses/staff who looked after the men, were led by Doctor Candy, a local GP in Bookham. He administered the injections, issued the prescriptions and was overall medically in charge. However, the nurses were not registered nurses, and were not Red Cross nurses.

A photograph of the nurses at Polesden Lacey show that while they were dressed as nurses, they do not belong to any particular hospital or group. Some, we understand, were members of Maggie's staff (maids). In one of the existing photographs there is one man who is a military orderly. Maggie may have employed additional staff to help run the hospital.

Maggie had officers staying in her house; they all had to lead their men "over the top" (there was never any choice – that was their job). If possible, they had to be made well enough to go back and do just that. They were often less well armed than some of the soldiers they were in charge of. A number of Canadian and Australian officers found their way to Polesden Lacey.

Any criticism of Maggie for not having enlisted soldiers at her home should be dispelled, on the grounds that the officers she did have to stay were all (as far as possible), being prepared to go back and lead their men.

Maggie continued to entertain at the weekends at the house in 1915 and 1916, and some of the officers who were well enough were invited to her dinner parties, frequently.

Some officers recuperating at Polesden Lacey survived; some went back to the front; some did not survive after being sent back. Some lived a long life but never forgot what they had experienced. I do not list all of the names of the men in this chapter. All of them mattered; all of them made a huge difference to the outcome of the war. A full list of the names is held at Polesden Lacey.

We have precise dates for the officers staying at Polesden Lacey in 1915. The dates for 1916 are not precise, but we do know Maggie had officers at the house until she closed it at the end of 1916.

Eighty-six men arrived from regiments[152], which varied widely geographically. I name some regiments, to demonstrate that the men were from all four countries of Great Britain, and from abroad. Men arrived from many other regiments in Great Britain, and also from other regiments abroad. In a special article or book about the men, all of the regiments would be listed.

1st Black Watch & Royal Highlanders & 6th Perthshire Battalion; Scots

Guards; the Gordon Highlanders; Highland Light Infantry; Royal Field Artillery; The Royal Regiment of Artillery (RA); Irish Fusiliers; Dublin Fusiliers; 2nd Battalion Welsh; Border; East Yorkshire; Northumberland Fusiliers; Coldstream Guards; Royal Engineers; Royal Garrison Artillery; Royal Field Artillery; Royal Flying Corpse/ Royal Air Force; Royal Navy; Remounts Depot; Royal Army Service Corps; Duke of Cambridge's Own & Middlesex; King & Liverpool; 12th Durham Light Infantry; Lucknow Volunteer Rifle; India Volunteer Corps; King's African Rifles, and were looked after at Polesden Lacey.

The time spent in recuperation in such a peaceful setting, with staff from the house working as nursing staff, contributing to some comfort for them, must have been such a sharp contrast to where these men had come from, and to where they were being sent back, if they were able enough. I provide some short background details of a few of the men.

Some of the men, such as Thomas Fairfax Ross (1897–1960), were career soldiers. He was in the Rifle Brigade as a second lieutenant from 1914, and in 1915 as an acting adjunct (assistant to a senior officer) he was wounded in the leg and was sent back to England. His release document from King Edward VII Hospital stated he was to have massage and exercise. While he was recuperating at Polesden Lacey, he became friendly with Sonia Keppel (Alice Keppel's daughter and Maggie's goddaughter). They remained friends forever. Sonia appeared to be quite smitten with him.

Maggie liked him too. He returned to front-line duties. He was sent to Egypt. He was awarded the Military Cross in 1916. By the end of the war, he was made a captain. He retired as an honorary brigadier in 1945; he held a place on the Supreme War Council at Versailles and became a stockbroker. He fought in World War II. Thomas came to stay at Polesden Lacey a number of times after the war, to see Maggie, bringing his wife once.

Some were lawyers: Kenneth McFarlane Gresson (1891–1974) from New Zealand, who initially enlisted in the Territorial Force as a lieutenant in 1911 and by 1914 as a captain in the 1st Canterbury Company. He was in action in Gallipoli (Dardanelles Campaign/Straits) and was badly wounded; he was at Polesden Lacey in 1916. He returned to New Zealand in 1917 and became a lawyer, and was a lecturer from 1923 to 1947. He became a judge in the Supreme Court.

James Oscar Fitzalan Harley McConnell Orr (1892–1992) was also a lawyer, from Canada. He studied law in Vancouver, where he enlisted in the 29th Canadians. He was wounded on 16th July 1916, hit between the eyes by a piece of shrapnel. His only acquaintance in England arranged for him to be taken straight to King Edward VII's Hospital, on his arrival at Charing Cross Station. He was under Sister Agnes's care, at the hospital and his operation was successful. He spent some time recovering at the Duke of Norfolk's home in St James Square, London (demolished in 1938), before he arrived at Polesden Lacey to recuperate.

He described his war experience with clarity: "We young soldiers, had a common saying, that the life of a subaltern in the PBI [*poor bloody infantry*] was ninety days. I did not make it... At the 'Bluff' Ypres salient, 16th July 1916, I caught a piece of 5.9-inch high explosive between the eyes." (The Bluff was a mound near St Eloi, south-east of Ypres in Belgium.) He was at Polesden Lacey for a while in 1916. Later he returned to Canada and became a judge in Vancouver.

Robert Uchtred Eyre Knox (1889–1958) was commissioned into the Indian Army in 1911. Following this, he moved to the Suffolk Regiment, and as a lieutenant he was awarded a DSO on 21st January 1916. He was wounded and survived the war, and ran the probation service after the war (in a wheelchair). as an amputee. He became a civil servant at the Treasury, and one of his jobs was overseeing the honours system. He died in 1958 in London.

Francis Moreton Smith (1891–1961) was a Rhodes scholar at Exeter College, Oxford; he joined the King's Horse Regiment; he moved to the York and Lancaster Regiment. He was wounded in 1915 at Loos, February 1916 Somme, Arras 1917. He transferred again to the RAF in Hastings. He became a solicitor after the war in Durham. He contributed to managing a number of improvements in the law courts at Durham. He died in 1961.

Major Oliver Stuart (1896–1976) was commissioned as Second Lieutenant in the Middlesex Regiment in October 1914. He transferred to the RAF in 1915, where he was promoted to flight commander, then major, 1918. He was a flying ace (five or more aerial victories). He was awarded a Military Cross. He retired from service in 1921, and he became an aviation journalist and wrote a number of books. He died in 1976.

Edward Clifford Smith was at Polesden Lacey in 1916. He joined the East Surrey regiment in 1915. He was wounded on 29th September 1915. He was patched up and returned to the front and became, temporarily, a captain.

Some men were at Polesden Lacey for a considerable time.

Maurice Peel (1873–1917) recuperated at Polesden Lacey from 18th June to 17th July 1915. He was a descendant of Sir Robert Peel, Prime Minister (1834–35,

1841–46), and he was Vicar of Tamworth, Staffordshire, before joining the army as a chaplain, with the 1st Royal Welsh Fusiliers. Some Anglican chaplains were criticised when they were on duty, because they did not all go "over the top".

This could not be said about Maurice. He was wounded at the battle of Festubert in May 1915. He had asked permission to go over the top to join his men in order to help them. He was shot and brought back to England and recuperated at Polesden Lacey. He returned to the Western front in 1917. He received the Military Cross for his work with wounded soldiers and rescued many men.

On 14th May 1917 at Bullecourt (second Battle of Bullecourt, which ceased finally on 15th May), he went into the trenches to aid his men. He carried his officer's stick and the Bible. He was unarmed. He was shot though the stomach and died on the battlefield. Maurice Peel was among a list of men who benefited from being at Polesden Lacey, and who were sufficiently well enough to go back to the battlefields, and who died there.

The list of men who died in addition to Captain The Rev. The Hon. Maurice Berkley Peel, who died on 14th May 1917, were: Lieutenant Reginald Seymour Lardner, 9th May 1918; Captain Harry Eustace Herrick, 11th May 1917; Lieutenant John Richard Jarlath MacHales, 24th March 1918; Herbert Cyril Ramsey, 22nd April 1918; Douglas William Arthur Nicholls, 10th April 1917; Geoffrey Thomas Trafford, 23rd July 1918; Herbert Victor Moffett de la Fontaine, 5th August 1917 at Passchendaele (close to Ypres).

The thunderous barrage and mass slaughter, the horror and bitter suffering of World War I, brought to an end the world as it had existed until 1914. An Australian officer, Lieutenant Wilfred Barlow, who was "a volunteer, schoolteacher, husband and father of four", was killed at Bullecourt on 12th May, literally smashed to pieces by an artillery shell."

Shortly before his death he wrote to his wife, "I hope the war will soon be over because it is destroying the best men and everything that is beautiful and civilised in life."

First Maple Leaf Club in London at 11 Charles Street – 1915 to 1919

"The Maple Leaf Club, just off Berkeley Square, is doing a… great little work. It gives the Canadian soldier a *pied a terre* in the centre of things; saves him from cinema headache, from too long a course of restaurant-feeding; and above all, from the Lonely Officer Advertiser in the Agony Column. It is a pleasant place for luncheons and teas; and it does something – here is an important point – for the Americans who are serving in the Canadian Contingent. They more than most of our visitors, are apt to find themselves lost during leave; they are half-shy of having got into the great scrap at all when they find how very much like strangers they can feel in London until they discover No 11 Charles Street" (Sketch, 15th March 1916).

After Maggie's father died in 1913, Maggie decided to extend and refurbish 16 Charles Street for her own use. She used the services of Mewes & Davis. Higgs & Hill were the builders, employed to execute the building work.

16 Charles Street, London

© Leanne Smith

No 16 Charles Street backs on to 14 Hays Mews, which gave Maggie the space for a large ballroom to be installed. This building work lasted one year. 16 Charles Street is magnificent and an impressive house. It provided a home for Maggie and a large entertaining space (the new ballroom), and lots of space for guests. Once the building work at 16 Charles Street was completed (by the end of 1914), Maggie was able to move into No 16. Maggie still owned the lease of No 11 Charles Street.

Canada legally entered World War I on 4th August 1914, when Great Britain declared war against Germany. The British declaration of war on 4th August, automatically brought Canada into the war, because of Canada's legal status as a British Dominion. During the 1914–18 war, approximately 470,000 Canadian men and women served overseas with the Canadian Expeditionary Force (CEF). In 1914, the first group of Canadians to arrive in Great Britain (varying numbers quoted from 25,000 to 30,000/33,000) began their training on Salisbury Plain. By 1915 Canadian units were stationed through England and Scotland. The number of Canadian troops who came to Great Britain was over 131,000 by the end of 1916.

While there was concern by the Canadian government and military, about how the Canadian troops spent their leave time (from wanting good old-fashioned home comforts to more troubling men who "wanted to have a good time"), a decision was made that the government would not become involved in how the troops (men and women) spent their spare time. This resulted in benefactors and volunteers providing precisely what official sources would not do, which was to establish Canadian-only social clubs in London. (London was of interest to most Canadians for their free time.)

Volunteers raised funds in Canada, because of their morality, duty, patriotism and philanthropic spirits. Lady Julia Drummond, having been successful in Montreal with fundraising, turned her attention overseas and offered her services to the Canadian Red Cross in England. She came across to Great Britain, and she was the lady who at that time made a difference, and brought much-desired help to Canadian troops.

In London, Lady Drummond organised an "information bureau"; various associations also helped (YMCA+), but accommodation was not so far supplied. Clubs such as the RAC Club and others opened their doors to officers. But enlisted men were not offered much. Cheap hotels filled easily, and most of those were too costly for many soldiers. Lady Drummond's appeal for help with this scheme, attracted a number of prominent/important Britons in addition to benefactors in Canada.

In 1915, Maggie Greville offered Lady Drummond the use of 11 Charles Street for the first Maple Leaf Club (for Canadian soldiers) in London.[153] Some help was provided by Rudyard Kipling and his wife Caroline. It was opened on 4th August 1915. Maggie and Lady Drummond became friends. Lady Drummond stayed twice at Polesden Lacey, 9th–11th October 1915, and again 9th September 1916.

Canadian troops (private and non-commissioned officers) "would have a warm welcome, congenial companionships and board and lodging at a reasonable rate". The Canadian Prime Minister Robert Borden, Canadian High Commissioner Sir George Perley and Rudyard Kipling were present at the opening ceremony. Funds were not provided by the Canadian government, although some funding came later from the government of Ontario.

11 Charles Street provided sleeping accommodation, two dining rooms, a lounge, a smoking room and a billiards room for the men. It was a Canadian club opened, managed and financed by Canadians, but with Maggie's gift of the use of the house.

The Club offered men who had "leave passes" the comfort to get cleaned up, good food, hot baths, bed and laundry taken care of, and a safe place to store their kit. Breakfast and lunch cost from eight pence each, dinner from a shilling. The club was supported by King George V and Queen Mary. The club offered its services from August 1915 until August 1919.

Many Canadian troops were stationed in France and Belgium, fighting alongside the British soldiers. When leave time was granted, there were no pre-planned arrangements for soldiers off duty. For Canadians who had no homes in Britain, including those Canadians coming back from France or Belgium for a few days, the choices available to offer respite were negligible.

Initially this First Maple Leaf Club could offer accommodation for fifty to sixty men. Within a short timescale the number of beds was increased to 110.

By 1916 two additional Maple Leaf Clubs were created, both located near to Marble Arch; one offered 126 beds, also later in 1916 the second club offered four hundred beds. Later still, the government of Ontario provided funds for five new houses to be acquired near Victoria Station, thereby providing another 350 to four hundred beds. Most of the funding had been contributed voluntarily, and the people working in the Maple Leaf Clubs were volunteers and some Canadian military personnel.

By 1918 there were thirteen club buildings. Yet more space was required for Canadians coming back from the war, and who often had two weeks' leave at a time. A total of five huts (so without accommodation) were opened by the Maple Leaf Club from 1918 as canteens, providing recreational and lounge areas in London for Canadian troops, prior to their return to Canada at the end of the war. The Maple Leaf Club at 11 Charles Street closed its doors in August 1919.

Maggie's gift was incredibly generous. Yes, other benefactors existed and added to the ability of the Maple Leaf Club to expand. Maggie did not have to offer number 11 Charles Street in one of the most fashionable and expensive areas of London (then and now), as a base for Canadian troops to recoup. Queen Mary and George V were supportive of this scheme. But Maggie's decision to allow her house to be adapted and used by troops is an outstanding kindness. Maggie had lived in number 11 Charles Street from the 1890s, not long after she married Ronnie (it was not her first home as a married lady in London; that was in Deanery Street, and was also provided by her father), but 11 Charles Street was her home for more than twenty years. She could have sold the lease. Maggie made a difference to so many Canadians.

Maggie got to know Sir Max Aitken (by 1917 he was Lord Beaverbrook), who attended the opening ceremony at 11 Charles Street, and he was a donator, among a number of notable Canadians. Maggie's friendship with Max Aitken was not close or personal. They were never real friends; no doubt her style of entertaining was not his. Maggie's Salon included royalty, maharajahs and aristocrats, most of whom would not have interested Max Aitken.

However, he must have respected Maggie because of her generosity. Maggie's contribution in providing number 11 Charles Street as the first Maple Leaf Club, would have meant a great deal to him. While Max Aitken himself would not have wanted to spend time with Maggie and her inner circle, he appreciated that the comfort offered to Canadian soldiers on their short stay away from the front at 11 Charles Street, was incredibly generous.

Maggie received a thank-you letter from the Headquarters, Overseas Military Forces of Canada, based at Argyll House, 246 Regent Street, London, dated 30th June 1919, at 16 Charles Street, which said:[154]

"Dear Mrs Greville,

Now that the majority of the Canadian Expeditionary Force has returned to Canada, and the Canadian London Clubs are preparing to close, I wish to take this opportunity on behalf of the Non Commissioned Officers and Men of the Overseas Military Forces of Canada, in conveying to you our great appreciation for the kindness and assistance you have so freely given to us during the past war.

The Maple Leaf Club, which has occupied your residence on Charles Street, has afforded a splendid home to our men while on leave in London and has helped them in many ways to enjoy their holiday."

(The last part of this letter is missing.)

Maggie disposed of the lease of 11 Charles Street in the early 1920s; it is remarkable that she held on to the house for so long. Sir Frederick Lewis (director/owner with a consortium of shipping lines, Furness Withy & Co.) acquired the lease, and he lived at 11 Charles Street for almost twenty years until World War II began. A footnote to 11 Charles Street. This house was used in World War II by the American Red Cross Club and functioned as a club for nurses. The American Red Cross Club also used number 10 Charles Street (literally next door) during World War II.

Later, as discussed below in Chapter 17, Maggie donated the cost of the Spitfire in World War II to the government. At the time, Lord Beaverbrook was Minister of Aircraft Production in Great Britain, and his real job was to get Spitfires manufactured, hence his continuing respect for Maggie as a benefactor.

Importantly Maggie's contribution to World War II, was significant in providing Polesden Lacey as an ammunition base, and providing accommodation in the grounds for serving soldiers, and for officers in the house (as already discussed).

Maggie's DBE was awarded in 1922. The Court and society column listed in *The Times* on 23rd January 1922 stated that the *London Gazette* announces that "the King has appointed Margaret Helen Anderson, the Hon Mrs Ronald Greville, to be a Dame Commander of the Order of the British Empire". It was awarded to her for her services in World War I, providing Polesden Lacey as a Convalescent Home, and for providing 11 Charles Street as the home of the Maple Leaf Club from 1915 to 1919.

One of the occasions when Maggie wore her DBE, was for the Italian ball she hosted on 26th May 1924 in aid of the Italian hospital in London, which needed funds.[155] Among the guests attending this ball were the Prince of Wales (not often one of Maggie's guests), the Duke and Duchess of York, Princess Marie Louise and the Prince of Piedmont, and the Marchesa della Toretta and Princess Mafalda.

The Italian ambassador, Maggie and the organiser of the ball, Count de la Feld, received the guests. Maggie wore the pale purple ribbon of Dame of the British Empire across her shoulders, and the badge was pinned to her bodice. She was also wearing stunning jewellery. The staircase was decorated with rambler roses and white lilies. The fireplaces were filled with banks of roses, lilies, carnations, hydrangeas, pelargoniums and calceolarias, with green and white maple and other foliage. The tables in the dining room where supper was served were decorated with white lilies, red and white carnations and green foliage, making up the Italian colours.

One thousand two hundred guests were received with difficulty, as the stairway was impassable. The Prince of Wales eventually reached the ballroom. Crowd control by the police outside broke down several times.

Mr Luigi Naintre paid many of the expenses, including the cost for Ambrose and his band to play (being excused from the Embassy Club) in order to raise lots of money.

An overwhelmingly successful event, but guests were overnumbered and this must have been somewhat overwhelming. Maggie, as always, was more than generous.

The *Sunday Express* published an article on 31st May 1931 – "The Wealthy Woman" – stating that, "The woman who understands most in this country about finance is the Hon Mrs Ronald Greville, who is extremely wealthy. She, on the other hand, is a large spender and likes entertaining. I often wonder why Mrs Greville never became a journalist, because she has; (1) Business capacity; (2) A craving for news; and (3) Liking for power. As it is she contents herself with having people of importance around her. The wonder to me is that she has not become terribly bored."

Maggie's kindness to children, in addition to her care for her godchildren, was provided consistently, locally. Every Easter, the children who lived on the estate were given an Easter egg hunt. The area covered with eggs was from the south side of the bailiff's cottage up to the north side of the tennis court.

An annual Sunday party was held for the children of St James Church school, at the end of the summer school term in July. The younger children were brought to Polesden Lacey by bus, but the older children walked up from the village, although Maggie on some occasions also sent down her cars to help bring up the children. A merry-go-round, Punch and Judy, coconut shies and swings were set up east of the house, on the flat ground at the end of the golf course. Each child was given a pre-packed tea and a threepenny piece. Maggie joined in some of the children's games (her early years at Polesden Lacey). These children's parties were held up to and including 1937.

In January each year, a separate Sunday school treat was provided by Maggie at the Old Barn Hall in Bookham. There was a substantial tea, followed by entertainers: magic, conjurors and jugglers. The prizes (two prizes per class) were presented by Maggie, and every child was given an orange to take home. In addition, the children of the staff at Polesden Lacey were given presents at Christmas, along with their parents.

Maggie gave help, real help on a number of occasions, without this necessarily being made public. An unhappy situation for one of her servants, which was labelled a sensation locally, provides a sad story. Without Maggie's support this would have been become a disaster of unparalleled magnitude. It was already a tragedy when Maggie heard what had happened to Joyce. It was a debacle, but without Maggie, Joyce would have been destroyed totally; one life was already lost.

It is understood from information at Polesden Lacey that in October 1916, a maid named Joyce commenced work at Polesden Lacey.[156] She was the fifth under housemaid. I name her as Joyce. I do not provide the real name of the maid, in order to avoid upsetting any of her descendants.

On the night of 23rd/24th April 1917, Joyce shared a bedroom with Ethel-Franklin (fourth housemaid) and Ruby James; they had gone to bed at ten o'clock. At about 1am, Ethel heard a noise, as she thought someone had moved the door handle to the bedroom. Joyce replied, "It is only me." Ethel went to the next bedroom, Joyce's real bedroom, and found Joyce, who said she was unwell. Ethel said she would make a drink of hot water and ginger for Joyce. A short while later, Joyce returned to the shared bedroom.

The head housemaid, Annie Sessions, appeared (she had heard noises) and wondered if someone was unwell. Ethel told her that Joyce was unwell. Annie talked to Joyce, who returned to the shared bedroom. A short time later Joyce got out of bed again, saying, "I must go to the lavatory." Joyce switched off the bedroom light as she went out of the bedroom. Ethel fell asleep. At approximately 3.30am, Ethel woke up and realised that Joyce was not in bed. Ethel talked to Joyce through the door of the next-door bedroom. Joyce said something (not one hundred per cent audible). Joyce then returned to the shared bedroom wearing a raincoat. They then both went to sleep again.

At 6.30am Ethel got up. Joyce said although she felt better, she would like to stay in bed for a bit. At 8.15am Ethel took Joyce a cup of tea. Joyce was not in bed in the bedroom she had been sharing, but was back in her own room. Ethel and Joyce talked briefly. Joyce remained upstairs in her own bedroom.

After Ethel had eaten her breakfast, she told Annie (Head Housemaid) that she did not think "everything was quite right with Joyce". Annie went upstairs and talked to Joyce and returned, then told Ethel that she should go down to Great Bookham, and make a request for Doctor Candy to come to Polesden Lacey.

Ethel cycled down to Great Bookham at about 9.30am. Doctor Candy arrived at 10.45am. Doctor Candy realised that Joyce was frightened, emotional and incoherent. He also worked out that Joyce had recently given birth. There was a locked tin trunk at the bottom of the bed in Joyce's room. The key was found (in a chest of drawers) and inside was a dead female baby. It was apparent that the baby had been strangled. It was clear that "the neck was restricted by two pieces of tape".

On Wednesday 25th April the post-mortem was undertaken by Doctor Candy and Doctor Potts, at the Leatherhead mortuary. On Thursday 26th April 1917, an inquest was held at Leatherhead into the baby's death.

The coroner announced that the jury had decided that they believed Joyce was guilty of "wilful murder", while "she was in a state of frenzy at the time". The jury decided to "hand over their fees to the funds of the Leatherhead Red Cross Hospital".

On Monday 7th May 1917, at the Epsom Petty Sessions, Joyce was charged with "the wilful murder of her female child". Mr AH Tritton was the magistrate, with additional magistrates attending. A decision was made to remand Joyce in custody. She had, up until the 7th May, remained working/living at Polesden Lacey. Remand was granted for one week and she was and committed for trial at the next Assizes. There was a discussion as to whether the baby was alive more than momentarily, or in the legal sense. Mr Roland Oliver, barrister, said that Joyce "would plead not guilty and would reserve her defence".

At the Surrey assizes on 6th July 1917, Joyce "was indicted for the murder of newly born female child at Great Bookham on 24th April 1917". Her defence lawyer was Sir E Marshall Hall, KC, accompanied by Mr Comyne Carr.

Maggie had instructed Sir E Marshall Hall (1858–1927) to defend Joyce. He was an English barrister who had a formidable reputation as an orator. He successfully defended many people accused of notorious murders, and became known as the "Great Defender". He became famous, because the public enjoyed reading about sensational legal cases which were reported in the popular press, in the late nineteenth century and early twentieth century. His fee must have been substantial. Maggie paid for all of the legal costs.

Marshall Hall's defence for Joyce was that the child had fallen on her head, as she was born. Given the state of mind Joyce had at this time, it was not likely she could have deliberately decided to kill the baby. He pleaded for leniency because a soldier "had forcibly taken advantage of her".

The jury decided that Joyce was "guilty of manslaughter" and "strongly recommended her to mercy". The sentence passed by Mr Justice Darling was of six months' imprisonment – the least he said he could impose. Joyce collapsed and had to be helped out of the dock.

Maggie paid for Doctor Candy to visit Joyce every day after the baby was born, while she remained at Polesden Lacey. Why? Maggie hardly knew Joyce. Possibly Maggie had noted Joyce worked well from October until the April birth? But Maggie was not obliged to help Joyce. Did Maggie recognise the extreme distress in Joyce? With Maggie's infinite amount of money, Maggie could afford to help.

But not everyone, or many employers in such a situation, would do so much, especially as Joyce had been in her employment for a short time. The legal costs must have been substantial. Currently we do not have any knowledge of Joyce returning to work at Polesden Lacey.

This is one sustained example of Maggie "stepping out from being the rich lady who lived on the hill" at Polesden Lacey, and of doing so much more. Just possibly Joyce's situation allowed Maggie to ponder that, if her father had refrained from looking after her mother so well (and therefore Maggie herself), what would have become of Maggie, all those years ago?

There are many more times when Maggie did more than help out.

Maggie often lent her house at 16 Charles Street for charity events. In World War II she hosted the weekly "Hospital Supply Working Party for the Ladies Diplomatic Corps". As a member of the Ladies Grand Council, she was one of the ladies ensuring free pure milk was given to children at a hostel in the East End of London.

Maggie supported a list of charities: events for the Theatrical Ladies Guild (1935); by opening the gardens at Polesden Lacey for the Queen's Institute and District Nursing Fund (1935/36); and a gift she provided in June 1940 of £1,050 to the Lord Mayor's "Red Cross and St John's Fund, for the Sick and Wounded".

However, Maggie did not allow anyone to use her or try to extract money from her, just because she was a rich lady living on a hill. As she received many written requests for money (begging letters) from people she did not know at all, her reply in writing, which was always sent out to them, stated the following:[157]

"Dear Madam/Sir,

For the following reasons I am unable to meet your demands. I have been held up, held down, sand bagged, walked on, sat on, flattened out and squeezed by the income tax, super tax, tobacco tax, beer tax, motor tax, purchase tax and every society, organisation and club that the inventive mind of man can conceive for Red Cross, Double Cross and every bloody cross and hospital in the country.

The Government has governed my business until I do not know who the hell owns it. I am inspected, suspected, examined, informed, required and condemned so that I do not know who I am.

I am supposed to have an inexhaustible supply of money for every need, desire or hope for the human race, and because I will not beg, borrow or steal money to give away, I am cursed, discussed, boycotted, talked to, talked at, talked about, held up, rung up, robbed and damn near ruined.

The only reason I am clinging to life is to see what the bloody hell will happen next.

I am,

Yours faithfully."

Amusing? Yes. This does not detract from Maggie's incredible continuous kindness to so many people. It does emphasise that she would not be taken for a fool, and that her charity was given to those whom she knew, employed or became aware of through organisations. A similar comment was often made about Lord Beaverbrook – anyone Lord Beaverbrook knew who was in trouble was helped immediately. Maggie may have had her obstinacies, but anyone who contributed to her smooth-running success, and knew her well and needed help, was cared for.

FIFTEEN

Formal Offer to George and Mary in 1914 of Polesden Lacey

As already discussed, King Edward VII's kindness to Maggie – including her in the Marlborough House Set, after Ronnie died – was demonstrated by the King coming to stay for the weekend at Polesden Lacey.

Alice Keppel and fifteen more guests in the Marlborough House Set arrived for the weekend of June 5th and 6th 1909 (more than a year after Ronnie died). This enabled the continuity of Maggie's place in the Marlborough House Set, the King's Set! This gesture guaranteed Maggie's successful continuation in the Royal Court, with all that this meant.

Because of Edward's incredible kindness to Maggie, she decided in 1914 to make an "offer" to King George V and Queen Mary. The reason behind this gesture, seems to have been to express how thankful Maggie was to Edward VII.

In June 1914 an agreement was made, whereby Maggie would leave Polesden Lacey to one of George and Mary's children. On 14th June 1914, King George and Queen Mary were at Polesden Lacey (recorded in the Visitor Book).[158]

The offer had been made in writing. Edward, Prince of Wales (future Edward VIII), would inherit the palaces and the houses. Balmoral and Sandringham always have to be discussed/negotiated, as they do not come as an inclusive package for the new king or queen. The second son and other children of a monarch do not automatically receive houses – although there is most often a gifting/offering of a property made to such children, when they marry.

It was agreed that Bertie (Albert Frederick Arthur George) would be bequeathed Polesden Lacey in Maggie's Will. After the 1914 date, Bertie was included in invitations to Maggie's house in Charles Street, and for weekends at Polesden Lacey.

Maggie's friendship with the British Royal family was enduring and reaped many benefits. Maggie, King George and Queen Mary were friends. Maggie and Queen Mary were particularly close as they could talk to each other unaccompanied (without courtiers being present).

Maggie was a friend of Princess Beatrice (Queen Victoria's fifth daughter and last child); from that relationship sprung Maggie's huge friendship with Queen Eugenie of Spain. Maggie's relationship with Bertie (1895–1952) grew from 1914, and was extended by his marriage to Elizabeth Bowes-Lyon (1900–2002) in 1923, and became one of Maggie's most important links with the Royal family.

The Duke of York was not expected to inherit much property. From King George and Queen Mary's view, the gift of Polesden Lacey was a sensible solution. Maggie was delighted; this bond drew her closer to the Royals. Maggie began to include the Duke of York more and more, into her invited guest list.

Bertie met Elizabeth in 1920. He grew to love her and twice asked her to marry him, and was twice refused. On the third occasion in January 1923, Elizabeth accepted Bertie. Their engagement was announced. Maggie had sometime earlier suggested (more than once) to Bertie that Polesden Lacey, was a place he might like to "come to on his honeymoon".

The part of the honeymoon Bertie and Elizabeth spent at Polesden Lacey, must have been tinged with extra pleasure, knowing that the house and grounds would become their property one day (their wedding was 26th April 1923).

Maggie changed her mind, and in March 1942 a new Will was created, although this was not disclosed to Bertie and Elizabeth.[159] The bequest of Polesden Lacey and more to the National Trust, surprised the Queen Mother. The jewellery bequest to the Queen Mother (instead of Polesden Lacey) in the new Will, written in March 1942, also surprised the Queen Mother.

Maggie stated that she loved the Queen Mother as the daughter she did not have (in tears running down her cheeks), talking to Beverley Nichols, when he visited her not too long before she died in 1942, and she was in bed at the Dorchester Hotel. Yet Maggie remained silent about her new Will.

The closeness of the relationship between the Queen Mother and Maggie was often demonstrated. When Elizabeth returned home after her state visit to Paris with Bertie in July 1938, Elizabeth visited Maggie promptly to cheer her up (Maggie was unwell and in bed at Charles Street). Elizabeth popped round to Maggie's house in Charles Street immediately, to give her the news and gossip from her time in Paris.

An obvious reason for the change in the bequest exists, but it is surprising that Maggie did not advise Bertie and Elizabeth.

The Queen Mother wrote in a letter to Osbert Sitwell on 27th September 1942:[160] "It is terribly sad to think that she has gone" and "Do you remember those wonderful weekends at Polesden" and to Queen Mary dated in a letter 13th October, Elizabeth said, "I will miss her very much" and "I must tell you that Mrs Greville has left me her jewels" (both prior to publication of Maggie's Will January 1943).

The bequest Maggie passed to Queen Elizabeth the Queen Mother in 1942, allows our connections to the British Royal family to continue, as the jewellery has now passed to the Queen, and will continue to Prince Charles and the Duchess of Cornwall, and to Prince William and the Duchess of Cambridge.

Three Honeymoons at Polesden Lacey – Marquis and Marquess of Carisbrooke (Mountbatten), 19th July 1917

I provide an explanation to the change of name for the British Royal family and follow this with confirmation of three honeymoons spent at Polesden Lacey.

On 17th July 1917 George V's proclamation announced that, all German Royal family surnames were to be changed from that date to English names, as anti-German feeling ran high in World War I. The House of Saxe-Coburg and Gotha was changed to Windsor. George V removed German titles from his family, who were British subjects.

The Battenberg family name became Mountbatten. Prince Alexander of Battenberg (1886–1960) was the son of Prince Henry of Battenberg and Princess Beatrice (Queen Victoria's ninth and last child), and he was sister to Queen Victoria Eugenie of Spain.

On 17th July 1917 Prince Alexander's name was legally changed to Alexander Albert Mountbatten, and he became Marquis of Carisbrooke, Earl of Berkhamsted and Viscount Launceston on 18th July 1917.

He married Irene Denison (1890–1956), daughter of the 2nd Earl of Londesborough and Lady Grace Adelaide Fane, at the Chapel Royal, St James's Palace, on 19th July 1917. On her marriage, Irene became Marchioness of Carisbrooke.

The Marquis and Marchioness of Carisbrooke spent their honeymoon at Polesden Lacey, from the 19th July until their departure on 27th July 1917.

Twenty years after their marriage, they were among Maggie's close friends; the Marquis and Marchioness of Carisbrooke were guests for the weekend of 24th/25th July 1937 at Polesden Lacey. They had one daughter, Iris (1920–82).

Alexander held a number of posts in the navy, army and air force. He received no state allowance, and he was the first member of the Royal family to work in commercial companies including Lazard Brothers and Lever Brothers. Alexander and Irene are buried at St Mildred's Church, Whippingham, Isle of Wight.

George V issued Letters Patent on 30th November 1917, and Whitehall announced the Letters Patent on 11th December 1917, and they appeared in the *London Gazette* on 14th December 1917 and declared that, the King restricted the style of "royal highness" and the titular dignity of "Prince (or Princess) of Great Britain and Ireland" to the children of the Sovereign, the children of the sons of the Sovereign and the eldest living son of the eldest living son of a Prince of Wales.[161]

The Letters Patent also stated that "the titles of royal highness, highness or serene highness, and the titular dignity of prince and princess shall cease except those titles already granted and remaining unrevoked".

Second Honeymoon – Bertie and Elizabeth, 26th April 1923

Bertie met Elizabeth Bowes-Lyon in 1920. He was very much in love with her, and she accepted his offer of marriage in January 1923 (as stated earlier).

Maggie had told Bertie as a young man, on an occasion when he was being entertained by her, that that if he ever "met the right lady" Polesden Lacey could provide a perfect setting for part of their honeymoon.

Maggie the great traveller was away in the winter of 1923. She was in Johannesburg in March 1923. Maggie sent a telegram from Johannesburg to Frank Bole, Head Steward, in charge of all of Maggie's staff/servants at Charles Street and Polesden Lacey in March 1923, which read as follows: dated 29th March 1923:[162]

"TO BOLE

"DUKE OF YORK 'SPENDS' HONEYMOON POLESDEN

"SO GO PALACE SEE GREIG REGARDING ARRANGEMENTS = GREVILLE."

Frank Bole did go to Buckingham Palace and he met with Louis Greig.

The telegram (above) Maggie sent to Frank Bole (January 1923) from Johannesburg, saying "Go Palace. See Greig. Arrange Honeymoon", was the springboard, for Frank Bole to arrange the first ten days of Bertie and Elizabeth's honeymoon at Polesden Lacey.

On 26th April 1923 the Duke and Duchess of York arrived at Polesden Lacey at about 5.30pm.[163] They were married in Westminster Abbey. And they lunched at Buckingham Palace, departing from the Palace just after 4.15pm. The Prince of Wales, Princes Henry and George stood to one side of the Palace gates, and the bridesmaids stood at the other side and threw quantities of confetti at the newly married couple. They drove down the Mall, which was full of well-wishers, to Waterloo Station.

At Waterloo they were met by Herbert Walker, General Manager of the Southern Western Section of Southern Railway. Bertie and Elizabeth boarded "a special" to Bookham from Waterloo. A carriage on the train had been especially prepared for them, and the train was driven by Mr Wiggs. Security was provided by Chief Inspector Emmett. The couple arrived at Bookham Station, which had been spruced up for the occasion. The Chief Constable of Surrey welcomed them both to Surrey.

Bertie had arranged for one of his chauffeurs to be in place, waiting for them at the station, in one of Bertie's own Armstrong Siddeley cars (Bertie had more than one of these cars).[164] They were driven to the centre of the village of Bookham, which had been dressed with flags and streamers. The car stopped, as arranged, by the church (St Nicholas). The couple were welcomed to Bookham by the Rector, Rev GS Bird, and the Chairman of the parish council, Mr DW McFarlane. The Duke of York spoke to the villagers near to him and thanked everyone for their welcome.

Then, the car proceeded to the gates of Polesden Lacey, where the car stopped again. Frank Bole (Maggie's Head Steward) welcomed the Bride and Bridegroom on behalf of the estate tenantry, who were ranged round the gates. Some detectives accompanied the couple; they remained at Polesden Lacey during the time the couple were in residence, in order to deter "any invaders".

The Duke (later George VI) and Duchess of York on their honeymoon at Polesden Lacey, nr Dorking, Surrey, from the Country House Album

Bertie and Elizabeth were given the private suite of rooms which were/are known as the King's Suite (after Edward VII's stay at Polesden Lacey). This included, in addition to their bedroom, a sitting room, a bathroom and dressing area.

The suite was described in detail in a huge number of magazines, journals and newspapers, both before and after the wedding. Repeated articles appeared in so many different publications. The public learnt so much detail of the layout of the Royal Suite, which Bertie and Elizabeth occupied.

The Illustrated London News, 28th April, showed photographs of the inside of the suite, including a photograph of the main bedroom with King's bed on show (Edward VII).

The *Liverpool Daily Courier*, 28th April 1923, stated that, "The Bridal couple will occupy the Royal Suite on the first floor, which is furnished throughout with unrestrained luxury. From every window of this suite, there are wonderful views of the Surrey Hills and the famous gardens with their pergolas, statuary with clipped box hedges."

The *Evening Standard*, 27th April 1923: "The Duke and Duchess are occupying at Polesden Lacey the suite used by King Edward."

Bertie, of course, was used to his own suite of rooms at Buckingham Palace, and both of them needed space. Catherine, the Duchess of York's maid, needed to bring in the clothes for Elizabeth at different times of the day. Bertie's valet would provide in turn his required clothes. They both wrote letters to family and friends, and a desk/s would provide them with various writing materials. Their sitting room and bedroom were filled with flowers. A drinks tray was laid out, and also fresh fruit provided.

Elizabeth the Queen Mother confirmed that she spent much of the morning (27th April) in bed, the day after her marriage, reading the newspapers and only emerged dressed, in time for lunch downstairs. She still felt exhausted and did not get up till lunchtime.

From Polesden Lacey, Elizabeth wrote to her mother, the Countess of Strathmore, and Kinghorne (mother) on 27th April 1923 – the morning after the wedding. William Shawcross, in his book, *Counting One's Blessings*, included this letter:[165]

"My Darling Angel… I stayed in bed all this morning to rest and read the papers, and am just going down to lunch in my old blue tweed! poor Catherine is miserable because I won't wear anything new – I hate new things!

This is a delicious house, & the food is too marvellous, & it seems too funny not to be dashing about! I think the wedding went off alright, don't you? Do write angel, from your very, very loving Elizabeth…"

Catherine was Elizabeth's maid. The official photographs prove this comment about her clothes.

Bertie also wrote to Elizabeth's mother and he wrote to his parents, expressing his thanks for their kindnesses. King George V replied that he wished "to congratulate him [*Bertie*] on having such a charming and delightful wife as Elizabeth". King George also commented of Bertie: "You have always been so sensible and easy to work with… I feel we have always got on very well together (very different to dear David)".

George V was aware that his eldest son (Edward VIII-to-be) had many shortcomings. George V said of Edward "After I am dead, the boy will ruin himself in twelve months". A portentous warning.

As Bertie's right-hand man for many years, it was inevitable that while Bertie and Elizabeth were enjoying their honeymoon at Polesden Lacey in 1923, Bertie wrote a letter to Louis Greig.

Geordie Greig (the grandson of Louis Greig) has stated that, "The honeymoon was spent at Polesden Lacey, an imposing mansion in the countryside, lent to the couple by Mrs Ronald Greville, a rich brewing heiress with an unmatched appetite for royalty. While there, Albert wrote Louis an affectionate letter to thank him for all he had done."

The tone of Bertie's letter was relaxed and intimate and indicated that Bertie was enjoying every possible aspect of married life. Quoting from Bertie's letter, "We arrived here safely though very tired and the sudden peace & quiet of this place was too marvellous. I must send you all my thanks for your wonderful work and half [sic] during the long and busy time which has at last come to an end. Please tell Carruthers & Miss Heaton Smith how much I appreciated all they have done as well. It is now 12.45 and I have not had a bath yet!! Everything was plain sailing, which was a relief. You know what I mean. I was very good!! Ever yours, Albert."

On Thursday 3rd May on a visit to London by Bertie and Elizabeth from Polesden Lacey, an argument took place between Elizabeth and Louis Greig. The cause is not known, although Elizabeth was already beginning to show criticisms of her husband's principal aide.

"Throughout the Duke and Duchess' honeymoon spent at Polesden Lacey, there were plain clothed police at every entrance, the lodge gates were kept locked, within the gates there were plain clothed men from Scotland Yard by day, and uniformed police by night. There were also rangers from Windsor patrolling the estate."

For Bertie and Elizabeth enjoying the first part of their honeymoon at Polesden Lacey, and knowing that Polesden Lacey was going to become their own home, must have been very special indeed. The stunning view from the King's suite on the south side was a perfect way to relax away from town.

King George V thoughtfully ensured Bertie was managed by Sir Louis Greig (1880–1953), CVO, KBE, for a number of years.[166]

In 1909, Dr Louis Greig was the assistant medical officer at Osborne Naval College (which Bertie attended), and he became Bertie's support structure and friend. Bertie was transferred to HMS *Cumberland* in 1913; Greig was the ship's surgeon. Bertie suffered from ill health and had an appendectomy, which he hoped would cure him (1914). In 1916 Bertie participated successfully at the Battle of Jutland on HMS *Collingwood*, but he was soon back in bed with a duodenal ulcer, which was after three years diagnosed, but not treated until November 1917, due to risk. Louis persuaded the medical team to carry out the operation. Because of Louis' help, Bertie said that Louis was responsible "for saving his life".

When Bertie left the navy (unsuitable) and joined the RAF, Louis accompanied him. Later Louis was assigned to look after Bertie, when he was at Trinity College, Cambridge, then as an equerry to Bertie, and finally Comptroller of Buckingham Palace. While Louis had been the support system for Bertie, ever since George V asked Louis to look after Bertie, Louis' power at the Palace diminished after Bertie married Elizabeth. Gradually Elizabeth became Bertie's mentor. It appears that Elizabeth preferred to remove the influence Louis Greig had exerted over Bertie, even though Louis had given immense service to her husband prior to their marriage. Gradually Elizabeth managed to erode Louis Greig's influence, and she became Bertie's mentor full time.

Third Honeymoon – John Anderson and Ava Wigram, 30th October 1941

John Anderson, 1st Viscount Waverley (1882–1958), married again in October 1941. He had married Christina Mackenzie in 1907 and they had two children. Christina died in 1920. John Anderson married Ava Wigram (1895–1974) on 30th October 1941. Their honeymoon was from 30th October 1941 to 4th November – a weekend only.

He served as Home Secretary, Lord President of the Council and Chancellor of the Exchequer. Anderson shelters are named after him, as he was the minister responsible for initiating the idea, and signing the document to establish them. The corrugated shelters were made available for people to have them in their gardens in World War II, hence the name the Anderson shelter.

He was a National Independent Member of Parliament.

Ava was a political and social hostess who networked successfully. Winston Churchill thought she "had more influence than any woman of her generation", which Maggie must have found interesting. Successful as John Anderson was in his career, (as an important member of the government in World War II) he was quieter than Ava, whom he adored.

Ava had a son, Charles, who was disabled, by her first marriage in 1925 to Ralph Follett Wigram. Ralph died in 1936. Her son Charles died in 1951. The bride was given away by her brother Major Josselin Bodley, and the groom's best man was his son, Alistair.

After their wedding at Chapel Royal, St James, they came to Polesden Lacey for four days for their honeymoon.

"The weekend honeymoon of four days was spent at Polesden Lacey, lent by the Hon Mrs Ronald Greville. Afterwards Sir John and Lady Anderson returned to London and have settled in the house in Lord North Street, where the new Lady Anderson made her home for some years with her late husband."

SIXTEEN

The Year of Three Kings

George V died on 20th January 1936: his death was hastened by Lord Dawson of Penn (doctor to George V) at 11.55pm; one of the reasons being, he was looking after the King's dignity, so the death could be reported in the morning edition of *The Times* "rather than in less appropriate… evening journals".

Edward Prince of Wales became King Edward VIII immediately after his father's death. Edward's planned Coronation date of 12th May 1937, was used for the Coronation of George VI.

January 1936 was the beginning of a year's unparalleled history in Great Britain, for the British monarchy. The year of three kings.

Maggie had tried earlier in her life to be friends with Prince Edward, but this had not worked, as I have said. Maggie was certainly the backer of the right people. The stress caused to Bertie and Elizabeth over the abdication was huge. Maggie as a friend was able to be kind, supportive and inclusive, further enabling her closeness to the Royal Court. Maggie really did love Elizabeth (as the daughter she did not have) and she also loved Bertie.

Maggie did not like Lady Emerald Cunard. Maggie sometimes entertained Emerald when it was deemed necessary, but she was definitely not a friend. Emerald cultivated Edward VIII and Wallis Simpson to an incredible degree. It was known by everybody in society that Emerald hosted dinner parties for Edward and Wallis often, and ensured that they were Emerald's special friends.

Emerald was hoping for a position as Mistress of the Robes in Edward and Wallis's new Court.

On 9th December 1936, the King informed the government of his irrevocable decision to abdicate. On 10th December 1936, the King signed the Instrument of Abdication at Fort Belvedere (at about 10 am), witnessed by his brothers Prince Albert George (Bertie), Prince Henry Duke of Gloucester and Prince George Duke of Kent. The document was drawn up by the King's close friend and adviser, Sir Walter Monckton. A few hours later, Prime Minister Baldwin informed the House of Commons.

His Majesty's Declaration of Abdication Act 1936, was given Legislative Assent by the Act of Parliament on 11th December 1936, and at that time, the Duke of York became King George VI and the Duchess of York became his Queen Consort. At 2pm, the King's abdication was publicly announced.

His Royal Highness Prince Edward Duke of Windsor made a BBC radio broadcast on the evening of 11th December from Windsor Castle, having abdicated. Immediately after the speech, the Duke of Windsor drove to Portsmouth and boarded HMS *Fury* at 2am (12th December) to commence his journey into exile, initially to Austria. Edward's reign had lasted 327 days, the shortest of any British monarch, except the disputed reign of Lady Jane Grey over 450 years earlier.

Winston Churchill had polished Edward's speech to ensure it was moderate, when he spoke about his inability to do his job "as I would have wished without the support of the woman I love".

Emerald Cunard had, for the past year, spent a huge amount of time with Edward and Wallis Simpson. Emerald had entertained them frequently, and accompanied them all round London. Maggie invited Emerald for the evening of 10th December to Charles Street, and this invitation was the first for eighteen months.

Emerald said to Maggie on arrival:[167] "Maggie, dearest, do tell me about this Mrs Simpson – I have only just heard of her!" A surprising comment when Emerald had been hoping to become Mistress of the Robes in the new court! But on the evening in question, Maggie did not bother to reply. Later Emerald lamented, "How *could* he do this to *me*?" Maggie, of course, had backed the winners!

Everyone in society knew how Emerald had not only curried favour with the pair of them, but had actually been sycophantic at every possible moment in the preceding years.

When Maggie heard Emerald being so illogically silly, by her pretence, she could easily have pricked her false bubble, but she said nothing. Later, Maggie being Maggie, she took the opportunity to repeat Emerald's hypocrisy to some of her society friends.

Maggie had more than a slight understanding of the 1936 abdication crisis. Her closest Royal friends (apart from Queen Mary and Princess Beatrice) were Bertie and Elizabeth. From 1935, Scotland Yard's "best detective", Special Branch Superintendent Albert Canning, was asked to monitor Wallis and her behaviour, contacts and activities. He usually checked up on communists and trade unionists, but he was put on the case. "On 25th March 1935 a brief report landed on the desk of the Commissioner of the Metropolitan Police, Sir Philip Game, and without doubt this was discussed with the Home Secretary, Sir John Simon."

One of Maggie's close friends was Sir John Simon, the man who had asked to marry her (as she described to Robert Boothby) "on the floor of the Saloon" at Polesden Lacey. Maggie ensured she knew nearly every bit of gossip about everyone in society, and we can be sure that she knew much more than she let on.

Instead of answering or commenting on Emerald's ludicrous comments to her, Maggie remained quiet. Maggie's friends who were in government were many; Maggie could have obtained any information she required from them about the abdication, if she thought she was missing anything!

Maggie never hesitated to ring up Winston Churchill, or other politicians serving in the government (she knew so many well), if she wanted to discuss a person or situation. If Maggie wanted information, she knew who to ask and could easily do so. If Sir John Simon had not offered Maggie the information of his own volition, she would have sounded him out to get it. Also, of course, her other political friends would have offered much background as to what was happening.

Maggie's intimate friendship with Bertie and Elizabeth was paramount to her; the handling of the understanding Maggie enjoyed in this friendship, precluded any chance of Maggie being without information or failing to have a clear view of the real situation. Maggie entertained/dined with Bertie and Elizabeth during 1936. Close friendship equalled knowledge, particularly in this case.

Additionally, Maggie's dislike of Emerald was "long born". Emerald always wore a lot of make-up. Some years earlier, Maggie made a cutting comment to

Queen Mary about Emerald, saying she "wasn't half as bad as she is painted". Emerald's make-up was quite strange, and this was known in society.

Maggie's close friendship with Bertie and Elizabeth, and also with Osbert Sitwell (who was a close friend of Elizabeth's), allowed Maggie to be on intimate terms about what was happening in 1936 prior to the abdication. When Edward and Wallis were on board the *Nahlin* in the summer of that year, Maggie was socialising with Bertie and Elizabeth.

After becoming King on 11th December 1936 (after the abdication of his brother on 10th December), Bertie announced Edward's title on 12th December as the Duke of Windsor as the first act/decision of his reign, although all of the formal assent documents were not signed until March 1937. A new year ahead, 1937, for Maggie and her close friends. A coronation to look forward to.

One amusing and true story provided a diversion for Elizabeth (and possibly Bertie too), in addition to Maggie and some of her friends, about the abdication in 1936. Osbert, being such a good friend of Maggie and Elizabeth, was an author. He wrote a book, entitled *Rat Week* (a long poem, seventy-nine pages) after the abdication, denouncing close friends and followers of Edward and Wallis. He wrote:

"Where are the friends of yesterday
That fawned on Him,
That flattered Her;
Where are the friends of yesterday,
Submitting to His every whim,
Offering praise of Her as myrrh
To Him?
What do they say that jolly crew,
So new, and brave, and free and easy,
What do they say, that jolly crew,
Who must make even Judas queasy?"

Osbert had worried that although he was a real friend of the Queen, she might have thought he was being impertinent, so he did not send Elizabeth a copy of the book directly. The opposite was true; Elizabeth managed to get a copy, and she adored it and wrote to Osbert, "I must tell you first of all, that we thought your satire absolutely brilliant. It really is perfect – it hits hard (and never too hard for me) and is wickedly amusing."

Elizabeth also expressed to Osbert in a letter dated 19th February 1937[168] what a relief it was, to have his amusing and friendly letter "amongst the vast amount of begging letters, complaints, appeals, warnings, lunatic ramblings etc. which go up to make one's daily postbag… So you can imagine how one falls greedily on the few friendly letters that come, and yours was very welcome!"

Interesting friendships, Maggie, Elizabeth and Osbert; Maggie was also friendly with Osbert's brother Sacheverell, not so much his sister Edith.

Maggie was ready and able financially to adapt to new advances if she recognised their advantages and uses. London in the 1930s was becoming modern, with electric lighting rather than gas in the main streets. By the thirties motor cars were more in evidence than horse-drawn vehicles.

London Transport was created (the Underground and the Metropolitan Railway became part of the London Passenger Transport Board, which included all of the capital's railway, bus, tram, trolleybus and coach services in 1933).[169] The Post Office completed the automation of London's telephone exchanges (the Strowger system was adopted by the Post Office by the spring of 1924).[170]

Strowger exchanges became the backbone of the UK telephone network, and remained a key component for over fifty years. The last Strowger exchange at Crawford, Scotland, was not removed from service until 23rd June 1995.

In 1929 the stock market crash, which originated in America, set off the Great Depression in Great Britain and many parts of the world. The effect of this economic downturn for Great Britain was dramatic. Britain's world trade dropped fifty per cent. By 1932, unemployment was about 3.5 million people in this country.

The areas which suffered the worst problems were understandably the North of England, Scotland, Northern Ireland and South Wales, where coal mining, shipping and steel production were concentrated.[171]

Unemployment in some of these areas reached seventy per cent. Sadly, Jarrow as a northern town was one of the most affected places (Jarrow March highlighted this emphatically), as soup kitchens became a normal way of life for far too many people. Despite their abysmal treatment, the Jarrow marchers achieved their aim of raising public awareness and generating sympathy. The town gained new engineering and ship-breaking work, later in the decade.

Although a national unemployment and health scheme existed, it provided payments to people according to their contributions (and only for fifteen weeks), but too many people were too poor to contribute, and it cannot be exaggerated how dire life must have been for everyone who was unemployed.

However, London and the South East suffered less so, although anyone unemployed anywhere in Great Britain experienced severe hardship. By the mid-1930s unemployment began to fall in the South East, though the North and parts of Wales, experienced the Depression for most of the decade.

In 1934 the government passed the Special Areas Act. The Act identified South Wales, Tyneside, West Cumberland and Scotland as areas with special employment requirements, and invested in projects such as the new steelworks in Ebbw Vale.

Success of the Act was limited because the level of investment was not high enough, and it was not until the late 1930s that the shadow of unemployment lifted from Britain, thanks in part to government investment in rearmament. Spending on goods and services, and in particular spending on building new houses and roads (particularly in the South East), helped the country to pick itself up.

The south saw new developing industries such as the electrical industry; houses and industry were being electrified. Mass production methods brought new products, such as electrical cookers and radios to the middle classes. Industries which produced these prospered. Nearly half of all new factories that opened in Britain between 1932 and 1937, were in the Greater London area.

Did Maggie notice or consider what was happening throughout the country during the 1930s? The depression which affected many industries in Great Britain, did not seriously upset London so much or so quickly.

In 1931 Ford opened a new large factory in Dagenham. One day when Maggie was walking down Regent Street, she spotted a red Ford van for sale in a showroom. She popped into the showroom and bought this van, and as she said to Beverley Nichols afterwards, "it always pays to have cash".[172]

This was a practical purchase, as the van was used to take produce from Polesden Lacey to the London house, without having the more laborious use of delivering items to the local station, followed by collecting them from the station in London, and transferring them to Charles Street. I have confirmation from Ford UK, that at this time, Ford managed their Head Office in Regent Street, with a showroom on the ground floor. A pragmatic expense, coupled with the amusement of Maggie having enough money in her handbag, to buy a van for cash!

By 1938, there were nearly forty thousand factories in London, employing over three quarters of a million people. Light industry factories were established on the west side of London, including Hoover and EMI. On 12th March 1935 a speed limit of thirty miles was established in built-up areas, and on 31st May 1935 the driving test became compulsory. Not that Maggie was worrying about driving tests, with her five chauffeurs and even more cars.

On 30th July 1935 Penguin Books was established by Allen Lane, thereby opening up the mass market for reading. London's theatres were very busy, and at the Palace Theatre Cole Porter's *Anything Goes* ran for 261 performances.

Department stores such as John Lewis, Harrods, Whiteleys and Selfridges had been trading successfully for many years, providing the latest designs and products. Life in London could be full of fun![173]

Maggie had enjoyed electricity at Polesden Lacey from 1907, when the house was ready for entertaining her guests in the country. The provision of en-suite bathrooms seemed normal to her, and also central heating. These changes in society were welcomed, and made life, shopping and entertaining more fun for anyone with money.

Maggie always had more than enough money, for everything she required. Her generosity and charity work, as detailed in Chapter 13, was her way of helping anyone she knew or came across who needed help, including assistance to so many charities.

Maggie's health began to deteriorate in the 1930s. Maggie returned from India in 1934, having become extremely unwell prior to her departure from Bombay. She had several bouts of illness in 1937, '38 and '39. Her health problems included ear, eye, throat, phlebitis and more ailments. She was given considerable attention from her physicians, who were members of the medical profession who mattered in London. As soon as she recovered, she hosted some stunning events from her house in Charles Street.

Examples include a wedding reception for the Lampson wedding in December 1934, which was an enormous gathering. Charity receptions and balls were held at the house. Dinner parties which included royals and maharajahs, were staged at both Charles Street and Polesden Lacey.

Having recovered, Maggie accepted once more society invitations, and travelled again. In 1938 Maggie was allowed to use the Royal entrance to Royal Ascot, so her car could draw up at the entrance to the Royal Box, which made life more comfortable for her, after a period of illness. In 1939, an invalid carriage was loaded onto a train at Calais, so she was in reasonable comfort en route to Monte Carlo.

SEVENTEEN

Pre-Second World War

Maggie's predisposition to Germany and the Nazis (for some duration, before reality educated her) fell into line, with many aristocrats, politicians and some of the government's thinking at the time. Maggie attended Hitler's 1934 Nuremberg Rally, and she was also at the August 1936 Summer Olympic Games in Berlin. While Maggie's attitude towards Jewish people was wrong while she sustained it, she was not alone. By 1937, her understanding of the Nazi Party had begun to change.

The Coronation of George VI on 12th May 1937 (the date that had been chosen for Edward VIII's Coronation, so not to waste a plan) enabled Ribbentrop to excel in his courtship of royalty, politicians and aristocrats. The day following the Coronation, Ribbentrop held a vast reception at the German Embassy. Fourteen hundred people were present.[174]

Otto Horcher, the famous restaurateur, from Berlin catered lavishly; he was incredibly close to the hierarchy of the Nazis and the food was of the highest standard. The large terrace of the German Embassy had a canvas awning erected, to accommodate so many guests. Barnabas von Geczy and his orchestra (he was a violinist, composer and bandleader and favourite of Hitler and Goebbels) entertained everyone, with stars from the Berlin Opera. The effect made the Court ball at Buckingham Palace the evening before, seem positively shabby.

Present were the Duke and Duchess of Kent; Crown Princes of Belgium,

Greece, Japan and Saudi Arabia; leading members of the British government, civil service, armed forces; the headmasters of Eton, Harrow and Westminster, most of the diplomatic corps and aristocrats Ribbentrop had come to know, in London society. Not everyone attending this event could be described as pro-Nazi Germany, but they were comfortable as guests.

Maggie attended the Coronation of King George and Queen Elizabeth as a favoured guest, alongside so many important people, among royalty, aristocrats, dignitaries, politicians and international service personnel. Ribbentrop used the timing of this occasion to provide two lunches in honour of Blomberg, War Minister (who had been favoured by Ribbentrop, German Ambassador to Great Britain from 1936), against Goering and Neurath.

The two lunches followed the huge reception (already detailed above) held at the German Embassy. At the first (large) lunch, "he invited the people he considered most important to himself in London". Those present at the first lunch included "the Archbishop of Canterbury, the Baldwins, Edens, Vansittarts, the Londonderrys, Lords Lothian and Derby, the press barons Rothermere, Kelmsley, and the hostess Maggie Greville".

The second lunch included "the Neville Chamberlains, the Duff Coopers, the Samuel Hoares, the Halifaxes, Sir Thomas Inskip, the Winston Churchills and Emerald Cunard".

Ribbentrop and his wife Frau Anna Elizabeth's popularity, reigned high in London society. In fact, Ribbentrop's wife was more popular than he was. As Chamberlain (an appeaser) became Prime Minister on 28th May 1937, Ribbentrop believed this would serve him well in negotiations. But Ribbentrop failed in his attempts to demand that Britain sign the Anti-Comintern Pact, and have former German colonies in Africa returned, which created his bitterness towards Britain. By early summer, Ribbentrop realised he was a failure, socially and politically; he felt snubbed and became seriously antagonistic to the country, and represented Britain as a most dangerous enemy to Hitler.

This does not excuse Maggie for her support of the Nazis at all. That it may have been fashionable amongst some people is totally unforgiveable. But for a while, Maggie erroneously supported a regime which became responsible for one of the worst, if not the worst atrocity ever perpetrated by one nation against human beings. However, appeasement was the approach taken by Chamberlain's government, until he finally gave way to Churchill on May 10th 1940.

Maggie was wrong to suggest (prior to World War II) that Nazism was acceptable. She was not alone. She was among a group of pro-Nazi sympathisers, including Lord Halifax, Lord Brocket, Lord Redesdale, Duke of Westminster, Duke of Wellington (5th) and Lord Londonderry.

Other notable Nazi supporters included the Duke and Duchess of Windsor (although not Maggie's friends), and Oswald Mosley and Unity and Diana Mitford, in addition to members of the government. Ribbentrop was entertained not only by Maggie, but by aristocrats and some of the Royal family. Maggie's visit to Nuremberg in 1934 has been documented.

However, her attitude did not prevent her from entertaining Winston Churchill (who disagreed with her wholeheartedly), or even the critical Harold Nicolson. Friendship supersedes argument, if it is real. Maggie's understanding of reality fortunately emerged in time to aid World War II, by her donation of the P8643 Spitfire to the government, and she provided a major contribution by offering Polesden Lacey for troops in World War II, and provided other charitable gifts and fundraising activities

As a lady who ceaselessly entertained, travelled, learnt and discussed affairs of the world so that when she visited a country (certainly in Europe), "heads of state formed the impression that Mrs Ronnie Greville was an important woman", Maggie's inability to understand reality with respect to Nazism is surprising. The list of politicians and aristocrats who erroneously believed that Hitler would provide peace, is long.

How long did Maggie keep up her pro-Nazi support? Given the number of Jewish friends Maggie had, why was she so bedazzled by the Nazi propaganda? Why could she not see what was really happening until rather late? This was an important mistake she made.

Maggie was a lady whose character has been described by many of her friends and acquaintances. The commentators, some praised her, while some criticised her, as they accepted her hospitality, but all of them helped to display her incredible ability to understand people.

She had the intelligence "to sum people up in an instant", one of her close friends Osbert Sitwell said. She was curious about anyone who contributed to society.

Professor Lindemann (he became one of Maggie's friends) was responsible for bringing some key Jewish scientists to Great Britain (Kurt Mendelssohn, Nicholas Kurti, Heinz and Fritz London, Franz Simon, Erwin Schrodinger, Heidrich Kuhn), although initially they had reservations about leaving their home country. The British government's attitude to Germany prior to World War II, was one of conciliation, of appeasement.

Recognising Maggie's attitude to Germany and Jewish people as a race, prior to World War II, how did her friendship with Lindemann flourish? Did he respect her? Did he enjoy her hospitality? As a teetotal man (except on rare occasions when Churchill persuaded him to have a brandy) and a vegetarian, it cannot be for food and drink, that he came to stay or see Maggie.

I discuss Lindemann more in the final chapter, in reviewing how political Maggie's Salon was. Her friendship with Lindemann, although he was not Jewish, must have caused him some unrest, given his own views were diametrically opposed to Maggie's. However, being at the centre of society, socially for Maggie and politically for Lindemann, brought their separate spheres together at times.

Who Were Her Jewish friends?

Some extremely successful and wealthy friends of Maggie were Jewish. Many of them stayed at Polesden Lacey or dined at Charles Street.

I list some of Maggie's Jewish friends; the list is too long to list all of them; some were at Charles Street more than at Polesden Lacey. Maggie did know some of them very well:[175] Sir Ernest Joseph Cassel (3rd March 1852–1921) and Wilhemina Cassel (1847–1925); Sir Edward Albert Sassoon, 2nd Baronet (1856–1912); Sir Sigmund Neumann, 1st Baronet; Clarissa Bischofscheim (1828–1923); Rufus Daniel Isaacs, 1st Marquess of Reading (1860–1935), who stayed at Polesden Lacey often, and his first wife Alice Edith Isaacs (née Cohen); Dorothy Mathilde de Rothschild (1895–1988) and James Armand Edmond de Rothschild (1878–1957); Sir Philip Sassoon, 3rd Baronet (1888–1939); Marie Louise Eugenie de Rothschild (1892–1975); Andre Maurois (1885–1967) and Leslie Hore-Belisha (1893–1957); Albert Maximillian von Goldschmidt-Rothschild (1879–1941).

What would such friends think of Maggie's attitude? Most of the list above stayed at Polesden Lacey, but only once or twice. Sir Ernest Cassel stayed eight times and Rufus Isaacs (Lord Reading) stayed sixteen times. However, for some of them, their dates of death precluded them from knowing anything about Maggie's pre-World War II Nazi support. When did Maggie realise the truth?

The Spitfire P8643 Maggie donated to the government in World War II

© Crown Copyright IWM

Change of Mind Politically

In 2012, with a colleague, we identified precisely the P8643 Spitfire which Maggie donated to the government.[176] This plane was on active service from 21st May 1941 until it was scrapped on 30th December 1944.

Finally, if not prior to Kristallnacht (November 9th–10th 1938) then certainly afterwards, Maggie understood what was really happening in Germany. There were a few lines of information filed at Polesden Lacey, from which we were able to build up more details about this plane.

We talked to the Imperial War Museum research department (who were very helpful); for the first time, we identified the actual plane, and we collected the photograph the museum held. in 2012. It had been folded for many years, so there is a crease down the centre of the picture, and we brought it back home to Polesden Lacey. This gift shows Maggie finally understood reality! What took her so long?

The photograph of the plane, a Mark IIb, numbered P8643, was taken while it stood on the hard stand at Castle Bromwich. The date is either March or April 1941. The Imperial War Museum cannot be more precise. The plane was an early mark and much more efficient Spitfires were produced as the war proceeded. The plane was used for sweeps, circus and rhubarb sorties.

This plane was built because of Maggie's generosity. Lord Beaverbrook had taken over as Minister of Aircraft Production on 14th May 1940, and this plane was one of many, Lord Beaverbrook oversaw while he was in charge. Beaverbrook continued in this post until June 1941, when he was moved, and he took over as Minister of Supply (aircraft production had by then been transformed by Beaverbrook's energy, intellect and organisational ability; Churchill wanted Beaverbrook to make "the same difference" in supplies). Spitfires varied in cost from around £5,600 to £12,000 each, depending on the type/year of their build.

Joseph Mitchell was the designer of the Spitfire plane; sadly, he died in 1937. Joseph Smith took over as chief designer; he was responsible for the further development of the Spitfire, including mass production. Mitchell's design was so sound that, the Spitfire was continually improved throughout World War II. Over twenty-two thousand Spitfires and derivatives were built. Twenty-four marks with sub-variants produced.

The P8643 Spitfire was manufactured as a Mark IIb and fitted out with a Merlin Mark XII engine.[177] On 29th April 1941 the plane was flown to Maintenance Unit (MU) 12, Kirkbride, Cumbria, where it was fitted with radio and armaments, including 2x20mm canon. On 21st May 1941 the plane was flown from Kirkbride to join 222 (Natal) Squadron, at Coltishall, Norfolk.

The 222 (Natal) squadron operated from several airfields; while the plane was based at RAF Manston, the P8643 suffered category C damage on 24th June 1941, while Sergeant AO Sharples was flying it by an overshoot on the ground. The plane came to rest in a gun emplacement.

On 4th July 1941 the damaged Spitfire was repaired at Air Surface Training Ltd. The maintenance team at RAF Manston did not have suitable engineering facilities to repair the plane. The plane was repaired and delivered by 12th August 1941 to 37 MU at Burtonwood, near Warrington, Lancashire, for reissue to a squadron.

On 3rd September 1941 the plane was assigned to 266 (Rhodesia) squadron at Wittering and reassigned to 266 Squadron at RAF Wittering (Cambridgeshire & Northampton Borders) and used again for Rhubarb Runs and Circus Sweeps, with substantial success.

On 8th October 1941 the P8643 suffered Category B damage while on active service, and on 11th November 1941 was sent for repairs to 5MU at

Kemble, Gloucestershire. On 17th July 1942 the plane was delivered to No 1 Coastal Artillery Operational Unit at Thorney Island (for many years Thorney Island had a Hampshire postal address, but it is actually in West Sussex). Later in 1942 the plane was based at RAF Langham (Norfolk Civilian Anti-Aircraft Co-Operation Unit).

On 29th January 1943 Flying Officer Jimmy Gee flew the P8643 on an offensive patrol "a low-level attack on transport, train busting over France". He hit a tree but managed to fly back and made an emergency "under carriage up" landing at Rye, East Sussex.

The plane sustained Category B damage and was repaired at Westland Aircraft Ltd at Yeovil. Flying Officer Jimmy Gee was injured.

By 11th February 1943 the plane was sent to Westland Aircraft Ltd at Yeovil for repair, and then sent to Air Service Training Ltd. for further repair work on 23rd March 1943.

By 5th September 1943 the plane was repaired and sent to 33 MU at Lyneham, Wiltshire. Unfortunately, a flying accident (Category E) happened on 12th November 1943. The plane was repaired again; it was an old mark; better, stronger Spitfires were now being built.

The plane was sent to several more maintenance units: 9MU at Cosford, then 61MU at Rednal and finally the plane arrived at 45MU at Kinloss in Scotland on 11th September 1944. A decision to scrap the plane was made in September, and she was actually scrapped on 30th December 1944. Maggie's plane was battered and out of date in 1944, but the plane had provided much successful service in World War II.

Definitions of operational sweeps, rhubarb runs and circus by the RAF, and damage categories, are supplied in the Endnotes.

Maggie finally understood and helped Great Britain in World War II

Maggie certainly changed her view prior to the beginning of World War II. As discussed in Chapter 8, British troops were billeted for two years on the estate at Polesden Lacey; there was even an ENSA established to entertain the troops. In 1939 there is proof that British officers stayed in the house as guests, while some of them were also in huts on the estate. Canadian troops were billeted along the woods, leading to Bookham.[178]

Maggie helped RAF badly burnt aircrew, by offering some hospitality while they were at Headley Court. They were invited to spend the day at Polesden Lacey, have tea and return back to the care of Headley Court.

Adding in Maggie's benevolence in providing Polesden Lacey in World War II for British troops, and officers staying in the house, and the whole of Polesden Lacey grounds being made available to the troops for training with space for accommodation, this was a fine and honest turnaround of her views, and finally an understanding of international warmongering.

Added to the Polesden Lacey Convalescent Home in 1915–16, and the Maple Leaf Club 1916–19 with her house 11 Charles Street providing the premises, not many people could have done more to help Great Britain individually. Yes, as already stated, she was wrong for a while. But she certainly made up for it.

Maggie Greville was one of a number of owners of country estates who were taxed after the budget in 1939, by the need to fund World War II. In 1881 probate duty was established on all personal property and included house, land, contents, including jewellery.

By 1894 estate duty was set at eight per cent on properties valued over one million pounds. In the 1930s inheritance tax/death duty increased and reached forty per cent. Maggie had sufficient money to continue to live well.

John Simon (a close friend of Maggie's and Chancellor of the Exchequer) rang her up after the budget and told her of the taxes which he had been obliged to introduce. Whilst on the telephone, Maggie made a "swift calculation" and this "seemed to show that, from all sources of taxation she would now have to pay a £ in the £". Maggie "retorted that Sir John would ultimately be the loser. For she would henceforward be obliged to live on capital".[179]

Maggie was clearly displeased, but she was unlikely ever to run out of money.

The National Trust was able by the National Trust Act 1937 (and additional legislation) to acquire country estates, which meant that families donating their property to the Trust did not have to pay death duties. Under the National Trust Country Houses Scheme, the donor families could continue to live at their property, rent-free, for two generations, and afterwards pay a market rent. Part of the property was required to be open to the public by this scheme. Maggie did not have the problem of ensuring family continuity at Polesden Lacey.

EIGHTEEN

Fourth Death

Many aristocrats who wished to be in London in World War II stayed/kept rooms or suites at some of the London hotels. They felt more secure in hotels which benefited from modern building developments of concrete and steel construction, rather than staying in their brick-built houses. The Dorchester was completed in April 1931.

The Ritz Hotel was designed by Mewes & Davis (Maggie's architects who oversaw the refurbishment and extensions at Polesden Lacey in 1907–08) and was completed in 1906 after the removal of two hotels, the Walsingham and the Bath Hotel. The Ritz was among the first concrete and steel hotels buildings in town (the Savoy had earlier used steel in 1903–04).[180]

Maggie moved into the Dorchester hotel, during the war, but she was still entertaining at Charles St, in February/early 1940. She may have felt the Dorchester Hotel was more central for her visitors – not much of a distance to either the Ritz or the Savoy. Being just around the corner from where her house was, and closer to the Queen Mother and her other friends living in Mayfair, made the arrangement particularly comfortable.

On 30th April 1942 Maggie gave a lunch party at the Dorchester Hotel in her suite. Among her guests were Lord Louis Mountbatten (by then Chief of Combined Operations), the Duke and Duchess of Kent, the Duchess of Buccleuch, and Mr Chips Channon. Maggie by this time was not well, and used a wheelchair for much of the time. However, she wore (as you may expect) some of her famous priceless jewels. She made a comment at the beginning of lunch, saying, "Chips is my only vice." No doubt referring to his anecdotes and gossip. He was known to have always kept diaries, something which scared many people who knew him throughout his life, although not Maggie. The first volume of three of *Chips Channon's Unexpurgated Diaries* was published in March 2021.[181]

The Funeral

Maggie died on 15th September 1942 at the Dorchester Hotel, London. Frank Bole and Adeline Liron were with her at the hotel.[182]

On 18th September 1942 the funeral of Maggie Greville took place at St Nicholas Church, Bookham.[183] Members of society attended the funeral, along with some of Maggie's staff. King George VI and Queen Elizabeth were represented by Sir Eric Mieville (Assistant Private Secretary to the Duke of York). The Bishop of Guildford (John Macmillan), assisted by the Rev A Maby, officiated. Maggie was buried afterwards at Polesden Lacey, in her own plot in the Ladies' Garden.

Later, Maggie's grave was designed by Sir Albert Edward Richardson (1880–1964) who was an architect, scholar and lecturer. James Lees-Milne described the grave as looking "like the top of an old-fashioned servant's trunk, half buried in the grass". Richardson was an architect, who was President of the Royal Academy from 1954 to 1956. He was also Professor of Architecture at University College London. He was an eccentric by any standard (having immersed himself in Georgian architecture and its restoration, and in the 1930s he liked to travel by horse-drawn carriage or sedan chair when dining out). Any visitor to Polesden Lacey can view Maggie's grave in situ.

The Memorial Service for Maggie took place on 23rd September 1942 at St Mark's North Audley Street (the church in which Maggie married Ronnie).[184] The Archdeacon of Wells and the Rev KH Thorneycroft officiated. Queen Mary was represented by Major the Hon John Coke, Princess Beatrice by the Marquess and Marchioness of Carisbrooke, Princess Arthur of Connaught by Mr F Blunden, and Princess Helena Victoria and Princess Marie Louise (both granddaughters of Queen Victoria) by Mrs Hugh Adams. The Memorial Service was attended by a huge number of distinguished friends and relatives whom Maggie had entertained and known for years. Some of the staff also attended this service.

A new Will was written by Maggie in 1942, which (fortunately) provided the magical gift to all of us of Polesden Lacey; members or visitors to Polesden Lacey can benefit forever from this bequest. Maggie's Will was made in the same year she died, 1942. On 27th March 1942, when Maggie Greville's new Will was signed, the changes made, benefited the National Trust, Polesden Lacey and so many people. The Will was formally registered in the High Court on 5th January 1943 for probate.

The National Trust received a fine legacy.

The Queen Mother and Bertie did not know that Maggie had written a new Will in March 1942; this was more than a surprise to the Queen Mother. Whether Bertie was surprised is not known, as he had been aware that Polesden Lacey was being gifted to him from 1914. The Queen Mother understood that the house, contents and land were being gifted to both of them, sometime after meeting Bertie (post-1920) and certainly from 1923 when they married, and spent the first part of their honeymoon at Polesden Lacey.

I provide details in the next chapter of Maggie's substantial bequest of jewellery to the Queen Mother. Other major bequests were: £20,000 to Princess Margaret, and £25,000 to Queen Eugenie of Spain.

In 2020 we celebrated the seventy-eighth anniversary of Maggie's death. Maggie was one of the most beneficial donors to the National Trust. In addition to the bequest to the National Trust, and of gifts to the Royal family, the bequests to close family and friends were of major importance to Maggie.

The actual value of Maggie's bequest (gross) was £1,564,038.8 shillings and 3 pence, and the net value amounted to £1,505,120 and 5 shillings and 10 pence.[185]

In real terms the National Trust was given Polesden Lacey, the contents, and the land; the lease on 16 Charles Street and the contents; and half a million pounds.

Maggie Greville was one of the most beneficial donors to the National Trust.

Clause 16 (3) of the Will stated that "I DIRECT that my Trustees shall not invest in the stocks and shares funds securities or other investments in Australia". This was a reference to the shares William McEwan had owned in BHP Billiton (the Australian mining company, originally the Broken Hill Proprietary Company), which was registered in 1885 in New South Wales and was his only real investment loss. Maggie chose to emphasise in her Will this direction to the trustees because her father, William McEwan, had said she should never trust or do business with Australians.

Fourth Death

Maggie's continuing friendship with both William McEwan's family and the Greville family continued throughout her life. In spite of losing her husband Ronnie in 1908, Maggie was able to include her relatives with royalty, maharajahs, politicians and other guests throughout her years as a hostess.

Some relatives predeceased Maggie: in addition to her father William McEwan, 1913; Sir Sidney Robert Greville, 1925; Auriol Camilla Horne, 1930 (Ronald Greville's niece); and William Younger of Ravenswood, 1925. Among some of Maggie's relatives who were entertained during her later years were, Charles Beresford Fulke Greville, Robert Younger (Baron Blanesburgh), Ralph Younger and William McEwan Younger.

What is apparent is that at no time were any of Maggie's relatives on her mother's side visible. Maggie's success in society was made possible by the marriage of William McEwan to her mother Helen, which established her social position. Maggie did not show any contact in any way publicly with the Anderson family. Generous as Maggie was to royalty, relatives, friends, godchildren, and institutions and organisations, it can be noted that in Maggie's Will there is no mention of any member of the Anderson family in her lists of bequests. It appears that Maggie had no communication with any of her mother's family, once she had grown up. Nor is it known while Maggie was growing up, if contact by Helen (Maggie's mother) was ever made to her own family. Certainly, there is no mention in any documents so far of any contact. A little surprising that there were no small bequests at all.

Maggie was godmother to thirteen children: six girls and seven boys.[186] Maggie's bequests in her Will signified how much she cared for her family, friends and staff. The size of the bequest signified the love/care she held for each person.

Four of Maggie's goddaughters were given five hundred pounds each, including Sonia Keppel's daughter Rosalind (the Duchess of Cornwall's mother). Alice and George Keppel's daughter, Sonia Rosemary Keppel, was bequeathed £2,000. Maggie adored Sonia Keppel; Maggie wanted to adopt Sonia, but the request was refused by Alice. Sonia's sister Violet did not receive a bequest. One goddaughter, Margaret Anne Mackay, was bequeathed £5,000, far more than any other godchild.

Five of Maggie's godsons were given £500 each. Two other godsons, Reresby (Reresby, as per will) Sitwell and Robin Warrender, were given £1,000 each. Reresby was the son of Sacheverell Sitwell and Georgia Doble. Maggie was very fond of Sacheverell and Osbert Sitwell (brothers).

Maggie bequeathed £10,000 to Osbert – he was not a godson, but she really enjoyed his company and his humour (along with the Queen Mother). Maggie herself stated in her Will while writing of other bequests, that they were given "as a small reminder of her friendship".

Maggie's obituary in *The Times* included a separate statement from Osbert Sitwell commenting on Maggie's character.[187] Osbert said of Maggie that in addition to being a great hostess, more importantly she "loved to be in the company of the young, in some way of her own, won their confidence and hearts immediately, and was able to return their confidence. She liked in them, I think, the qualities upon which she set the greatest store – quickness, courage, directness and freedom from affectation and pomposity. Pretensions enraged her and sometimes she set out with an almost Elizabethan gusto to combat them and vanquish those who indulged in them. As for people she loved people of all sorts, as long as they were genuine. Her grasp of politics and business was masculine, it is true, but the way in which she went to work in everything was most essentially feminine".

Maggie was not liked by everybody, but she lived at the centre of things, knowing what was taking place and judging it with accuracy (mostly). As a result, her advice was invaluable and she was consulted by many people of importance

Some of Maggie's servants were individually rewarded in her Will when she died.

Frank Bole, Head Steward, was bequeathed a legacy of £1,000 and an annuity of £500 a year, plus the modern household silver.

Adeline Liron (the Archduchess), employed as a personal maid (gradually she became Maggie's companion), was bequeathed the use of all of Maggie's apartment forever, when Maggie died; some of Maggie's possessions "which do not exceed £100 each in value" and they included Fabergé and Cartier "trinkets, two rows of pearls, all my wearing apparel" and a legacy of £50 per month; plus £100 per year to care for Maggie's dogs during their lifetime. Adeline died in 1959.

Sydney Smith, the Head Chauffeur, was bequeathed an annuity of £200 per year for life, and "all my motor cars with accessories and the garage furniture at 11 Hays Mews". George Moss was given an annuity of £100 per year for the rest of his life.

Gladys Yealland (Maggie's maid) was given a legacy of £500.

Maggie directed her trustees to give other servants (indoor and outdoor), including charwomen who had been employed for more than six months, had not received an earlier monetary gift or were not under notice to leave and were employed for less than eight years, two years' wages in addition to wages due. If they were employed for more than eight years, they received in addition to wages due, seven years' wages.

After Maggie's death on 15th September 1942, Maggie's bequest of Polesden Lacey, the contents and the land, plus the contents and lease of 16 Charles Street, and the wine cellars from both houses to the National Trust, was considerable.

By October 1942, James Lees-Milne (Secretary to the National Trust Committee) met with the executors of Maggie's Will (Lords Ilchester, Bruntisfield and Dundonald, and Captain Terence Maxwell) to begin the process of agreeing what to do with the contents of both properties.

On 11th January 1943, the General Purposes Committee for the National Trust met in London. James Lees-Milne stated that "they agreed to let me do what I thought best with the contents, subject to Clifford Smith and Kenneth Clark endorsing my opinion". Lees-Milne also said that "Sir Edgar Bonham-Carter urged, sensibly I thought that we keep Polesden looking like an Edwardian lady's country house, and not a museum".

Clifford Smith (Former Keeper of Furniture and Woodwork at the V&A) provided the report "on the furniture and other works at Polesden Lacey".[188] Clifford Smith made recommendations as to what was "to be kept and what was to be sold" in his report, having visited both properties. His report was dated 1st February 1943.

Specialists, Mr Abbey from Christies and Trenchard Cox (of the Wallace Collection), agreed that the furniture and paintings at Charles Street were "not of a very high standard", but Mr Abbey considered that some of the silver was valuable – "notably a few James II porringers, Queen Anne salvers & Georgian teapots".

Clifford Smith visited Charles Street on January 20th, 21st and 22nd 1943. He inspected furniture, silver and other works of art; he was looking for objects deemed worthy enough to be exempted from death duties, "being of national, scientific, historic or artistic interest", which would enable them "to be accepted by one of the country's national museums, or, as in this case the National Trust". He commented: 16 Charles Street "was furnished with French furniture and contained little Old English furniture. It had however, a small number of fine eighteenth-century chairs. An Adam-Chippendale lacquer commode valued (moderately) at £200, is the outstanding piece of furniture in the whole collection".

Regarding silver, he said, "the forty pieces of old English silver (valued at £3,395) mainly of the period of Charles II, James II, William and Mary and Queen Anne, together with the Georgian pieces, are all of outstanding quality and importance".

"The blue & white K'ang Hsi" (Kangxi 1661–1722), he regarded as "fine and important pieces".

Sixteen panels of tapestry, "folded up and inaccessible", were to be examined later. He rejected copies of silver, French furniture, mirrors and a clock. He said much of the French furniture was "of average quality". He charged thirty guineas for two days' work, rather than the three.

From 1936 James Lees-Milne (1908–97), as Secretary to the Country Houses Committee of the National Trust until 1951, brought together a number of houses and gardens under the direction of the committee. The purpose of the National Trust was to enable "promoting the permanent preservation for the benefit of the nation of lands and tenements (including buildings) of beauty or historic interest and as regards land for the preservation of their natural aspect features and animal and plant life".

The National Trust was founded by Octavia Hill (1838–1912), Robert Hunter (1844–1913) and Hardwicke Rawnsley (1851–1920) on 12th January 1895.[189] James Lees-Milne was an employee of the National Trust, executing the wishes of the National Trust Board of Trustees. He was active in accepting properties to the ownership of the National Trust, but only as/when agreed by the Board.

On 31st August 1943 Druce & Co (London-based cabinet maker/sellers of second-hand furniture in Baker Street) collected from Polesden Lacey what was deemed to be "the secondary furniture". Druce was established in the 1840s and listed in the Marylebone Trade Directory of 1853 as "Furnishers, Upholsterers and Upholders for clients of discernment".

Lees-Milne was involved with art and antique experts, until Polesden Lacey was organised and opened as a visitor attraction (1948). In November 1944 Lees-Milne was awarded a bonus of £200 for his work.[190] It seems he asked the finance committee of the National Trust to allow him to take £200 worth of furniture from Polesden Lacey instead of cash (as he would have paid tax on the money). This seems to have been agreed. But gossip and facts are not always the same. This remains speculative.

Today, the number of people who visit Polesden Lacey has grown substantially. For the financial year 2019 to 2020 (end of February), over 420,000 members and visitors arrived at Polesden Lacey to enjoy the house and grounds.

Maggie stated in her Will, referring to the grounds, "That it may be found convenient and suitable to provide for a Kiosk or Kiosks in this park where refreshments can be procured".

The Margaret Greville Rose was launched in 2017 at Chelsea Flower Show, and we can always appreciate the magical gift of Polesden Lacey to the National Trust on each anniversary of Maggie's death on 15th September 1942. Polesden Lacey's success as a venue, has grown beyond what anyone could have conceived.

NINETEEN

Donation of Jewellery to the Queen Mother

The jewellery Maggie acquired on her wedding day includes some stunning items. There is not absolute proof or references to this jewellery, but a number of newspapers confirm the descriptions, and it appears that the following details provide a reasonably accurate picture of the gifts she received.

Maggie received the following on her wedding day on 25th April 1891.

William McEwan gave Maggie a beautiful tiara, which was composed of three rivieres (necklaces) "made of the largest and finest stones". Plus "there are five diamonds down the centre of the tiara, each the size of a sixpence".[191]

William McEwan gave Maggie a large diamond spray in a design of creeper leaves, which "measured quite half a yard in length" and also described as "containing nine enormous brilliants, set in an equal number of diamond oak-leaves".

Helen McEwan gave Maggie a stunning travelling bag: "it is in dark crocodile skin, fitted with every conceivable article that could be needed for the toilet, as well as writing materials. Even a tiny Etna [*box for storing small treasures*] and a pair of sweet little candlesticks are among the contents of the numerous silver-gilt boxes, the lids of which are hammered a series of little circles intersecting each other" (*The Truth*, 30th April 1930).

Ronald Greville gave Maggie five diamond stars which fastened on her veil, and a diamond and ruby heart.

Lord Greville (Ronnie's father) gave Maggie a diamond and emerald bracelet. Lady Greville (Ronnie's mother) gave Maggie a necklace which was an antique cross cut from an enormous turquoise, set in brilliants.

It is interesting to understand that Helen McEwan's jewellery was bequeathed in trust to Maggie, not given directly to Maggie. I have proved that when Maggie's mother (Helen McEwan) died on 3rd September 1906, Helen bequeathed most of her inheritance to Royal Chelsea Hospital and to the Gordon Boys Home.

I have talked to both of these institutions. I have written confirmation from the Royal Chelsea Hospital, who were extremely helpful and provided precise details to confirm that Maggie purchased her mother's jewellery (thereby overriding the terms of Helen's Will) which had been "left in trust to Maggie" and which otherwise would have meant that, the jewellery would have to be returned for the benefit of both institutions when Maggie died.

The outright purchase of the jewellery was agreed by the executors at valuation and consisted of "watches and jewellery". The sum of £491 were each given to the institutions. Maggie paid £982 in total, but there is no known exact list to describe these items.

Maggie gave the Duchess of York a triple (short) row of natural pearls as one of her wedding presents, when she married Bertie. The Duchess of York wore the pearls almost constantly for a long time. Pearls were considered to be very valuable, more so than diamonds and other jewels, until the method of producing cultured pearls was established (from 1928).

Approximately one hundred years ago, William Saville-Kent discovered while working in Australia (close of the nineteenth century) the method of "culturing pearls".[192] His system was taken up in 1916 (patent granted) by three Japanese men: Dr Tokichi Nishikawa (1874–1924), a marine biologist; Tatsuhei Mise (1880–1924), a carpenter without a scientific background; and Kokichi Mikimoto (1858–1954), a vegetable vendor who became a pearl farmer. From 1928 cultured pearls were commercially produced. There are several types of cultured pearls, including Akoya, South Sea, Tahiti and modern freshwater pearls (Edison) available today. Natural pearls (located by diving) are restricted to preserve the oyster beds and are now traded as antique jewellery and command very high prices. Natural antique pearls sell at very high prices, whereas cultured pearls (of similar high quality) sell at various prices. Size, shape, colour, lustre, surface quality, nacre thickness and being matched, affects the price.

Modern cheaper cultured pearls are widely available today. Real pearls remain valuable, but they are not usually worth more than diamonds in today's market, although when Maggie boasted about their value (pre-1928), they were.

Maggie's interest in jewellery was well known during her life and has been acknowledged since she died, due to Maggie's gift to the Queen Mother.

Maggie bequeathed her real jewellery to the Queen Mother in her Will (presented in a black tin trunk). This jewellery links Polesden Lacey to the British Royal family today. The jewellery is spectacular. What work was carried out to alter any of the pieces of jewellery in Maggie's tin trunk is currently unknown, though there is evidence that Maggie used Boucheron for a number of changes to some of her jewels.

Where did she obtain so much, and such stunning and valuable jewellery?

Boucheron and Cartier proved to be endearing sources of supply for Maggie's high-end requirements. We have some of the listings and details of the jewellery, which was gifted in the black tin trunk, labelled with Maggie's initials and old spelling of Polesdon Lacey. We do not have knowledge of all of the spectacular pieces of jewellery in this trunk.

Pierre Cartier opened his salon in 1847, when he took over a shop at 29 Rue Morgueil in Paris.[193] His son Alfred ran the business from 1874, and Alfred's three sons – Louis (Paris), Pierre (New York) and Jacques (London) – established Cartier as a world-famous jewellery brand. Jacques gained the Royal warrant in 1904 in London. Cartier items – the Festoon necklace, the Chandelier earrings, the Pear-Drop earrings, the Ivy-Leaf clips and the Scroll brooch (all owned by Maggie) – provide illuminating examples of the finest quality.

In 1858 Frédéric Boucheron opened his first boutique in the Galerie de Valois underneath the arcades of the Palais Royal, which at that time was the centre of the Parisian luxury trade.[194] In 1893, he was the first jeweller to open a boutique in Place Vendôme, one of the finest jewellery salons ever created.

The history of Boucheron is fascinating: covering purchases by the Russian Royal family from 1860; the purchase by Frédéric Boucheron of many of the French Royal family Crown jewels in 1887 (at auction); an incredible order by the Maharajah of Patiala in 1928; the appraisal of the Shah of Persia's (Iran's) Imperial treasures in 1930; the opening of the Bond Street Salon in London in 1903, to other international venues.

A photograph of Maggie's Boucheron diamond tiara created in 1921 (the third change to Maggie's tiara as detailed below), was recently on show on the Boucheron website in the history section, described as "exceptional" and confirmed as one of the Queen Mother's favourite items.

Both companies were successful more than a century ago, and continue to be the first point of call for wealthy international purchasers today.

Donation of Jewellery to the Queen Mother and Bertie, and Elizabeth's Shock of Losing Polesden Lacey

The black tin trunk in which Maggie's jewellery collection was stored and gifted to the Queen Mother, contained over sixty pieces of jewellery with initials MHG on the front, and Polesden Lacey, spelt as Polesdon.

From 1899 to 1925 Maggie's name appears more than forty times at Boucheron; six or seven times were for alterations or repairs; this was for new and antique jewellery. The contents of the black tin trunk are fabulous, unique and extremely valuable. Maggie was an enduring client of both Boucheron and Cartier.

We have only some of the details of the jewellery gifted to the Queen Mother. The mystery continues over the contents of Maggie's small black tin trunk when Maggie died.

I list some items below: it has to be a list. The references for the jewellery are from Sir Hugh Roberts, the Queen's Diamonds.[195] Additionally, some jewellery is listed from Vincent Meylan, Boucheron, the Secret Archives.

- The Bow Brooch, 1900 (according to Sir Hugh Roberts), Boucheron.
- The Greville Chandelier Earrings, Cartier, one pair of earrings, but with changes, 1918, 1922 and 1929, London.
- The Greville Scroll Brooch, Cartier, 1929, London.
- The Greville Festoon Necklace, 1929 and 1938, Cartier, London. Diamonds! Maggie ordered the original two-row necklace in 1929, which had a back chain in silver. In 1938 she ordered a separate three-row diamond necklace to be made (so diamonds all round). At that same time, Maggie requested that the 1929 version of the original two-row necklace was altered, so the silver chain at the back was removed and it was made into an all-diamond necklace. This necklace can therefore be worn as two rows, three rows or five rows. Camilla Duchess of Cornwall has worn this a number of times, whilst wearing the Greville diamond tiara (Boucheron).

- The Greville Ivy-Leaf Clips, before 1930 and 1937, Cartier (Sir Hugh Roberts). The first clip was made prior to 1930. The second clip was made in 1937. The earlier clip was modified to match the 1930 clip.
- The Pear-Drop Diamond Earrings, Cartier, New York and London (Sir Hugh Roberts) These earrings were acquired from Cartier New York prior to May 1938. The completed record for them appears in Cartier, London, on 31st May 1938. According to Sir Hugh Roberts, Vincent Meylan misattributes these earrings. Sir Hugh confirms them to Cartier.
- The Greville Diamond Tiara, 1953 version (as altered by the Queen Mother), is on show in Sir Hugh Roberts' book. Please note that three styles of this tiara had been created while Maggie was alive, as listed by Boucheron for 1901, 1919 and 1921, and are confirmed for Maggie. The fourth version of this tiara was created by Cartier in 1953, for the Queen Mother, which provided raised peaks of diamonds. This tiara was frequently worn by the Queen Mother, and is/has been worn by Duchess of Cornwall on a number of occasions.

Precise details of the Greville diamond tiara are that, on 12th November 1901 Maggie ordered the diamond tiara in the shape of papyrus leaves.[196] It formed a circular crown on a platinum base. It was designed to be worn on the centre of the head, as a royal crown is worn.

In March 1919, Maggie requested Boucheron to open up the original tiara in order that she could wear it as a headband lower on her forehead, as was the new fashion. Seemingly, this modification was insufficient.

On 8th January 1921, Maggie returned the tiara to Boucheron, and requested that it was dismantled, and made into the art deco geometric shape (there were no raised diamonds at this stage).

At the time of writing, this tiara remains in the Queen's ownership; the Greville jewellery collection will pass to Prince Charles and the Duchess of Cornwall, and later on, to Prince William and the Duchess of Cambridge. While the Duchess of Cornwall does not yet own this tiara, she does have total control/management of it. It is maintained at a London jeweller, and it is understood that no other member of the Royal family may wear the tiara.

The Duchess of Cornwall wears some of Maggie's jewels: at the (formal) State Opening of Parliament and Her Majesty's State dinners. On 12th July

The Duchess of Cornwall wearing the Greville Tiara and the Festoon necklace.

© Photo y "Pool/ Getty Images Entertainment via Getty Images"

2017, King Felipe VI and Queen Letizia of Spain were received at Buckingham Palace for a formal banquet, and she wore this Greville tiara.

In 1907 Maggie purchased the Boucheron Ruby and Diamond necklace, which was given to our Queen by Bertie and Elizabeth, when she married Prince Philip.[197] This necklace was worn (as Princess Elizabeth at first, and later as the Queen) from 1947 until 1983. The necklace has not been seen since 1983, when the Queen wore it on a state visit to Sweden. In 2017, King Felipe and Queen Letizia of Spain made a state visit to England, and the Duchess of Cambridge wore this necklace for the first time, at the formal State Dinner the Queen held.

Two square pieces of diamonds and rubies were removed for the Queen; if the Duchess of Cambridge wishes to wear this necklace more often, it may well suit her to have the two pieces added back into the necklace, as the Duchess of Cambridge is taller than the Queen. The necklace was placed on show with Princess Elizabeth and Prince Philip's wedding presents in 1947. Over a hundred years after Maggie purchased the necklace, it is being worn again by the Royal family.

Additionally, when Princess Elizabeth married Prince Philip, Bertie and Elizabeth (Queen Mother) gave Elizabeth, Maggie's Chandelier Earrings from the tin trunk.[198] The earrings were ordered at Cartier in December 1918; in September 1922 six marquise and six batons brilliant were added to lengthen them; in February 1929 Cartier supplied "ten assorted diamonds" the third stage and final amendment. The earrings consist of sixteen stones each.

In 1910 Maggie ordered a separate/different lighter headband, with foliage motif set with 293 diamonds (Boucheron).

In 1918 Maggie bought two pear-shaped diamonds mounted as pendant earrings at cost of 355 francs. In 1925 Maggie had these extended with two baguette cut diamonds. Maggie continued to purchase and have work undertaken at Boucheron throughout her life.

In 1921 Maggie gave some diamonds (number unknown) to Boucheron to have them remounted according to the latest fashion. The Paris showroom created a double parure (two sets) made up of a short pendant necklace, and a long necklace in the form of a bailiff's chain. Both on show in Meylan's book.

Maggie talked about her pearls frequently. Comments about them appeared in newspaper articles. Every year Maggie deposited her sautoir (long strings) of 210 pearls and her three necklaces (a four-strand, three-strand and a single strand) with Boucheron for restringing. Currently we do not have any known information to state that Boucheron sold Maggie these pearls, but she is unlikely to have them restrung by the company, if they had not sold them to her originally.

Maggie boasted to Gladys Yealland, lady's maid (from 1931–42), that they would "buy the whole of Piccadilly". The suggestion exists (in later years) that Gladys was responsible for taking the pearls for restringing to a jeweller, and that Gladys had to wait at the jewellers while they were restrung. It seems Gladys went out shopping, as she was sure she could trust the jewellers, and returned to collect them, then wore them on the way back in Maggie's car.

In 1922, Maggie added to her parure of pearls (set) by purchasing a pair of pendant pearl earrings set with two one hundred-grain pear-shaped pearls at cost of 150,000 francs. Among Maggie's orders were: hair pins, lighters, pins for veils, rings, each decorated with a rectangular diamond mounted on platinum, or a lozenge-shaped diamond.

I have a reference to an emerald and diamond necklace Maggie purchased, which reputedly had belonged to Marie Antoinette and was in Maggie's tin trunk.[199] In Russia Princess Nadezhada Tereshchenko married Vladimir Vladimirovich Mouravieff on 21st January 1909 (Vladimir Mouravieff-Apostol-Korobyine) They had three sons, Vadim, Andrew and Alexis.

Prior to the 1917 Russian Revolution, the family brought to England most of their fortune, including beautiful emeralds and diamonds (the Tereshchenko Blue Diamond), and also a necklace which had reputedly belonged to Marie Antoinette. Princess Nadezhada and her husband came twice in 1917 and once in 1918, to stay at Polesden Lacey (as confirmed by the Visitor Book).

Seemingly, Princess Nadezhada had obtained a necklace which Marie Antoinette had owned. The suggestion exists that Princess Nadezhada sold this necklace to Maggie. The Marie Antoinette necklace, and another necklace (emeralds and diamonds) owned by the Empress Josephine (but not owned by Princess Nadezhada), were apparently gifted in Maggie's black trunk to the Queen Mother.

Vincent Meylan confirms that "at one time Maggie took one small and one large emerald necklace to be made into one necklace by the firm" (Boucheron). Doubt remains as to whether the above-named necklaces were kept intact after acquisition, or altered or sold, This, raises questions. It is conjecture (not totally proved so far) that the necklace which was once owned by Marie Antoinette, and was in Maggie's tin trunk, was sold to Maggie by Princess Nadezhada, but there is an understanding that Princess Nadezhada had obtained a necklace, which Marie Antoinette had owned whilst she and her husband had spent time in France.

In 2018, a piece of spectacular jewellery was confirmed to be in Maggie's box, known as the Kokoshnik Tiara – emerald and diamonds and created by Boucheron in 1921.[200] In 1921 Maggie purchased a diamond bandeau, decorated with an emerald of 93.7 carats from Boucheron, known today as the Kokoshnik Tiara, but not named as such by Meylan. The reason for the Russian title is due to the halo or crescent-shape design, which was popular with Russian royalty prior to 1917.

A photograph of this tiara being worn by Maggie in 1937 has been located.

Maggie wore the tiara while attending a concert at the Austrian Legation (now an embassy) in 1937 in London, at a Richard Tauber concert.

We now have documentary proof of this tiara, which has never been seen or worn, we understand, since Maggie died in 1942.[201]

The photograph of this tiara was tracked to Berlin (see references), and was taken by Erich Salomon, who tragically died in Auschwitz in 1944. This tiara was worn for the first time since 1942 by Princess Eugenie when she married Jack Brooksbank in 2018, and it is absolutely stunning.

The value of such a piece (conjectured by the press incorrectly) is extremely high. The large central emerald is cabochon in style; the quality is superb. It is impossible to value this tiara, unless it were ever to be sold (most unlikely).

In 1923 Maggie ordered pendant earrings – pear-shaped cabochon emeralds suspended from a line of four detachable diamonds – to complete her emerald parure (set).

We have confirmation of a number of items of jewellery which were in the trunk, but not all. Many additional pieces of jewellery which were present in the trunk remain unknown. A formal request was made in 2019 to discover more about the contents. We have been unable (so far) to obtain this.

Some Other References re Maggie's Jewellery

In letters to Osbert Sitwell on 27th September 1942: "It is terribly sad to think that she has gone" and "Do you remember those wonderful weekends at Polesden".

A letter the Queen Mother wrote, about passing on the jewellery she had inherited from Maggie (should anything happen to her in World War II), was provided by William Shawcross book, *Counting One's Blessings*. It was the first letter the Queen Mother wrote referring to Maggie's jewellery after being advised she had inherited it, and was dated 13th October 1942.[202] The letter was written from Balmoral Castle (one month after Maggie died) to Queen Mary.

"I must tell you that Mrs. Greville has left me her jewels, tho' I am keeping that quiet as well for the moment! She left them to me 'with her loving thoughts', dear old thing, and I feel very touched, I don't suppose I shall see what they consist of for a long time, owing to the slowness of lawyers and death duties, etc, but I know she had a few good things. Apart from everything else, it is rather exciting to be left something, and I do admire beautiful stones with all my heart. I can't help thinking most women do."

An important (known) letter the Queen Mother wrote in World War II and quoted by William Shawcross (dated 27th June 1944) to her daughter Elizabeth, was regarding her own personal assets/jewellery.[203] "This is just a note about one or two things in case I get 'done in' by the Germans! I think I have left all my own things to be divided between you & Margaret, but I am sure you will give her anything suitable later on – such as Mrs. Greville's pearls, as you will have the Crown ones. It seems silly to be writing these sort of things, but perhaps it would be easier for you darling if I explained about the jewels." There is no further reference to the pearls/jewellery in this letter.

I understand the Queen Mother was given a short three-strand pearl necklace by Maggie when she married the Duke of York. In the letter above, the Queen Mother is referring to the three different long strings of pearls which had belonged to Maggie.

The *Evening Standard*, 21st June 1938, said in talking about Maggie, "Her jewels, particularly her pearls, are fabulous and she has often said that she will leave them to the Queen in her Will." There are many references to Maggie's pearls.

Camilla the Duchess of Cornwall is the great granddaughter of Alice Keppel, who was Edward VII's last mistress for the last ten years of his life. Alice was also one of Maggie's lifelong friends. Alice Keppel had two daughters, Sonia and Violet. Sonia married Roland Calvert Cubitt, 3rd Baron Ashcombe, and had a daughter named Rosalind, who gave birth to Camilla.

It is fascinating to understand that the wealth Maggie bequeathed, has provided and continues to provide, such direct connections to the British Royal family today for Polesden Lacey. Maggie's jewellery being worn by the Duchess of Cornwall prior to her inheritance of it, as Prince Charles's wife, offers a spectacular connection to the history of the baby who was born in unusual circumstances and who became a key player in international society.

Some additional references to newspaper articles are listed below and they help to identify the range of Maggie's jewellery. Many more exist.

- *Queen*, 21st May 1910. "Mrs Ronald Greville often wears a set of black diamonds." I have heard about these, but no real confirmation as yet.
- *Queen*, July 1914. "Mrs Ronald Greville wore an immensely tall and very handsome tiara of diamonds."
- *The Sunday Times*, 25th July 1928. "Maggie wore a lemon-coloured dress with her magnificent diamond and emerald necklace."
- *The Sunday Times*, May 1933. At a dinner and reception given by Sir John and Lady Simon, "Mrs Greville had on her empire-shaped tiara of diamonds and emeralds, and many more of these same stone on her dress of maize-coloured satin."

- *The Sunday Times*, 1st June 1934. "Her emerald and diamond tiara looked lovely with her dress of green lace."
- *The Sunday Times*, 2nd December 1934. At the Royal wedding (29th November 1934) of Princess Marina and the Duke of Kent, *The Sunday Times* references Maggie: "The Hon Mrs Ronald Greville's emeralds and diamonds, long chain, earrings, brooches, bracelets, tiara and necklace [*which belonged to the Empress Josephine*] were things at which to marvel."
- *Evening Standard*, 1936. "Mrs Ronald Greville blazed with diamonds, a diamond tiara on her head, huge diamonds round her neck and more round her wrists."
- The Sunday Times, 29th May 1938. At a dance given by Lady Baillie for the debut of her daughter Miss Pauline Winn, "the Hon Mrs Greville wore pale green satin and her lesser emerald necklace."
- *The Sunday Times*, 12th June 1938. "Mrs Greville wore pale grey with some of her fine ropes of pearls."
- 18th December 1940. "Lovely jewels – including an enormous diamond ring, diamond shaped as on a playing card."

Beverley Nichols, in his book *The Sweet and Twenties*, said of Maggie when she was in her suite and in bed at the Dorchester (1942) not long before she died:[204] "On her hands the fabulous diamonds still sparkled, though she was now so thin that she had to clench her fingers to prevent them slipping off."

The media have suggested (but as yet there is no proof) that the Duchess of Cornwall's engagement ring was originally one of Maggie's diamond rings, and the stones have been reset for Camilla. This remains a possibility.

There have also been a number of comments about Maggie owning black diamonds.

Maggie owned more jewellery than I have listed. No details of her rings are known, apart from mention of diamonds and emeralds, but no doubt there were other stones also.

There is much more to discover. No research is ever complete.

TWENTY

The Closure of a Star Performance

From a gossip view, an example of Maggie's discretion occurred in 1912, when Maggie arrived in Cannes for one of her many visits. Many, many foreign royals and aristocrats entertained each other for several weeks a year whilst in France, the South of France being the one of the most popular destinations (except when buying jewellery or clothes in Paris) for the weather, hotels and, importantly, for meeting up with friends. On one of Maggie's visits, having only just arrived, she received a request from a doctor she knew asking for advice about a client.

One of the doctor's clients was Mathilde Kschessinska, who had been the Principal Dancer of the Imperial Ballet in Russia. Mathilde had enjoyed a friendship with Nicholas (the future Czar, pre-1894), but his mother ensured the relationship ended. Nicholas married Alix of Hesse.

Mathilde became the mistress of Grand Duke Sergei Michaelovich. Mathilde did not love Sergei, but she welcomed the protection he gave her, and his patronage. Mathilde met another man, Andrei Vladimirovich, and lived with him but managed to maintain her relationship with Sergei.

Both Sergei and Andrei (they both knew of each other's relationship with Mathilde) believed that they were the father of Mathilde's son Vladimir (nicknamed Vova). It seemed that Vova was often unwell. Mathilde usually travelled with a doctor. On one occasion, Mathilde arrived in Cannes without her travelling doctor, and needed to find a local doctor who was able to attend

Vova. Mathilde had told both her lovers that Vova had been treated by this doctor. The doctor was surprised to discover that both men had written to him, and both men had sent cheques to pay for Vova's treatment. The doctor needed Maggie's advice and sought her opinion as to his dilemma. Maggie's advice was, "Accept both cheques. Never impugn a woman's honour." We know Maggie could be discrete!

Who Were Maggie's Real Friends? Who Really Mattered to Maggie?

Lord Reading (Rufus Isaac) was one of Maggie's real close friends. She had many friends, but she adored Lord Reading. She knew Lord Reading for a very long time. She entertained both Rufus and Alice (they were married for forty years) in Charles Street and at Polesden Lacey. When they were in London, Lord and Lady Reading lived in Curzon Street, close to Charles Street. Alice was unwell for many years, and after she died, Maggie may have wished that her relationship could have become even more important to Lord Reading. However, Maggie with her wealth, her circle and her own fiefdom, may not actually have wanted to share, or alter her status.

However, when Stella Charnaud, a lady who had previously helped Alice with secretarial work, became engaged to Lord Reading, Maggie wrote a note to Lord Reading, saying: "Stella struck me as a charming clever woman, but I think she is lucky to have won you, as we all know how wonderful you are and how unselfish."[205]

Sometime later, Stella established the Women's Voluntary Service, now known as the RVS.

One important moment which proves Maggie's friendship with Lord Reading mattered so much was the time Lord Reading was considering the role of Viceroy of India which he had been offered. Robert Boothby related in his book *Recollections of a Rebel* that one day at Polesden Lacey, Maggie said, "Rufus Reading came down to Polesden alone in order to ask her whether he should accept the Viceroyalty of India."[206] Boothby said, "This was difficult to believe, and I asked the date, which she gave me. Early next morning I went downstairs in my pyjamas to look at the Visitor Book. There it was. The single signature 'Reading'."

Lord Reading stayed at Polesden Lacey on 11th December 1920 and departed on 12th. He accepted the role of Viceroy of India, and he became

Governor from April 1921. We know of how fond Maggie had been of Lord Rufus for so long.

Who Were the Most Important People to Maggie? Royalty? Other Friends?

In addition to Lord Reading, Maggie had a number of close friends. Possibly she placed them in categories. Edward VII, Princess Beatrice, Queen Mary, King George, Bertie and Elizabeth, Queen Eugenie of Spain, Princess Alice, and the Earl of Athlone, and more international royals, including maharajahs, were her real friends.

Maggie needed her own confidantes. Adeline Liron had been Maggie's personal maid and became, as time passed, her personal companion, so she too was in Maggie's inner circle.

Some of Maggie's close friends were: Professor Lindemann (surprisingly), Robert Horne, John Simon, Osbert Sitwell, Beverley Nichols, Henry Harris, Beverley Nichols, Alice Keppel, Sarah Wilson (Winston Churchill's aunt), Austen and Ivy Chamberlain. Maggie's relationships with some key people enabled her to have thirteen godchildren, all of whom mattered to Maggie (they each received a bequest in Maggie's Will).

Did Maggie Actively Dislike Anyone, Yet Entertain Them?

Maggie's dislike for Emerald Cunard has already been discussed in Chapter 15!

Maggie disliked Edward VIII and Wallis Simpson, although in the 1920s Maggie had tried to become one of Edward's friends. While Maggie was on a tour to India, 1921–22, she managed to be for some of the time in exactly the same place as Edward, particularly while staying at the Viceroy's house (Lord Reading was in residence) in Delhi. This particular time was complicated by the arrival of Edwina Ashley to be with Louis Mountbatten (aide de campe to Edward).

Edward did not like Maggie, although he attended some of Maggie's parties in London (usually after a Ball elsewhere), possibly because "everyone was going on to Maggie's". Edward's dislike of Maggie, was because he knew she was a good friend of his mother Queen Mary. Edward realised that Maggie would tell Queen Mary when she got home, about Edward's various affairs/bed hopping/pursuit of ladies. He definitely thought she was a gossip, and in this case, he was probably correct.

How Political Were Maggie's Salons at Polesden Lacey and Charles Street?

Baron Kenneth Mackenzie Clark (1903–1983), author, broadcaster, art historian and museum director, stayed with Maggie at Polesden Lacey several times in the '30s, and said "we visited her once a week: I can't think why" (in London), with his first wife Elizabeth, known as "Jane".

Clark was born at 32 Grosvenor Square, an only child with rich parents – a successful Scottish family in the textile trade. Clark's great-great-grandfather invented the cotton spool and the Clark Thread Company of Paisley was a huge business. Clark's Scottish connection, and the earlier trade connection, may have appealed to Maggie.

Clark's career was astounding; he was in charge of the Ashmolean Museum aged twenty-seven, the National Gallery aged thirty and was knighted aged thirty-five. Clark wanted art to be "available" to everyone. He became a life peer in 1969. He and his wife lived and entertained in considerable style in a large house in Portland Place. "The Clarks in joint alliance became stars of London high society, intelligentsia, and fashion, from Mayfair to Windsor"; his personal influence and success would be an attraction for Maggie.

Clark stated that, "The conversation at these dinner parties was not even about money, mere generalities. But afterwards Mrs Greville would draw aside Sir John Simon, Sir Sam Hoare or some other of her regulars, and talk to them seriously. She sat back in a large chair; as a Phoenician goddess, while the cabinet minister or ambassador leant forward attentively. I have no doubt she had considerable influence".

Maggie Greville enjoyed talking to, manipulating and trying to influence politicians. Kenneth Clark also said of her: "She was immensely rich and the only hostess who had any political power, not simply on account of her wealth but because she was a shrewd and forceful personality."[207]

Maggie lived not far (in the country) from Lord Beaverbrook, who resided for much of his life at Cherkley Court, Leatherhead. But their worlds did not meet or cross often. Both of them entertained politicians profusely. Lord Beaverbrook did so because he was, for much of the time, persuading, manipulating and influencing many of them to take political decisions and execute manoeuvres to obtain what he wanted to be put in place. He was a member of the Cabinet in two world wars. Beaverbrook, in addition to hosting his guests at Cherkley Court, which included his friends, businessmen in finance, newspapers and politicians, did not court royalty, as Maggie did.

Beaverbrook was not one of Maggie's friends, but he must have given her some respect for her part of providing 11 Charles Street for the first Canadian Maple Leaf Club in London (as above). Additionally, for her gift of the P8643 Spitfire to the government (World War II). Also, for providing Polesden Lacey in World War II as an ammunition depot and having troops billeted there, including officers staying in the house, along with other military activities taking place. Plus, Canadian troops were given space in the woods for their camps at this time.

Maggie's approach was different to Lord Beaverbrook; the royalty she hosted, including maharajahs, friends and politicians, covered an area of social activity in which Beaverbrook had no interest. While politics mattered to Maggie, she believed she had some influence, possibly achieving or facilitating political changes. Maggie was not an integral player, as Lord Beaverbrook. Maggie brought together at Polesden Lacey politicians who had total privacy, and could meet, and discuss away from town, the most current situations which were developing. Maggie did manage to elicit some change/s with regard to certain politician's places in society.

One example of this was evident after Maggie returned from a trip to Egypt. She told Beverley Nichols that George Lloyd (High Commissioner) had not been kind to her when she was in Cairo.[208] "That dreadful Lord Lloyd had the impudence to think he might be Viceroy, but I soon put a stop to that!" She made this comment in the company of Lord Reading (a close friend, and previous Viceroy of India). Lloyd was removed from his role in Cairo in 1929 by Arthur Henderson (Foreign Secretary).

Beverley Nichols recorded in his book *The Sweet and Twenties* that in 1931 Maggie offered him cash: "Once Maggie offered me a great deal of cash… but I refused it."[209] Maggie had asked Beverley to stand against Duff Cooper, Conservative candidate for Westminster, as an independent candidate. Maggie did not care for Duff Cooper.

Maggie said, "I will pay all your expenses." A pause. "And a great deal more." Beverley's reply was, "And in any case I shouldn't get in." "Perhaps not. But at least you would split the vote." After, some thought, Beverley did not take Maggie up on her offer. She accepted the refusal, but as Beverley remarked, she often said to him, "Dear Twenty-Five, so unworldly."

Winston Churchill was not a close confidante/friend of Maggie's, but she numbered him among her friends.[210] Professor Lindemann (1886–1957) was in charge of the Clarendon Laboratory at Cherwell and was the scientist Churchill relied on for his information. During World War II Professor Lindemann was not listed officially, as one of Winston Churchill's inner members of the War Cabinet (though Lindemann was appointed the British Government's leading scientific adviser by Churchill); but Lindemann did attend War Cabinet meetings, and travelled with Churchill frequently to conferences abroad, and was in touch with Churchill daily. Lindemann stayed at number 10 Downing Street often during the war (always accompanied by his valet Harvey).

Prior to World War II, in August 1934, Lindemann had toured Germany with Churchill. Together they saw the way Germany was rebuilding itself in terms of armaments, how men were being recruited and trained, tanks being built and aeroplanes. The original reason for the trip was to tour the Duke of Marlborough battlefields, so Churchill could gain first-hand knowledge of his ancestor's achievements for a book he was writing. They both understood what the Nazis were doing and what their intentions were.

Maggie had many sides to her character. She was shrewd, she was wrong sometimes (as per the build-up to World War II), until she finally understood what was really happening), but not often.

Somehow, Maggie mattered to Lindemann. He was a fascinating man, but not everyone liked him. He was arrogant. Lindemann was born in Germany; his mother Olga (American) was attending a health clinic in Baden-Baden. His father was from south-west Germany and was naturalised as a British subject circa 1871.

Lindemann had studied in Germany, but he hated the Germans and what they were doing to Jewish people, long before many other intellectuals recognised this. Churchill was one of the few politicians to challenge the complacency that existed prior to World War II.

Possibly after a large-scale test in 1934 of an air exercises held over Britain, which failed miserably, as any air defences that existed were totally inadequate, there was the beginning of some realisation that Great Britain had virtually no protection in the air, and little else to offer in strength. The public did not appear to be interested, and it took much longer for the government to begin to prepare at all for a war.

Maggie corresponded with Lindemann frequently from 1926 to 1940; she entertained him more than forty times between 1926–40 at Polesden Lacey and Charles Street. In her letters to Lindemann, Maggie expressed her dislike of Jewish people (though not individual Jewish people, as she stated to Lindemann in a letter dated 1st December 1933). Did Lindemann object to the attitude she displayed at the time? He must have struggled to accept her arguments at times.

Did Maggie wish to continue to be in the middle of inside knowledge of the government, and any major decisions that were made?

She managed to position herself in the middle of much that happened. Yes, she expected and hoped she had influence. A word here, or a telephone call to someone in Whitehall, was one of her usual approaches.

Lindemann was Churchill's right-hand man in terms of supplying Churchill the scientific information he required, frequently prior to Churchill making a speech.

Sometimes Lindemann was wrong. Lindemann had the idea in 1942 of "dehousing". Lindemann suggested that bombing "working-class people living in towns would break the spirit of the people" because they did not have large houses (unlike middle-class houses with land around them, where bombs were wasted) and they lived close together. This new approach to bombing resulted in, for example, the bombing of Dresden. It also produced the attack on Coventry Cathedral (14th and 15th November 1940) in retaliation; (Churchill was aware of the direction of where German bombs would fall, but not precisely where German bombs would reach, although he could not warn anyone at the time, because he would have shown the knowledge that Britain was able to read and decode German messages). Did Maggie know much of this background at the time, or only much later?

Maggie spent years cultivating politicians. While royalty, both in Great Britain and elsewhere in the world, provided her with a star-studded international guest list, she was as interested in being with politicians as she was with royalty, because ultimately, they did rule the world! Any insight to Maggie cannot ignore the (sometimes misguided) aspect of her foreign policy. Maggie travelled to so many places in the world, and met so many people who were in charge/running the country.

Maggie's involvement with royalty and maharajahs is well documented. Maggie's love of politics and her interest in manipulating a situation or a person to get the result she desired, was demonstrated a number of times.

Many politicians were regular guests at Maggie's table, both in London and at Polesden Lacey. Listing them all would be too much, but what can be recognised is that when Maggie hosted politicians away from London at Polesden Lacey, she provided time and space for them to continue their conversations away from the eyes of the world. Some of them are listed below.

Some of Maggie's weekends were political: the weekend of 23rd–25th July 1932 was clearly so;[211] Brendan Bracken MP, who had a number of political roles (MP, later Churchill's PPS and founder of the *Financial Times*) was added on to this weekend, with some of Maggie's regulars below.

This particular weekend was preceded by a royal weekend, 25th–27th June 1932, which was one of Maggie's regular thank-you weekends for Bertie and Elizabeth after Royal Ascot (each year) to provide them with a relaxing time. I can add that Anthony Eden and his wife Beatrice, Robert Horne (below) and Osbert Sitwell (author and good friend to both Maggie and Elizabeth) were also present. Everyone was, of course, vetted, so Bertie and Elizabeth were happy to be with the selected guests.

One of Maggie's most regular political guests was Robert Horne, Minister of Labour, President of the Board of Trade and Chancellor of the Exchequer – he stayed at Polesden Lacey more than fifty times and dined with Maggie in London at least one hundred times.[212]

Others were: Austen Chamberlain (Postmaster-General, Secretary of State for India, Chancellor of the Exchequer, Lord Privy Seal, Secretary of State for Foreign Affairs and First Lord of the Admiralty), who was a great friend (half-brother of Neville Chamberlain) and was a regular guest with his family, including frequently at Christmas; Stanley Baldwin (Financial Secretary to the Treasury, President of the Board of Trade, Leader of the Conservative Party, Chancellor of the Exchequer, Prime Minister); Arthur Balfour (First Lord of the Admiralty, Secretary of State for Foreign Affairs, Lord President of the Council, Prime Minister); Duff Cooper (British Ambassador to France, Chancellor of the Duchy of Lancaster, Secretary of State for War, First Lord of the Admiralty); Henry "Chips" Channon (member of Parliament only, but the "man with the diaries"); Sir Sam Hoare (Secretary of State for Air, Secretary of State for India, Secretary of State for Foreign Affairs, Home Secretary, Lord Privy Seal, and Secretary of State for Air once again); Viscount Hailsham (Member of the House of Lords, Lord Temporal, Attorney General for England and Wales, Leader of the House of Lords and Secretary of State for War, Lord High Chancellor of Great Britain, Lord President of the Council); Ramsay MacDonald, Prime Minister 1924, 1929–31 and 1931–35 as Head of

The Closure of a Star Performance

the National Government; Mackenzie King (Leader of the Liberal Party Canada, Prime Minister twice, 1921–26, 1926–30 and 1935–48); Richard Bedford Bennett (Prime Minister of Canada, 1930–35); Herschel Johnson (Democrat and Foreign US Service Officer and by 1941 Envoy Extraordinary and Minister Plenipotentiary to Sweden – later after Maggie's death US ambassador to the UN); Edward Mandell House (Democrat, an American diplomat and adviser to Woodrow Wilson during World War I and at the Paris Peace Conference in 1919); Professor Lindemann, (Paymaster General twice, Churchill's scientific adviser, who in spite of being a man who was not always liked, somehow maintained with Maggie a long friendship, including much correspondence); John Simon (Home Secretary, Foreign Secretary and Chancellor of the Exchequer, the man Maggie told Boothby, had asked to marry her).

The above politicians were Conservative (apart from clarifications above); however, Ramsay MacDonald was Labour and John Simon was a Liberal, although he moved from left-wing Labour to almost a Conservative later in life.

Maggie's servants were aware that political discussions were regularly conducted for many years (and including in World War II) in the Long Walk. This long stretch of the garden, gave politicians the chance to talk without being overheard at all. A relative of one of Maggie's maids, confirmed this in writing fairly recently. Polesden Lacey was a perfect for politicking away from London.[213]

Maggie was unlike Lord Beaverbrook, who enjoyed having diverse views from his guests at Cherkley Court, so he entertained not only Conservatives but members of the Labour and Liberal parties, whereas Maggie tended to be supplied by guests from the Establishment.

There are many occasions when Maggie called Churchill, to tell him or ask him, about something that had happened, which she thought required attention. Maggie entertained Winston Churchill at Charles Street, and at Polesden Lacey.

As the government had executed a policy of appeasement right up to the declaration of war in 1939, Maggie was not alone in her attitude to Germany. Lord Londonderry, Lord Halifax, Neville Chamberlain as Prime Minister, even Lord Beaverbrook, prior to the declaration of war, had been appeasers (for Beaverbrook, because he believed it would not happen), although Beaverbrook quickly adapted to his role in building Spitfires as Minister of Aircraft Production, and in being determined to beat the Nazis.

Can we blame Maggie for her pre-war attitude? Yes, because for a while she believed in accepting the idea of Nazism. Maggie and some aristocrats thought they would be safeguarded/keep their money and land, if Nazism was successful in Great Britain. Naïve! This was some acceptance of Ribbentrop's fawning and manipulation of prominent members of British society.

Previous enjoyable experiences travelling and visiting Germany – the country had been one of Edward VII's favourite places to seek a cure and other experiences – all helped to cloud Maggie's judgement, until, finally, clarity arrived. Neville Chamberlain did not help prior to war being declared. Let us not forget the climate of acquiescence and appeasement, which existed.

Anti-Semitism is not acceptable in any form, so Maggie did fall down on this point until finally she understood what was really happening in Germany and Europe. Given that Maggie was such a world traveller, and had met people in so many continents, and had Jewish friends whom she cared for (even more than care for in Lord Reading's case), it is surprising she was so wrong with this pre-World War II attitude. Especially as often she had helped so many charities and people, including staff with little income, by making a better world for them.

Yet she picked herself up, when she discovered what was really happening, as World War II began. How many other people gave so much in two world wars to the government and the country?

What Difference Did Maggie Make?

Being at the heart of political discussions meant she could influence (or try to and often succeed) and manage to elicit some changes which suited her. The amazing achievements of Maggie Greville on the world stage; her friendship with royalty, aristocrats and politicians; her charitable work throughout two world wars; and her route through her active years, was unparalleled.

The opportunities she gave to young people to get on in life. Her care and management for her staff. Her ability to meet, talk to and influence politicians and others, was substantial.

Maggie Greville made a difference to so many people, by using her money to improve education/students' grants, such as the Pretsell Scheme, started by her father. She donated to many charities, improving life for other people. Maggie gave to individuals who needed help, as long as they were prepared to make efforts to become successful.

Her character – often incredibly kind, sometimes acerbic, her intelligence, her shrewdness, her ability to understand situations both nationally and internationally (mostly correctly), her incredible inclusion into the British Royal family, her acceptance by many maharajahs, and her intrigue and gossip – made her one of the most fascinating people of the last century. Yes, her father's money eased her way, but money on its own is insufficient. Maggie was no doubt a genius of her time, and her influence made a difference.

The Polesden Lacey Convalescent Home in 1915–16, and the Maple Leaf Club, 1916–19, with her house 11 Charles Street providing the premises – not many people could have done more to help Great Britain individually.

Maggie's grasp of what was really happening as World War II commenced, meant that she quickly encompassed the situation, and once more gave to Great Britain. As stated in Chapter 8, British troops were billeted for two years in World War II on the estate at Polesden Lacey; there was even an ENSA established to entertain the troops. Canadian troops were billeted along the woods leading to Bookham in World War II. Maggie helped RAF badly burnt aircrew, by offering some hospitality at Polesden Lacey, while they were at Headley Court in World War II.

Yes, as stated above, she was wrong for a while.

But she certainly made up for it.

Beverley Nichols saw Maggie not long before she died. Beverley Nichols was one of her close friends, and Maggie was talking about Ribbentrop, while she was in bed at the Dorchester hotel. Beverley Nichols had dinner with her in her suite and realised that not long after dinner he should depart, as he realised that she was "very weak".[214]

"'Au revoir, Maggie.' She shook her head. 'I think not my dear Twenty-five [*Maggie's pet name for Beverley*]. I think it is good-bye.' Suddenly the windows rattled as a bomb fell unpleasantly near, in Hyde Park. 'That damned Ribbentrop,' she whispered. 'Thank God I told him what I thought of him, when he came to Polesden.' 'What was that, Maggie?' 'I told him that if ever there was a war, he might beat the English, but he would never beat the Scots.' Her eyes closed and she fell asleep. I had heard the last of Maggie's reminiscences."

Maggie Greville was one of a number of owners of country estates who were taxed after the budget in 1939, by the need to fund World War II. In 1881 probate duty was established on all personal property and included house, land, contents, including jewellery. By 1894 estate duty was set at eight per cent on properties, valued over one million pounds. In the 1930s inheritance tax/death duty increased, and reached forty per cent. Maggie had sufficient money to continue to live well.

What Did Maggie Bequeath?

Ronnie Greville's and William McEwan's graves are both in the grounds of the church at St Nicholas, Bookham. They can easily be located, as there are (open) railings around the graves. Helen's grave is, as already stated, at Highgate (Chapter 6).

Maggie bequeathed money: £150 per annum to the Rector of St Nicholas for the upkeep of both her father's and Ronnie's graves, and £100 per annum for the upkeep of her mother's grave at Highgate.

The details regarding the maintenance of the graves cover two pages in Maggie's Will (four clauses). Maggie was very concerned that the graves should be maintained, and she directed her trustees to withhold the monies if at any time they were in disrepair. She stated in her Will that "I particularly request that inspections are made to confirm that all three graves are kept in good order and condition" and if not, monies were to be withheld until proof of good maintenance was provided.[215]

Maggie said the following in her Will (reference the four clauses and one more clause relating to Adeline Liron): "I DIRECT that all pecuniary legacies and annuities bequeathed by clauses 4, 5, 6, 7 and 8 of my Will shall be paid or provided for in priority to my other pecuniary legacy bequeathed by my Will or any Codicil hereto."[216]

Unfortunately, in April 1978, new legislation freed rectors and commissioners of their obligations to look after such graves. The money Maggie had paid out herself directly, and any monies paid by the National Trust Trustees, remained in the Church Commissioners' general fund. In 1987 the Church Commissioners stated that diocesan funds would be made available to help take care of the graves. Since then, at one time, some scouts helped to tidy McEwan's and Ronnie's graves. Sometimes help to tidy the graves is provided by Polesden Lacey.

What Happened to Maggie's Bequest?

The actual value of Maggie's bequest (gross) was £1,564,038.8 shillings and 3 pence, and the net value amounted to £1,505,120. and 5 shillings and 10 pence.[217]

The National Trust was able by the National Trust Act 1937 (and additional legislation) to acquire country estates, which meant that families donating their property to the Trust did not have to pay death duties. Under the National Trust Country Houses Scheme, the donor families could continue to live at their property, rent-free, for two generations, and afterwards pay a market rent. Part of the property was required to be open to the public by this scheme. Maggie did not have the problem of ensuring family continuity at Polesden Lacey.

After Maggie died, an assessment by the National Trust was made of her possessions, as to what should be kept and what should be sold.

H. Clifford Smith's "Report on the Furniture and other Works of Art at Polesden Lacey" in 1943, to the Trust, included some comments and recommended many disposals.[218]

Recognition was given to the quality of much of the collection of the paintings, seventeen of which had passed to Maggie from her father. Maggie's paintings, added to her father's paintings, were assessed for what was to be kept and what was to be sold.

Clifford Smith stated that forty-eight coloured sporting prints (value £180), which were in situ in the Billiard Room, should be sold to provide wall space "for old master paintings, and for upright show cases for china, silver and other art objects". He said Maggie owned sixteen tapestries; many of these "will have eventually to be disposed of" or loaned to other National Trust houses, or to public buildings.

Some examples of his valuations of furniture which remain in place today at Polesden Lacey include, the Carlton House desk valued at £30 and the larger Regency writing table valued at £120 (library/study).

Referring to the Library and the Study, he remarked, "I would draw your attention here to the desirability of leaving the writing tables with their accessories and writing materials and all personal photographs standing upon them undisturbed."

Considering Maggie's porcelain, he said, "It is evident that only a portion of the Chinese porcelain should be kept and that the remainder will have to be sold. The same will have to be applied to the European porcelain – the English comprising mainly Chelsea groups and the European mainly Dresden and other tea-sets." Of the Italian maiolica he said, "The Italian majolica [sic] will have to be gone through in the same way with a view to the selection of the best pieces for the purpose of exhibition. There are 24 pieces valued at £542."

Clifford Smith argued heavily in this report that, every room at Polesden Lacey opened to the public should contain fresh flowers. He said flowers "should be a feature in every room: and at least some of the flower vases now in the flower room should be retained for roses". He said the main corridor was 108 feet long and 10 feet wide; he stated the east and west corridors were each 60 feet long, while considering display purposes. His suggested a list of paintings for the Dining Room, was followed precisely; in place today at Polesden Lacey are exactly his choice of paintings for this room.

He valued the silver (including pieces from Charles Street) as a total of "nearly 50" and value of "£3,550". Some items such as porringers were valued at £12 or £20 (seventeenth century); three circular tea caddies, seventeenth century, valued at £35; a pair of George III candlesticks were valued at £35, dated 1762. He suggested that a reduction of silver items would have to be made for display purposes.

Clifford Smith located in the strong room, some miniatures; many of these he decided were copies and not all were kept.

Additionally, he found in this room, "a miscellaneous collection of some 130 small decorative works of art". He decided which pieces should be kept, including several with the cypher of King Edward VII.

"Six others bear the signature of Peter Carl Fabergé (1846–1920), goldsmith and jeweller to the Czars Alexander III and Nicholas II of Russia." He said, "I put aside a group of thirteen little figures and animals and birds carved out of semi-precious stones and set with diamond eyes, which I recognised as the work of Fabergé, though unsigned."

His closing remarks in this report were, "Of special interest on account of the association of the donors with Polesden Lacey, is an oblong box of ebonised wood inlaid in silver with the Royal Arms of King George VI and Queen Elizabeth as Duke & Duchess of York." It has recently been proved that this box was sold, in the sales the National Trust asked Christies (Christies, Manson & Woods in those days) to execute in 1943.

On 11th January 1943, the Finance and General Purposes Committee of the National Trust (established in 1936), considered and agreed formally to recommend to the executive committee, that Polesden Lacey "was to be accepted". Additionally, at this meeting, it was agreed that the executive committee were to be asked to sell "chattels as are not required for furnishing Polesden Lacey principal rooms". It was at this meeting also it was agreed to ask Mr Clifford Smith to appraise the furniture and to ask Sir Kenneth Clark to assess the paintings. At the same time, it was agreed that James Lees-Milne may borrow some furniture "for his own use" from Polesden Lacey, with the intention of this being sold after the war.

The sales of much of Maggie's possessions by the National Trust took place on several days in 1943, from March to July. In fact, Maggie's goods were sold from Derby House, Stratford Place, because a bomb had landed on Christie's King Street premises.

The actual sale dates were: 3rd and 4th March, French Furniture; 9th March, Silver; 12th March, Pictures and Drawings; 22nd March, Wines; 13th May, Furniture; 30th June to 1st July, Furniture and Porcelain; 8th July, second portion of Furniture; 23rd July, Pictures and Drawings.[219]

I highlight only some of the sale dates below with some detailed items, as providing a full list would be too long. I can confirm precisely the following items were sold because, with a friend and colleague, I made a visit to Christie's King Street premises on 20th September 2018, and we were able to record the details below directly from Christie's Archives, which was a totally fascinating experience. We were given considerable help from the Archivists at Christie's.

On 4th March a carpet (runner) was sold, Lot 174, and was bought back by the National Trust for forty-six guineas.[220]

On 9th March a large quantity of solid silver was sold (by weight) and was removed from 16 Charles Street, including table forks, dessert forks, rat-tailed tablespoons, plain tablespoons, plain teaspoons, teaspoons with scrolls, salt spoons and a butter spade, a coffee pot with fluted spout, a plain oval tea kettle on a stand with a mount, a tea kettle engraved with a flower scroll work on a tripod stand with lamp.

On 22nd March Maggie's fine wines and spirits were sold from Charles Street and Polesden Lacey. "Non-dealers were forbidden by the Food Ministry's Wine and Spirits Order concerning auction to take part."

Maggie had a preference for Veuve Cliquot and Bollinger: fourteen dozen Veuve Cliquot champagne, 1928 and 1929, twenty-four dozen Bollinger 1928 and 1929. There was a note to the sale. Clients could not sample wines. Wines were not guaranteed. Additionally, there were some half bottles of Veuve Cliquot dated 1928, and two Magnums of Pommery and Greno dated 1921. Maggie definitely had a preference for Veuve Cliquot and Bollinger, and the years of 1928 and 1929!

Clarets were sold; twenty-four bottles of Chateau Pichon Longueville 1924 were sold at £6.10 shillings a bottle. "Ports without a name fetched £22.00 a dozen bottles; Hocks and Moselles reached £50/57 a dozen bottles. Brandies went at £5/£6 a bottle. Most expensive drinks of all were liqueurs. Four bottles of Cointreau were knocked down to £34 and four of Grand Marnier for £32."

"From the dealers' point of view the feature of the sale was the high price paid for clarets. A number of Chateau Ausone, Chateau Latour, and Chateau Margaux (1924) fetched 1,300 shillings a dozen, compared with 130 shillings normally. This sale realised more than £6,000."

On 13th May 1943. A collection of twenty-four mahogany chairs were sold (from Charles Street) with fluted legs carved with rosettes and partly gilt. The seats and backs were covered in silk damask. They were sold for £168.

On Wednesday 30th June a dark green figure of a fish with jewelled eyes (Faberge) was sold to Spink for £215.5 shillings. Some carriage rugs were sold on this day also, lined with mink for £63. Additionally, an invalid chair upholstered in green damask was sold for £7.16.6 pence.

On 1st July in the "Objets of Art & Vertu" sale, Lot 181 was sold, which was an oval stone tray with gold border chased with a laurel wreath by Faberge for 44.2 shillings. A pity so much more was sold; but at that time the view by the National Trust was limited and very different to today.

Christie, Manson & Woods in April 1943 (so after the sales had commenced, but not at the close of the sales) stated that, "We value for Probate the foregoing FURNITURE, SILVER, PORCELAIN, PICTURES, WINES etc. at the prices affixed making a Total sum of EIGHTY-NINE THOUSAND, NINE HUNDRED AND TWENTY-THREE POUNDS, TEN SHILLINGS, of which the items marked with an 'X' and valued at sums totalling FIFTY-TWO THOUSAND, SIX HUNDRED AND SIXTY POUNDS (and included in the above Total of £89,923.10) we recommend for EXEMPTION from DUTY under the provisions of SECTION 20 of the FINANCE ACT, 1896, as extended by SECTION 63 of the FINANCE(1909–1910) ACT and re-enacted by the FINANCE ACT 1930, as being of National, Scientific, Historic or Artistic Interest. The items marked with an 'K' valued at sums totalling THIRTEEN THOUSAND, TWO HUNDRED AND SIXTY-EIGHT POUNDS (and included in the above total of £89,923.10-) were EXEMPTED from DUTY on the death of the late Rt. Hon. William McEwan, M.P. in 1913."

The final total the National Trust earned by these sales (not currently known) was certainly in excess of expectations. The rest of the lease on 16 Charles Street was bequeathed to the National Trust, and this was sold between 1943 and 1946. *The Times* stated on 18th February 1946, that the Guards Club has bought No 16 Charles Street "as its future home", but variable dates exist. The National Trust banked more money from the sale of this lease.

Was Maggie's decision to gift the jewellery to the Queen Mother a master stroke? Did Maggie realise that by the provision of two of the most stunning bequests (house and grounds to the National Trust and jewellery to royalty), she was making a larger statement than her contemporaries, who were more inward-looking towards their families? Without children, the cause, the springboard and the lever to gift so much, was understandable. She made many other bequests; anyone who mattered to Maggie was taken care of (in most cases).

The surprise in Maggie's new Will, written in March 1942, was that the National Trust received an enormous bequest, rather than Bertie and Elizabeth. The gift of jewellery instead to the Queen Mother, means that Maggie's jewels continue to be showcased to the world; Maggie's friendships with British Royalty, and Bertie and Elizabeth particularly, ensured that such visual connections are maintained for future generations.

Maggie's gift to the National Trust allows an immeasurable number of people in Great Britain (who are interested in history and beautiful places) to enjoy one of the most spectacular destinations in the country, Polesden Lacey.

The influence of the profit from beer production travelled far. Maggie's contribution emphasises, that philanthropy mixed with money can be beneficial. William McEwan (the thinker and the planner), with his tutelage, management and careful guidance of Maggie, facilitated her place in history and provided her with the opportunity to shine.

The star Maggie became, was the result of her father's shrewdness, intelligence and determination for her to be successful, and was demonstrated in his business and personal/social life. Maggie used her father's gifts to her, and relished them until the closing stages of a life full of glamour, coupled with action, fortitude and ultimately accomplishments.

The magical world of Maggie Greville continues to flourish today: visibly in being able to see some of Maggie's jewellery worn by the British Royal family, and by her philanthropy, in donating Polesden Lacey as a place for everyone to visit.

Acknowledgements

Katherine Mills, General Manager of Polesden Lacey, has supported my work from the moment I talked to her about the book. I appreciate Katherine's help. I am extremely grateful for Katherine's encouragement, which has helped me enormously.

Alma Topen, Glasgow University Brewery Archives, for major and initial research, and longstanding enquiries into the real story of William McEwan and his family, and in particular his daughter Margaret Anderson (Greville). Alma's work provided the basis, for so much of the real story we have been able to prove.

Janet Durbin, for her significant contributions: re Polesden Convalescent Home, and correct details and biographies of soldiers staying at Polesden Lacey in World War I; for Janet's work on biographies for the Visitor Book at Polesden Lacey, and for her correct identification of photographs in Polesden Lacey's House and Collections website; for her work and mine on Christie's sales in 1943. For her research re Maggie's cars including information from the 20-Ghost Club, the Oldest Rolls-Royce Car Club in the world. For Janet's continuing help in research.

Tracey Parker, for her significant contributions of servant details from her studies/records and interviews, of both servants and descendants of servants who worked for Maggie Greville, including reminiscences by Edward Colling, grandson of Sydney Smith, Maggie's head chauffeur. For Tracey's work on the miniatures at Polesden Lacey (acquired from Tessiers); and for Tracey's continuing support and help with queries.

Bernice Forsyth, for her significant contributions: for work in "translating" the Visitor Book at Polesden Lacey. The importance of this book cannot be overstated. Bernice's work has made a huge difference. For "translating" Maggie's travels in 1899 around the Mediterranean, and for her work reference a maid in 1917 at Polesden Lacey. For research on Adeline Liron's Will and death; for establishing that Bertie and Elizabeth's gift of an engraved ebonised box with the Royal Coat of Arms to Maggie was sold at Christie's. For the background information re Princess Nadezhada Tereshchenko and her husband Vladimir Mouravieff Apostol-Korobyine. Additional research re Maggie's travels, including shipping lists. Census returns for Polesden Lacey. For "translating" Lindemann letters, transcript of letters written by Margaret Greville, held by Nuffield College, Oxford, files K131 and A28/F8.

Leanne Smith, for her significant work in locating images for *The Maggie Greville Story*. Leanne Smith for her significant contributions: re managing/clarifying and sorting thousands of documents at Polesden Lacey; for her thoroughness in tracking photographs, and in particular for the photograph of the emerald tiara Maggie owned, which was worn by Princess Eugenie in 2018 on her wedding day. For locating Maggie Greville's SY *Rona* journal, written on her travels in 1899 in and around the Mediterranean.

Roger Coleman, for his significant work and mine in evaluating the real beginning of Maggie's life, in conjunction with Alma Topen at Glasgow University, Brewery Archives. Roger Coleman, for his significant work and mine in identifying the P8643 Spitfire (Maggie's aeroplane) held at the Imperial War Museum, London, and for the location of the photograph by the Museum staff. Roger Coleman for his research, including the Greville Family line.

Alex Wigley, for his important help in researching my garden queries, and for his explanation and help, with titles of gardeners and garden and outdoor managers.

Significant and substantial contribution from David Lloyd, ex-trustee of the Spitfire Society. Information from operational records books and Air Ministry 1180 accident cards from RAF Museum supplied by Roy Nixon. Spitfire Aircraft Production. John Rawlings, *Fighter Squadrons of the RAF and Their Aircraft*. Eric B. Morgan and Edward Shacklady, *Spitfire History* (four editions).

Roy Vaux, for his important research of Frank Bole, Maggie's travels/shipping lists and census returns for Polesden Lacey.

Acknowledgements

Anthony Stephens, Conservation and Engagement assistant at Polesden Lacey, for research of Maggie's Jewish guests/friends, at Polesden Lacey and Charles Street.

Sir Hugh Roberts, *The Queen's Diamonds*: a major contribution to our "known" information regarding Maggie's jewellery given to the Queen Mother.

Jonathan Marsh, Head of House Collections, for his work on William McEwan's Archives and artefacts, as loaned from Glasgow University Brewery Archives.

Charlotte Burford, for her work on McEwan's papers from Glasgow University Brewery Archives, and Polesden Lacey Archives, Fountain Brewery and Fountainbridge Ledgers.

Elodie Fillon, for contributions to work on a number of topics at Polesden Lacey.

Significant contribution from Marion May: *The Ornamental Jacksons*.

Significant contributions from Aldith and Bernard Bruty: *Jackson's the Plasterers*.

Significant contributions from the Royal Hospital Chelsea, Martin Cawthorne, and Tom and David Lyall, Archive Office, Royal Hospital Chelsea.

Significant and important details provided by notes: in *The Memories of an Unnamed Soldier* (officer), including his time in World War II, staying at Polesden Lacey. Details of how the army used Polesden Lacey for troops/equipment and training. With additional details of Maggie's guests continuing to dine together with the officers.

Endnotes

One

1. Alma Topen's research work at Glasgow University (Brewery Archives of Scotland) in researching the history of William McEwen and his brewery, and the truth of Maggie's background. www.visionofbritain.org.uk Reference Alloa Academy.
2. The McEwan Family Ships, Coasting along. Glasgow University Brewing Archives. Alma Topen.
3. The Early Years, dated June 1994 at Glasgow University Brewery Archives. Research reference McEwan's papers, Alma Topen. Scottish Post Office annual Glasgow Directory 1844–45 re employer for William McEwan – TL Paterson.
4. The Early Years Travel. Glasgow University Brewery Archives. McEwan working for his uncles John and David Jeffrey at the Heriot Brewery. Alma Topen.
5. The Early Years. Glasgow University Brewery Archives. McEwan Papers. Census records. Wills of John and William McEwan and records at New Register House of Census Returns and Post Office Directories.
6. Glasgow University Brewery Archives. McEwan Papers. Financial Records 1856 +.
7. Individual letters McEwan dated, Brewery Archives. Glasgow Brewery

Archive, William McEwan, Letter Book SNNM 3/1 from William McEwan to suppliers/companies/agents/relatives/the bank, from his archive of letters (Glasgow Brewery Archive) and copies of which were in place at Polesden Lacey. Charlotte Burford, for her work on McEwan's papers from Glasgow University Brewery Archives, and Polesden Lacey Archives, Fountain Brewery, and Fountainbridge Ledgers. Jonathan Marsh, Head of House Collections, and Charlotte Burford, for their work on William McEwan's archives and artefacts, as loaned from Glasgow University Brewery Archives.

8   Alan Berridge. Significant research into McEwan's brewery at Glasgow University Brewery Archives, and in Edinburgh, into the real story of McEwan and Maggie.

9   Certificate of Incorporation of William McEwan and Company dated 24th July 1889.

10   Financial records analysis of the McEwan Brewery, with mergers over the years.

11   "Ale, Altruism and Art" by Julia Lloyd Williams (The Benefactions of William McEwan). *Apollo*, May 1994.

Two

12   Original research by Alma Topen Glasgow University re Anderson family.

13   Brewery Ledgers, Glasgow University Brewery Archives.

14   Birth certificate of Margaret Anderson, 20th December 1863 in London.

15   Baptism date for Margaret Helen Anderson dated 8th April 1864. Selkirk Old Parish Registers, Entry No 778/6 re William Murray Anderson's birth. Census returns 1871, Edinburgh (107 Fountain Bridge), re William Murray Anderson. Marriage entry for Murray Anderson to Wilhemina Campbell, 685/,1 Entry 111, Edinburgh 1893. Death certificate for Murray Anderson, October 1898 – 685/1 Entry 1109.

16   Census records, Edinburgh, including birth, marriage and death certificates.

17   Original research addresses Alma Topen. Compilation by R Coleman and Pam Burbidge. Map of Edinburgh dated 1893–94 for location of addresses. Post Office Street Directories, Edinburgh, for 1863–85 re

McEwan's residency. Census returns, 1871, Edinburgh, re Shandwick Place address, Reference No 685/1 book 59. Census returns, 1881, Edinburgh, Reference 685/1 Book 50 re McEwan's residency. Post Office Street Directories, Edinburgh, from 1868 to 1875, 1876 to 1885, re Helen Anderson's residency. Census records, 1871, Edinburgh, re Helen Anderson's East Maitland address. Census records, 1881, Edinburgh, re Helen Anderson's Atholl, Place address 685/1 Book 46. References: research of Old Parish Registers Dunfermline (424), vol 16 page 185, re Maggie's grandparents and mother. Census returns, 1871, Edinburgh (685/1), Book 43, re Maggie's grandmother.

18   History of 25 Palmerston House, Edinburgh. Archive documents. Glasgow University. Refs: www.conandoylecentre.com, re 25 Palmerston Place.

Three

19   William McEwan's Journal dated 25th July 1849, transcribed by volunteer Margaret Laidler, 2016.

20   Marriage certificate dated 26th November 1885, parish district of St Peter's Pimlico, Middlesex.

21   Report and valuation by Messrs George Trollope & Sons, licensed valuators, dated 21st June 1913. Additional inventory, Vol 549/060, of William McEwan's Will proved 21st July 1913 reference Charles Street lease.

22   Compilation of the Greville family line by Roger Coleman. Roger Coleman for his understanding/research of the Greville lineage, and for background to Ronnie's best man at his wedding (Homfray), and for additional research.

23   *Fulton County Journal* report, 25th January 1894, located by Mary Hunter, volunteer, reference Virginia Daniel Bonynge. New information, *Husband Hunters* by Anne de Courcy.

24   Marriage certificate dated 25th April 1891 at St Mark's, North Audley Street, London.

25   Confirmation from Rugby School obtained by Frances Wood, volunteer. Wendy Adams, Rugby School Ledgers, 27th April 2011, checked and reply to Frances Wood, Researcher at Polesden Lacey, reference Ronnie Greville's attendance at the school.

26   Archivist Pete Storer, Combermere Barracks, Windsor, confirmed

records. Nigel Lewis-Baker for his confirmed information of Ronald Greville's Army record in the 1st Life Guards and Household Cavalry.
27   *Bertie: A Life of Edward VII* by Jane Ridley and www.british-history.ac.uk
28   Alma Topen, Archives of William McEwan.
29   Wedding certificate of Margaret Anderson and Ronald Greville, dated 25th April 1891, as a magic key.
30   Marriage of Margaret Anderson. Wedding details of clothes and gifts. Newspaper articles of 1891. Newspaper cuttings from various newspapers/journals April 1891 re Maggie and Ronnie Greville's wedding: *The Scotsman, Vanity Fair, The Daily News, The Hawk, Country Gentleman*. References to jewellery given to Maggie Greville on her wedding day: number of newspapers: *The Scotsman* 27th April 1891, *Truth* 30th April 1891, *Woman's Magazine* (undated), *Worcester Herald* (undated) *Sussex Daily News* April 1891.

Four

31   Election manifesto dated 28th October 1896 and *Daily Mail* 11th November 1896.
32   *Bradford Observer* 18th January 1904, *Argus* 19th January 1904. www.britishempire.co.uk re Maggie in East Bradford.
33   John Barnes Vade Mecum www.barneshistorian and various newspaper articles re Ronnie Greville's political career: *Election Manifesto* 28th October 1896, *Daily Mail* 11th November 1896.
34   The *Rona* Journal written by Maggie Greville in 1899. Located by Leanne Smith and "translated" by Leanne Smith and Bernice Forsyth.
35   Image of Maggie Greville taken by Lafayette 5th October 1900 at his Bond Street studio. V & A picture Library, La Fayette Negative Archive Number (GP) 2517. Image Number 1000LF199-01.

Five

36   Conveyance of Polesden Lacey for the purchase of Polesden Lacey, dated 1902. Journal of the Royal Institute, Journal of British Architects, reference Ambrose Poynter Architect of Polesden Lacey 1902-

Endnotes

522/02/1907, Clare Prior (solicitor and volunteer) and Leanne Smith.

37 Surrey History Centre, Woking. Original legal documents/contracts of purchasers of Polesden Lacey, for centuries. Entries from 1847–1902.

38 Cambridge Architectural Research Company, Historic Buildings Analysis Report of Polesden Lacey, dated 2014.

39 Polesden Lacey Archives, reference Mewes & Davis work undertaken 1907–08.

40 Significant information from Marion May: *The Ornamental Jacksons. A Brief History of George Jackson Ltd.*

41 Significant information about Walter Stiles, Lead Modeller and Carver at Jackson's the Plasterers, by Aldith and Bernard Bruty.

42 Polesden Lacey archive listing work undertaken post-1960 fire, re the ceiling of Maggie's boudoir.

43 History of Charles Allom and White Allom by Diana Brooks. *Holloway White Allom*, by White Allom.

44 Letter dated 23rd February 1989, from Pauline How referring to her father who worked at Polesden Lacey in 1907–08 for White Allom. Dictionary of National Biography, *Rise and Demise of a Wren Church*, John Kenworthy-Browne (NT Yearbook, 1977–78).

45 Comment Maggie Greville made to Mewes & Davis, as her decorating request.

46 Polesden Lacey Visitor Book, 1907–42, "translated" by Bernice Forsyth.

47 Polesden Lacey Archives and research of churches built by Sir Christopher Wren. Union of Church Benefices Act of 1860.

48 Dictionary of National Biography, *Rise and Demise of a Wren Church*, John Kenworthy-Browne (NT Yearbook, 1977–78).

49 Wenham & Waters, Plumbing Fixtures, as labelled in the bathrooms at Polesden Lacey.

Six

50 Helen McEwan's Will (copy) from archives dated 30th December 1903.

51 Helen's death, 3rd September 1906: *Morning Post* 4th September 1906, *London Daily News* 6th September 1906. www.britishnewspaperarchive.co.uk

52 Royal Hospital Chelsea. Reference Helen McEwan's jewellery and

bequest: Royal Hospital Chelsea Archives Department, Private Funds of the Royal Hospital Chelsea. Confirmation details dated 20th November 2017, Martin Cawthorne, and Tom and David Lyall, Archive Office, Royal Hospital Chelsea.

53   Gordon Boy's School confirmation of receipt and distribution of Helen's bequest by Julie West, Gordonian Officer at Gordon's School. The Gordon Boy's School, Twenty Second Annual Report 1907, Legacies. Julie West, Gordonian Officer.

54   Death of Helen McEwan. Helen (Maggie's mother), Grave Number 36489 square 34 Western Cemetery, Highgate.

55   Ronnie's death, 5th April 1908. Ronnie's funeral from listed newspapers dated 6th April, *The Times*, *Irish Times*, *Daily Mail*, *The Court Journal*, the *Bradford Argus*, the *Daily Telegraph*, *Evening News*, *Bazaar*, *Surrey Advertiser*.

56   Ronnie's Will, dated 8th October 1906, obtained by Bernice Forsyth. Clare Prior (solicitor/volunteer) for analysis of the Will.

57   Ronnie's probate recorded 15th April 1908. Additional detail provided by a telegram dated 13th April 1908, by Jennie Cornwallis West, to Maggie about her return to the South of France on 14th April, to re-join her father.

58   King Edward VII's dog Caesar was buried in the grounds of Marlborough House in 1914.

Seven

59   A dinner menu from King Edward VII's visit to Polesden Lacey, 5th and 6th June 1909.

60   Impresario Andre Charlot. Details from Polesden Lacey Archives of artist listings as weekend entertainers.

Eight

61   Frank Bole. Originally Ronnie's manservant. Maggie's Head Steward (as he became) and friend.

62   Francis Crossley Bole, born 8th April 1879. Ancestry records, Bernice Forsyth and Roy Vaux. Baptism certificate dated 27th April 1879, Roy Vaux.

63 Address of Frank's parents after moving away from Somerleyton in 1891. Bernice Forsyth.

64 Frank Bole's passport (copy), Polesden Lacey Archives.

65 Addresses Frank lived at in London with his wife Evelyn and the three boys.

66 Addresses Frank and his family lived at in Surrey while he worked for Maggie Greville. Ancestry, Roy Vaux. Additionally, for his work establishing some confirmed details of Frank Bole's life and of Frank's family background. Also, Frank Bole's job titles and for his death and probate information.

67 Frank Bole's death at Epsom and Ewell Cottage Hospital, Epsom, 5th October 1954, including will. Ancestry, Roy Vaux.

68 Frank Bole's effects (London).

69 Garden information. References: *Liverpool Echo*, 5th October 1931, A Gardener's Life at Polesden Lacey (Garden Archives), local paper 1912. Arthur Thomson Groom, interview, 27th February 1988.

70 Walter William Bacon, known as the drunken butler. Various stories about him by Maggie's guests.

71 George Moss, senior butler, shipping lists, Bernice Forsyth.

72 A number of references following Maggie Greville's servants at Polesden Lacey, from the archives, and from contacts made and recorded by Tracey Parker, Volunteering and Community Involvement Officer, Polesden Lacey.

73 Robert Sydney Nash, Archive Files, Polesden Lacey, and images of Coverdale also on file. Robert Sydney Nash's memory, described by his son Robert/Bob of Maggie's generosity, in looking after Bob, by paying for the Convalescent home costs. Reminiscence by Robert Sydney Nash's son Robert/Bob, recorded 22nd February 1988 of arrangement by Edward VII, for Maggie to have a postman wait for replies to her mail. Interview with Donald Pirt, 14th April 2014, describing the continuing practice of this system.

74 Meghan Hill revisited Polesden Lacey for the first time in 1999 since she moved away in 1929.

75 Polesden Lacey Archives, reference Miss Lysaght Griffin's employment.

76 Visitor Book, Polesden Lacey, Bernice Forsyth.

77 Archive records and newspaper cuttings about Edward VII and Maggie, and the Marlborough House Set.

78 Adeline Liron, Maggie's personal maid, later companion and friend. Information sourced by Bernice Forsyth and Elodie Fillon. Passenger lists for shipping, and also Will and probate documents.

79 Adeline Liron, passenger ship information, Bernice Forsyth and Roy Vaux.

80 Beverley Nichols: quotation from *The Sweet and Twenties*.

81 Adeline Liron probate document, Bernice Forsyth.

82 Anecdote from the children of Frederick Henry Hart.

83 Research work and specific information located by Janet Durbin about Maggie's cars.

Nine

84 Polesden Lacey Garden Archives and additional research. Alex Wigley, Garden and Outdoor Manager.

85 Garden Conservation Plan, by Acta, for the National Trust, by Sarah Rutherford, dated 2011. Polesden Garden Character Area, Sarah Rutherford by Acta 2011.

86 Garden Archives at Polesden Lacey. References re gardeners at Polesden Lacey are: Young, 1998; Thompson, 1988; H Smith, 1979; Robertson, 1979; Currie, 1996. Plus, newspaper cuttings in archives dated 1913, 1916 and 1917, Twinn, 1932. Refs: (111 *London News* 28th April 1923) and other cuttings.

87 Garden Conservation Plan, by Acta, for the National Trust, by Sarah Rutherford, dated 2011. Garden Archives at Polesden Lacey.

88 Garden Archives documents, continuing. Plus, newspaper references to the gardens at Polesden Lacey at various times: RHS Show 22nd May 1917, *Daily Telegraph* 1st July 1922, *Daily Sketch* 21st July 1926, *Sunday Times* 21st July 1929, *The Queen* June 1938.

89 Head gardeners from Garden Archives at Polesden Lacey, continuing.

90 George Twinn, letter dated 3rd November 1932. Polesden Lacey Garden Archives.

91 Garden Archives, and a number of newspaper articles, confirmed Maggie's favourite flowers.

92 Henry Smith, Head Gardener for Maggie Greville from 1938, and after she died, until 1964.

93 David Smith's recorded statements and letters of his time growing up while living at Polesden Lacey, provide many valuable details of garden life and of Polesden Lacey, during World War II.
94 *Anthony Eden* by Robert Rhodes James.
95 *Cabinet's Finest Hour* by David Owen.
96 *Lord Beaverbrook* by AJP Taylor and additional research.
97 David Smith's continuing notes of life in World War II at Polesden Lacey.
98 Polesden Lacey Archives: the officer provided a written account of what life was like while staying at Polesden Lacey, in World War II. Located by Leanne Smith.
99 Reference to Visitor Book in World War II.
100 Polesden Lacey Garden Archives.

Ten

101 My Pictures by Maggie Greville.
102 Polesden Lacey paintings book entitled *The Pictures at Polesden Lacey*, dated 2017, National Trust, and Polesden Lacey Guidebook, dated 1999 and reprinted until 2007.
103 https://www.tate.org.uk/art/art-terms/b/bitumen, pages reference Sir Joshua Reynolds painting, "Nymph and Piping Boy", circa 1785–86.
104 Comment by Helen Taylor, House Steward (Conservation and Collection Care), at Polesden Lacey (2019) reference quality of Maggie Greville's paintings and Polesden Lacey Pictures Guide.
105 Polesden Lacey Guidebook, 1999 edition (full version), references carpets.
106 Silver described in the full version of 1999 Guidebook, and archive articles about silver at Polesden Lacey.
107 *Faberge's Animals* by Caroline de Guitaut, Royal Collection Publications.
108 Polesden Lacey Guidebook, 1999, and new research.
109 Furniture, Polesden Lacey Archives and Guidebook, 1999.
110 Clocks, Polesden Lacey Guidebook, 1999, and additional research.
111 References: www.thefrenchporcelainsociety.com compiled by Tamara Preaud Archivist, Manufacture National de Sevres 2003. www.designgallery.co.uk and www.iliadny.com and the Sevres Tea Set,
112 www.sothebys.com reference Kangxi porcelain.

113 Tancred Borenius, the Visitor Book, Polesden Lacey. https://www.arthistorians.info/boreniust and https://www.thehistorypress.co.uk/articles/the-secret-world-war-ii-peace-mission-of-tancred-borenius/

114 Jonathan Marsh, Head of House and Collections, and Charlotte Burford, Head Steward, reference, "Beyond the Dragon" Exhibition at Polesden Lacey, 2018.

Eleven

115 Passenger shipping list, Bernice Forsyth and Roy Vaux. Newspaper cuttings. Additional research. A–Z visitors' list, Charles Street and Polesden Lacey.

116 Images supplied by Maggie. Postcards also provided. Maggie's statements about her trip. Polesden Lacey Archive records of Maggie's South American trip. Passenger shipping list, Bernice Forsyth and Roy Vaux. Newspaper cuttings. Additional research.

117 Maggie's images and postcards; image of Renown arriving in Sydney, March 1927. Newspaper cuttings.

118 Notes, newspaper cuttings about Maggie's stay in Egypt, and being hosted by King Fuad in 1932. References: *The Egyptian Mail* 23rd March 1932, *African World* 9th March 1932.

119 Passenger shipping lists, Bernice Forsyth and Roy Vaux. History White Star Line and Cunard Line. Maggie's Travel. References: *Evening Standard* 28th October 1939, NT Act 1937.

120 *Women, Travel and Identity: Journey by Rail and Sea 1870–1940* by Emma Robinson-Tomsett.

121 Maggie's travel referencess, *Daily Express* 5th May 1933. Imperial Airways History.

122 Lord Reading: Maggie's favourite man. Background: *Lord Reading* by Denis Judd.

123 *Mountbatten* by Philp Ziegler, 1985, book club associates by arrangement with William Collins Sons & Co Ltd.

124 Reference to the background of Edwina Ashley. Number of books.

125 Copy of Maggie's letter to Lord Reading while staying at Viceroy House, 1922. From Marquess of Reading Letters from Mrs Greville, 1913–35, British Library.

126 The *People* newspaper, 1923. Number of newspapers reports of court case.

127   The Corfield Papers, University of Cambridge Centre of South Asian Studies. Reference Maggie in India, travelling with jewellery.

Twelve

128   Death of William McEwan: a list of newspaper articles, announcing the death and describing the funeral. Death of William McEwan: *The Daily Chronicle* 23rd June 1913, *The Yorkshire Herald* 23rd June 1913, *Medical Times* 28th June 1913.

129   Death certificate details, 12th May 1913.

130   William McEwan's Will dated, 13th July 1910. Details from various newspapers.

131   Precise details of McEwan's investments at the time of his death.

Thirteen

132   *The Last Season* by Anne de Courcy, Thames and Hudson. The description refers to 1939, but is applicable to earlier dates, for Maggie's style of entertaining.

133   Visitor Book, 1907–42. Bernice Forsyth.

134   Newspaper articles describing Maggie entertaining her "friends".

135   Details from McEwan's Will.

136   A number of newspaper cuttings.

137   Newspaper articles. Details from Charles Street dinner party book.

138   Maggie was always fashionable. *Sunday Times* 25th November 1928. www.telegraph.co.uk/luxurytravel and the biography of Harry Craddock.

139   Confirmed artist list: Polesden Lacey Archives.

140   *The Al Thani Collection* by Susan Stronge, V&A Publishing, 2015.

141   Newspaper cuttings described the guests arriving and departing from 16 Charles Street.

142   Visitor Book listings for the maharajahs. Much additional research into the history and the lives of the maharajahs.

143   Newspaper reports at the time. A number of recent website articles, including https://www.nottingham.ac.uk/research/groups/conferencing-the-international/index.aspx

144   A number of newspaper cuttings.
145   *The Recollections of a Rebel* by Robert Boothby Hutchison, 1978, reference "The Social Scene Between the Wars".

Fourteen

146   Copy of remarks made by Lady Chamberlain, Polesden Lacey Archives.
147   Polesden Lacey Archives. Polesden Convalescent Home with correct details and biographies of soldiers staying at Polesden Lacey in World War I. Full details from research by Janet Durbin. Newspaper cuttings. *Sister Agnes: The History of King Edward VII's Hospital for Officers, 1899–1999* by Richard Hough
148   *Canadian Military History* (Volume 20, Number 1, Winter 2011, pp45–60). Extracts by Sarah Cozzi. The Establishments of Canadian-Only Social Clubs for CEF Soldiers in London, 1915–19. "When You're a Long, Long Way from Home". Newspaper cuttings. References: PL Archives, http://www.canadianmilitaryhistory.ca/wp-content/uploads/2012/03/5-Cozzi-Maple-Leaf-Club.pdf
149   Details of World War II at Polesden Lacey are provided in Chapter 9.
150   Pretsell Scheme: *Edinburgh Evening News* 7th September 1937, *The Scotsman* 25th September 1937.
151   Christie's Archives, London, visit by Janet Durbin and Pam Burbidge 24th September 2018. Christie's Original Catalogues of 1918. *Daily Telegraph* 28th January 2011. www.redcross.org.uk
152   Research by Janet Durbin of officers who stayed at Polesden Lacey Convalescent Home in 1915 and 1916.
153   Lady Drummond: The Establishments of Canadian-Only Social Clubs for CEF Soldiers in London, 1915–19.
154   Copy of original letter dated 30th June 1919, thanking Maggie Greville for loaning 11 Charles Street for the first Canadian Maple Leaf Club in London. Polesden Lacey Archives.
155   The Italian Ball: *Daily Telegraph*, 27th May 1924, *The West Australian Perth Newspaper*, 28th May 1924.
156   The sad story of a maid who worked for Maggie. Research by Bernice Forsyth. Polesden Lacey Archives.
157   Letter written by Maggie on file: Polesden Lacey Archives.

158   Visit by King George V and Queen Mary to view all of Polesden Lacey. Visitor Book.

Fifteen

159   Maggie's new Will dated 27th March 1942.
160   *Counting One's Blessings, The Selected Letters of Queen Elizabeth the Queen Mother* by William Crawshaw. Letter written from Balmoral Castle.
161   Letters Patent issued 30th November 1917. Whitehall announcement and *London Gazette*.
162   Copy of telegram is on file: Polesden Lacey Archives.
163   Many Newspaper reports about the wedding, and arrival in Bookham and at Polesden Lacey. *The Star*, 1923, reference Bertie and Elizabeth's security for their honeymoon at Polesden Lacey.
164   Additional research with Armstrong Siddeley Club.
165   *Counting One's Blessings* by William Shawcross. Letters from the Duchess of York to Lady Strathmore, her mother, and reference to William Shawcross. The official biography of Bertie's letter to his father George V with the King's reply.
166   *Louis and the Prince* by Geordie Greig. 1999.

Sixteen

167   *Red Flappers* by Judith Mackrell. Emerald Cunard's remarks to Maggie about not knowing Wallis Simpson. *Illustrated London News* 6th July 1968.
168   *Counting One's Blessings, The Selected Letters of Queen Elizabeth the Queen* by William Shawcross. Letter to Osbert Sitwell.
169   https://tfl.gov.uk/corporate/about-tfl/culture-and-heritage/londons-transport-a-history/london-underground/a-brief-history-of-the-underground
170   www.britishtelephones.com/histuk.htm
171   https://www.nationalarchives.gov.uk/cabinetpapers/alevelstudies/1930-depression.htm
172   Ford Heritage Fleet administrator, public affairs, John Nevill, Ford Motor Company, Brentwood, reference red Ford van.

173 www.economicshelp.org/blog/7483/economics/the-uk-economy-in-the-1930s

Seventeen

174 *Ribbentrop* by Michael Bloch, 1992.
175 Anthony Stephens, conservation and engagement assistant, Polesden Lacey, above reference: Maggie's Jewish guests/friends at Polesden Lacey and Charles Street. *The Palgrave Dictionary of Anglo-Jewish History* by W Rubinstein and Michael A Jolles, reference Lesser's Art dealers.
176 Imperial War Museum re Spitfire P8643 – photograph number HU 88783. Maggie's gift to the nation. Definitions/explanations of the meaning of RAF terms are listed below the numbered references.
177 Significant and substantial contribution from David Lloyd, ex-trustee of Spitfire Society. Information from Operational Records Books and Air Ministry 1180 accident cards from RAF Museum supplied by Roy Nixon.
178 David Smith's recorded statements and letters of his time growing up while living at Polesden Lacey reference the Canadian troops.
179 Polesden Lacey Archives.

Eighteen

180 History of Mewes & Davis research. Architecture of the Entente Cordiale, Faculty of Architecture, Cambridge May 1971 relating to Mewes & Davis. History of London hotels.
181 *Chips Channon's Unexpurgated Diaries* by Simon Heffer. Polesden Lacey Archives.
182 Death of Maggie Greville at the Dorchester Hotel, 15th September 1942.
183 *The Times* Archives description of Maggie Greville's funeral. Polesden Lacey Archives. Information about Maggie's grave at Polesden Lacey: www.nationaltrust.org.uk and www.christies.com, and *Sir Albert Richardson – The Professor* by Simon Houfe, and to Peter Seabrook (volunteer) for this reference.
184 Additional *Times* archive description of memorial service.

185   Maggie Greville's Will dated 27th March 1942. Copy at Polesden Lacey Archives. *The Times* Archives. Maggie's Will with High Court approval of the Will 5th January 1943.

186   Details of bequests in Maggie's Will.

187   Published at the same time as the obituary of Maggie Greville in *The Times*, 16th September 1942. *Times* obituary for Maggie Greville, 17th September 1942, Osbert Sitwell.

188   Diaries and Ancestral Voices, James Lees-Milne; Clifford Smith Report, dated 8th April 1943. Furniture. James Lees-Mine diaries, reference contents of Polesden Lacey and Charles Street.

189   National Trust History.

190   A comment made a long time ago about James Lees-Milne. Possibly gossip?

Nineteen

191   Newspaper articles describing Maggie's wedding: *The Scotsman* 25th April 1891, *Vanity Fair* April 1891, *Daily News* 27th April 1891, *The Truth* 30th April 1891, Worcester Herald, The Hawk.

192   History of cultured pearls. www.jerseypearl.com

193   Cartier: a number of sources, augmented by a number of books and https://www.estatediamondjewelry.com/the-complete-history-of-cartier/ and other websites.

194   *Boucheron* by Vincent Meylan. "The Boucheron Archives" and https://us.boucheron.com

195   *The Queen's Diamonds* by Sir Hugh Roberts, published by the Royal Collection Trust, 2012.

196   Vincent Meylan's confirmation of details of work about Maggie's famous diamond tiara, gifted to the Queen Mother and now worn by the Duchess of Cornwall.

197   Boucheron purchase 1907 of the ruby and diamond necklace by Maggie Greville. More stunning jewellery items which were in Maggie's black tin trunk are listed and included in this chapter.

198   More stunning jewellery items which were in Maggie's black tin trunk are listed and included in this chapter.

199   Bernice Forsyth for the background information re Princess Nadezhada

	Tereshchenko and her husband Vladimir Mouravieff Apostol-Korobyine.
200	The emerald and diamond tiara worn by Princess Eugenie when she married Jack Brooksbank in 2018.
201	Leanne Smith's location and research of this fabulous tiara, purchased in 1921 from Boucheron.
202	A letter the Queen Mother wrote 13th October 1942, about passing on the jewellery she had inherited from Maggie (should anything happen to her in WWII), was provided in William Shawcross's book, *Counting One's Blessings*, p331.
203	Letter written by the Queen Mother to her daughter Elizabeth, 27th June 1942. *Counting One's Blessings* by William Shawcross.
204	*The Sweet and Twenties* by Beverley Nichols 1958. Weidenfield and Nicolson.

Twenty

205	Letter written by Maggie to Lord Reading. Polesden Lacey Archives.
206	*The Recollections of a Rebel* by Robert Boothby, Hutchinson 1978.
207	A number of references for Kenneth Clark. His own comments about Maggie. Polesden Lacey Archives.
208	*The Sweet and Twenties* by Beverley Nicolson, Chapter 6.
209	*The Sweet and Twenties* by Beverley Nicolson, Chapter 6. Maggie's offer to Beverley to stand against Duff Cooper for Parliament. Parliamentary Listings: Beverley Nichols and Duff Cooper: www.20thcenturylondon.org.uk and www.onthisday.com and www.overthefootlightsco.uk
210	*The PROF – The Life of Frederick Lindemann* by Adrian Fort.
211	Visitor Book, Polesden Lacey.
212	Politicians who visited Polesden Lacey regularly. Visitor Book.
213	Information regarding political discussions taking place in the Long Walk at Polesden Lacey, as supplied by Gladys Yealland to Tracey Parker.
214	*The Sweet and Twenties* by Beverley Nichols, Chapter 6. Maggie's final words to him.
215	Maggie's Will reference the maintenance of William McEwan and Ronnie's graves.
216	Direct reference from Maggie's Will, reference Adeline Liron. Adeline

Liron's Will and death certificate, re Bernice Forsyth.

217 Will of Margaret Greville, 27th March 1942. Total sum Maggie bequeathed. References: Claire Prior, solicitor. *Times* obituary for Maggie Greville, 17th September 1942, Osbert Sitwell.

218 Report on the furniture and other works of art at Polesden Lacey, near Dorking, bequeathed by the late Honourable Mrs Ronald Greville, DBE, H Clifford Smith, MA, FSA 1943.8.

219 Christie's sales dates for Maggie's possessions sold by the National Trust after she died.

220 Christie's Archives, London, visit 20th September 2018; Christie's original catalogues of 1918. Janet Durbin and Pam Burbidge 24th September 2018.

RAF Explanations

Imperial War Museum re Spitfire P8643 – Photograph Number HU 88783. Maggie's gift to the nation.

Explanations for Sweeps

As 1941 began RAF Fighter Command began to win some air superiority over France from the enemy. By May 1941, the squadrons based at the main air fighter fields operated together as combined fighter wings, under the tactical control of a newly created post of a "wing leader". Various types of short penetration fighter operational sorties were tried out, in a bid to draw the Luftwaffe into a war of attrition and to keep numbers of enemy fighters busy in the skies over France.

Explanation for Rhubarb Runs

These were operations when sections of fighters or fighter bombers took off, taking full advantage of low cloud visibility. The planes crossed the English Channel and dropped below cloud level to search for opportunity targets. These targets included railway locomotives, rolling stock, aircraft on the ground, enemy troops and vehicles on roads.

Explanation of Circus

These operations were bomber attacks with fighter escorts in the daytime/daylight. The attacks were against short-range targets with the intention of occupying enemy fighters and keeping their units in the area concerned.

Explanation of Damage Categories in World War II

A: Aircraft can be repaired on site.
B: Beyond repair on site, but repairable at a maintenance unit or contractor's works.
C: Allocated to constructive airframe duties (for ground training).
E: Write off.
SOC: Struck off (RAF) charge.

Further Bibliography

The Edwardians by Roy Hattersley.
www.legal-dictionary.thefreedictionary.com
Polesden Lacey Archives. Beer to Champagne,
www.lafayette.org.uk
www.thepeerage.com
Another Part of the Wood by Kenneth Clark.
All I Could Never Be by Beverley Nichols.
Daily Graphic, 19th July 1923.
Power, Grace and Decadence by Lawrence James, World War II timeline page.
Visitor Book, Parliamentary listings.
Imperial War Museum re Spitfire P8643 – Photograph Number HU 88783.
    Maggie's gift to the nation, reference P8643 Spitfire.
Evening Standard, 28th October /1939, National Trust Act, 1937.
Bookham Parish Magazine, 1909–15.
Evening Standard, 19th December 1930.
Additional research by Pam, 7th January 2019.
The History of 11 Charles Street, Mayfair.
Abdication 1936, *Rat Week* by Osbert Sitwell.
Gossip by Andrew Barrow, reference Maggie entertaining at the Dorchester
    hotel, London, Chapter 18 above.
Hansard, 1803–2005.